The Migration Mobile

CHALLENGING MIGRATION STUDIES

This provocative new series challenges the established field of migration studies to think beyond its policy-oriented frameworks and to engage with the complex and myriad forms in which the global migration regime is changing in the twenty-first century. It proposes to draw together studies that engage with the current transformation of the politics of migration, and the meaning of "migrant," from the below of grassroots, local, transnational, and multi-sited coalitions, projects, and activisms. Attuned to the contemporary resurgence of migrant-led and migration-related movements, and anti-racist activism, the series builds on work carried out at the critical margins of migration studies to evaluate the "border industrial complex" and its fall-outs, builds a decolonial perspective on global migration flows, and critically reassesses the link between (im)migration, citizenship, and belonging in the cross-border future.

Series Editors

Alana Lentin, Associate Professor in Cultural and Social Analysis at Western Sydney University

Gavan Titley, Senior Lecturer in Media Studies at the National University of Ireland, Maynooth

Titles in the Series

Radical Skin, Moderate Masks: De-Radicalising the Muslim and Racism in Post-Racial Societies, by Yassir Morsi

Contemporary Boat Migration: Data, Geopolitics, and Discourses, edited by Elaine Burroughs and Kira Williams

Race in Post-Racial Europe: An Intersectional Analysis, by Stefanie C. Boulila

The Undeported: The Making of a Floating Population of Exiles in France and Europe, by Carolina Sanchez Boe

Reproducing Refugees: Photographia of a Crisis, by Anna Carastathis and Myrto Tsilimpounidi

Disavowing Asylum: Documenting Ireland's Asylum Industrial Complex, by Ronit Lentin and Vukašin Nedeljković

Convivencia: Urban Space and Migration in a Small Catalan Town, by Martin Lundsteen

The Migration Mobile

Border Dissidence, Sociotechnical Resistance, and the Construction of Irregularized Migrants

Edited by Vasilis Galis, Martin Bak Jørgensen, and Marie Sandberg

ROWMAN & LITTLEFIELD
Lanham • Boulder • New York • London

Published by Rowman & Littlefield
An imprint of The Rowman & Littlefield Publishing Group, Inc.
4501 Forbes Boulevard, Suite 200, Lanham, Maryland 20706
www.rowman.com

86-90 Paul Street, London EC2A 4NE

British Library Cataloguing in Publication Information Available

Library of Congress Cataloging-in-Publication Data

Names: Galis, Vasilis, editor. | Jørgensen, Martin Bak, 1973– editor. | Sandberg, Marie, editor.
Title: The migration mobile : border dissidence, sociotechnical resistance, and the construction of irregularized migrants / edited by Vasilis Galis, Martin Bak Jørgensen, and Marie Sandberg.
Description: Lanham, Maryland : Rowman & Littlefield, 2022. | Series: Challenging migration studies | Includes bibliographical references and index.
Identifiers: LCCN 2022012016 (print) | LCCN 2022012017 (ebook) | ISBN 9781538165164 (cloth) | ISBN 9781538170984 (paperback) | ISBN 9781538165171 (ebook)
Subjects: LCSH: Europe—Emigration and immigration. | Border security—Technological innovations—Europe
Classification: LCC JV7590 .M8644 2022 (print) | LCC JV7590 (ebook) | DDC 325.4—dc23/eng/20220607
LC record available at https://lccn.loc.gov/2022012016
LC ebook record available at https://lccn.loc.gov/2022012017

♾️™ The paper used in this publication meets the minimum requirements of American National Standard for Information Sciences—Permanence of Paper for Printed Library Materials, ANSI/NISO Z39.48-1992.

Contents

PART I

Introduction

Chapter 1

The Migration Mobile

Border Dissidence, Sociotechnical Resistance, and the Construction of Irregularized Migrants

Martin Bak Jørgensen and Vasilis Galis

INTRODUCTION

Borders have been sites of contestations and struggles over who belongs and who does not, and who is and who is not allowed to move freely in transnational or national spaces. Embedded as they are in the bordering process, policing and security practices produce the irregularity and illegitimacy of the migrating subject. At the same time, border practices simultaneously imply processes of dissidence and resistance. Border infrastructures and resistance to bordering practices refer to dynamic and complex interactions between migrants and nonhuman others, namely a hybrid of material and digital technologies at the borderland and elsewhere (Dijstelbloem 2021). Border guards, EU officials, Frontex officers, activists, nongovernmental organizations (NGOs), and solidarity networks configure both hybrid alliances of humans/ nonhumans and new virtual and urban spaces in order to configure or resist bordering. Borders and (un)bordering practices constitute (or impede, for that matter) mobility by other means. Mobility in this context refers to (ir)regular movement of populations as well as the fluidity of the migratory space and the means to perform migration. The migration mobile, that is the fluid migratory space, is populated by a heterogeneous set of actors, both human and nonhuman, both pro-and against migration. The volume argues that even

3

in migration, migrants, borders, and technologies do not simply flow but are also fluid, "which means that they are open, uncertain, in process, both complete and incomplete in ways that are themselves open and uncertain" (Moser and Law 2006). People on the move do not have to be trying to cross through material borders to experience that they turn into aliens, noncitizens, someone who does not belong. Borders are physical, portable, and virtual (Lyon 2013) at the same time. Borders are also dynamic and unfixed entities that draw and re-draw lines of inclusion and exclusion in material semiotic terms. Fluidity here does not only refer to the porousness of the border, the migratory flows, and the dynamics of space but also to the flexibility of the migratory and bordering agency. Mobility changes shape and re-forms in relation to bordering practices. Thus we suggest that the study of migration should emphasize the fluidity of the border and actors that circulate within different migratory spaces, thereby co-creating them. The different spaces created by borders, migrants, border controllers, border technologies, solidarians, and so on have implications for the way we conceptualize migration, the processes and interactions that bring actors together, and the type of interventions that are made possible.

Current migration influx into Europe is characterized by an elaborate use of technological applications, both high-and low-tech, by nation-states to control mobility as well as migrants and solidarians to facilitate safe and free passageways (Darling and Bauder 2019; Dijstelbloem et al. 2011; Galis et al. 2016; Gillespie et al. 2016). Even the recent invasion in Ukraine by the Russian army, which has also pushed tens of thousands out of their homes, has been marked by the use of a digital platform: the first TikTok war (Chayka 2022). Internet culture scholar Aimée Morrison explains that while violent conflicts have been aestheticized on social media before, the TikTok coverage in Ukraine is going to radically change the way we think about conflict. While the killing of civilians and the influx of migrants have previously been characterized as the collateral damage of war, it is people's lives documented on TikTok that speak back now (Boseley 2022), constituting the loss of life and bordering practices as the center of attention.

Similarly, such usages have also affected research approaches, and over the last few years we have seen a techno-digital "turn" in migration research (e.g., Alencar 2020; Awad and Tossell 2021; Baldassar et al. 2016; Borkert et al. 2018; Gillespie et al. 2016; Leurs and Smets 2018; van Liempt and Zijlstra 2017; Ponzanesi and Leurs 2014). Research shows how techno-digital applications partly constitute the very migration routes; technology becomes a lens and a tool for shared decision-making and navigation among migrants.

This book investigates the complex entanglements of migration and technology by drawing on an interdisciplinary framework combining Critical Border and Migration Studies (cf. Casas-Cortés et al. 2016; Dijstelbloem

2021; Mezzadra and Neilson 2013; Papadopoulos and Tsianos 2013), Social Media Studies (cf. Rodríguez et al. 2014; Croeser 2014), European Ethnology (cf. Ehn, Löfgren, and Wilk 2016), racialization of surveillance technologies (Brown 2015; Parmar 2020), and Science and Technology Studies (cf. Dijstelbloem and Meijer 2011; Galis et al. 2016). These literatures have shown how borders are not fixed geographical entities but a set of fluid practices in a constant state of becoming; how technology transforms not only mobility but also forms of solidarity with migrants; how border crossing and everyday life can be studied; how surveillance is both a discursive and material practice that reifies boundaries, borders, and bodies around racial lines; show the multiple functions of borders and their racializing consequences; and how societies are influenced by the fact that we are producers and users of science and technology. By drawing attention to all kinds of technologies used at the borderland, we also point to the need to open up research to the low-technological artifacts that come to challenge high-tech surveillance technologies through their use for border crossing by migrants. Scrutinizing the co-construction of border technologies, sociotechnical resistance to borders and (irregularized) mobility first can help us understand how the global migration regime is changing in the twenty-first century, and secondly to raise critical questions regarding the implications of those technologies and how they potentially can remake migration and mobility. By tracing connections between various technologies and actors and highlighting the role of technology in controlling and enabling migration, an overall aim with this volume is to challenge the notion of migration.

The Migration Mobile therefore includes studies on the use of technology in the acts of imposing official power to control and limit migrations influxes, as well as the use of technology in protesting/circumventing power structures inherent in border technologies. The book likewise problematizes the fluidity of the concept of border and mobility. Building on existing literature that deterritorializes the concepts, contributions in the current publication will provide an orienting framework for understanding the multiple nature of the border as a geographical line, a technological apparatus, a boundary of protected identities and privileges, a classification filter, or a camp for "undesirable" bodies (Antonakaki, Kasparek, and Maniatis 2016; Millner 2011; Ploeg and Sprenkels 2011). Balibar (2002, 78) explains that a political border is never the mere boundary between two states but is always sanctioned, reduplicated, and relativized by other geopolitical infrastructures. The immediate effect is that the "border is everywhere" (Balibar 2002), portable, and virtual (Lyon 2013). Several chapters in this book focus on specific border-related infrastructures, both formal and informal.

This book is a collective product of an interdisciplinary research initiative called *DIGINAUTS: Migrants' Digital Practices in/of the European Border*

Regime that began in 2018. The project was based on the assumption that migrants' use of technology not only challenges our usual ways of thinking about migration but also subtly reconfigures the functioning of these technologies themselves. This publication addresses the use of technology in the configuration of migration. Several actors are partaking in enabling (or hindering) migratory mobility: the migrants themselves, smugglers, people in solidarity, law enforcement, border guards, policymakers, states, supra-states, and a plethora of technologies. Therefore, we aim to provide the reader with a pluralistic account of the practices and actors that co-produce migration and mobility and establish or subvert (temporarily or not) the border. The book aims to make a thematic account of these very different technologies implicated in border crossing and migration management. These technologies are embedded with both scripts of control and discipline as well as possibilities of resistance and emancipation (Sánchez-Querubín and Rogers 2018; Galis and Summerton 2018). We argue that we lack studies that relate and juxtapose border technologies to subjects shaped by these technologies. We also lack studies that juxtapose low-and high-tech border technologies. This does not mean that this volume simply adds low technologies of those who try to make it to Europe to the high technologies of those who try to prevent them.

We argue that we cannot properly understand the migrant subject without understanding the sociotechnical border practices in action. This means approaching technology not only in connection with the rhetoric of those who introduce it but also considering how it is materialized in human bodies through clandestine border-crossing practices and artifacts and/or digital appliances. The demarcation between superior and inferior technology, just like that between the inside and the outside of Europe, is not presupposed, but it constitutes, instead, the sociotechnical effect of this history (Galis et al. 2016). At the same time, the ways in which migrants repurpose, rather than simply use these technologies, have received limited attention. Further, existing studies neither problematize issues of navigation during the journey nor scrutinize the solidarity work at play in the migration process that technology enables or hinders. Hence, there is a need for a state-of-the-art publication that simultaneously examines how migrants are using technological applications and focuses on how their varied usage affects not only mobility but also the technologies themselves.

Another important aspect that this book addresses through the lenses of technology is that of solidarity with migrants, in a period when several voices have pronounced international solidarity dead, especially in regard to the inability of the EU member states to coordinate a common policy in terms of admission and integration (e.g., Agustín and Jørgensen 2019; Lahusen and Grasso 2018). Whereas previous research about actions taken in solidarity with irregularized migrants focuses on legal compliance, and how to allocate asylum seekers between member states (i.e., "internal solidarity," see Gerhards et al. 2019), this publication focuses on ground-up, self-organized solidary initiatives enabled by the use of technology. By focusing on "ground-up solidarity work," we aim at investigating the ways in which the migrants build and maintain relations and networks through techno-digital means including contact to aid workers and NGOs in the countries of transit and arrival (Cabot 2010). Such formations and actions constitute what we depict as solidarity networks (Rozakou 2016). In the context of this book, solidarity cannot be separated from the techno-digital actors that enable it. Therefore, we also reach a wider and fluid understanding of solidary acts and alliances that is sociotechnical.

ETHICAL POSITION

The issues we work with in this book call for both an ethical awareness and an ethical reflexivity in regard to how we (as researchers) collect data, how we engage with our informants, how we disseminate our results, and what we seek to achieve by and through our research (Fischer and Jørgensen 2021). This discussion is situated in a debate between the quality and objective of the research and thinking ethically (Zapata-Barrero and Yalaz 2020). In the literature, thinking ethically has been discussed through three ethical universal provisos: do no harm, respect autonomy, and ensure equitable sharing of benefits (e.g., Flick 2018; Krause 2017). When it comes to qualitative ethnographic work, there has been a long debate regarding the ethics of research with vulnerable groups. Migratory experiences characterized by vulnerability and precarity fall under this discussion (e.g., Pittaway, Bartolomei, and Hugman 2010). The book's chapters engage with this type of discussion from the perspectives of online ethnography and in our work with digital data and migrant strategies (Sandberg et al. 2021). Researching the entangled relations between digital technologies and migration, we not only have included migrants' practices, but also the activities of other actors, from solidarity networks to border control agencies. As discussed by Sandberg et al. (2021), digital technologies generate a whole new set of ethical and methodological challenges for migration studies: from data access to data interpretation, privacy protection, and research ethics more generally. There is surprisingly little research that reflects on these new challenges in digital migration research. In a recently published article, Maurice Stierl makes the case for an engaged scholarship that does not shy away from intervening in the contested field of migration with the intention not to fix but to amplify the epistemic and other crises of the European border regime (2020). Stierl criticizes the "do no harm" principle as being inadequate and asks if it should not also be expanded to engagements with policymakers. Stierl ends up discussing epistemic interventions that can produce counter-empirics in order to expose the violence of European Union's border regime. We see this as a form of activist engagement that can mobilize the production of critical knowledge on migration as well as one recognizing and promoting migrants' agency and autonomy in terms of capabilities and rights (also Fischer and Jørgensen 2021; Galis 2021).

CONCEPTUALIZING THE MIGRATION MOBILE

As mentioned earlier, the migration mobile is a site of contestation. When engaged productively, such contestations allow us to highlight some distinctive dimensions of the *fluidity* of mobility and migration. First, the chapters indicate that the contemporary politics of migration is constituted through various modes of power inscribed in bordering practices, technologies, authorities, groups, and individuals. Sovereign, biopolitical, disciplinary, sociotechnical, and resisting powers are assembled as part of a contestation to control movement, mobility, migration, and border making/crossing. Second, the actors implicated in the contestation are multiple, heterogeneous, and often unpredictable (Squire 2010). Migration, mobility, and border (un)making should be examined in relation to these actors, as well as the practices, systems, and institutions of which they are part (Trimikliniotis et al. 2014). The migration mobile is a fluid space. Fluidity here does not only refer to the flow of movement/migration. We are not merely interested in subjects and agency that move around and hold their shape. For this volume, what is mobile is also likely to be fluid. It is likely to change its shape. In short, migratory subjects change their shape and re-form themselves as they flow around (cf. Moser and Law 2006). Even the definition of the migrant is fluid, as we have observed during the war in Ukraine. Several European states' welcome of Ukrainian war migrants exposed a "double standard" for non-white migrants. Nation-states of the Global North that have for years resisted taking in migrants from wars in Syria, Iraq, and Afghanistan are now opening their doors to Ukrainians (Jakes 2022; Konotey-Ahulu 2022; Zaru 2022).

Through the metaphor of the migration mobile, we aim to address and capture not only the technicalities of bordering technologies and practices and/or the fluidity of migration flows. We also shed light on the relationships, interactions, adjustments, coordination, actions, and transformations among migratory subjects/objects. We have not sought to reproduce a study of migration and mobility as a "stopover in a linear process" (Wissink et al. 2013) or flows versus borders in a networked setting. The chapters focus on dynamic alterations. In this context, mobility goes on growing, changing, adapting, and working in places where it would never work if its relations were held stable, as in a network. And it also means that the migratory subjects perform fluidity. They contribute to enacting the fluid space within which migration achieves shape constancy (cf. Law and Mol 2001). Thus, mobility here refers to the constitutive agency of how migration and movement are simultaneously configured, re-configured, controlled, surveyed, enabled, impeded, and transformed. It also focuses on spatial aspects of movement and migration that are not necessarily or always material. In addition, the volume highlights instances of migrant digital space and interconnectivity and how they re-configure the border regime as well as emancipatory migratory practices.

STRUCTURE OF THE BOOK

This introductory chapter is followed by three sections, each with a set of chapters: Configuration of the Border Regime(s), Configuration of Migration Space, and Reconfiguring the Border Regime(s) and Emancipation of Space. The three parts emphasize different aspects of the migration mobile.

Configuration of the Border Regime(s)

The second part, "Configuration of the Border Regime(s)," investigates the configuration of the European border regime. Taking the lead from Tsianos et al. (2010), we understand the European border regime as a space formed by a "multitude of actors whose practices relate to each other, without being ordered in the form of a central logic or rationality" (p. 375), which at the same time reflects a regulatory (neoliberal) mechanism of control over individual mobility and production of irregularized "Others" embedded in specific technological apparatuses. It is the ambition of this volume to explore, position, and juxtapose the discussion on migratory mobility through the notion of the migration mobile, "in the mundane, imperfect, and noisy domain of shifting global mobilities and their negation and control in processes of bordering" (Mezzadra and Neilson 2012, 181). Moreover, the category of irregularized migrant is a legal and political construction developed and employed by authorities and border regimes. It puts forth a taxonomy of entitlement (i.e., who has legal access to protection, asylum, welfare, care, citizenship, and political rights). The dividing lines between so-called legal and illegal migrants are not clear, and people can enter a country through one category and end up in another. Policies change over time, often rapidly and drastically, and people become illegalized. This first section of the volume includes chapters that address the diverse bordering efforts of state and supra-state powers and the heterogeneous practices of bordering to control the unpredictable dimensions of migratory mobility. These bordering tactics, being antagonistic and mutually constitutive to the autonomy of migration (De Genova 2017), effectively configure the global border regime. On this account, we here include four chapters that show how the border regime creates subject categories and implements a simultaneous system of mobility and immobility.

Chapter 2, "The Embodied Identity of Migration and Border Biometrics" by Brigitta Kuster and Vassilis S. Tsianos, aims to outline some of the specific questions and problems that emanate from a new ontology of the body and its processing as a databased identity in the context of migration policy, based on control politics. Their discussion is in the sphere of the European dactyloscopic database Eurodac, which has been set up to identify asylum seekers and persons apprehended while illegally crossing an EU external border, and wants to contribute to the politicization of the constitutive instability of an embodied identity (i.e., of identification in general and above all via the body, as postulated by feminists such as Elizabeth Grosz, Stephenson/ Papadopoulos, and Kirstie Ball for the field of Surveillance Studies). In doing so, Kuster and Tsianos take up three exemplary media prominent stories, namely of Hussein K., Bilal C., and Franco A., that occurred in the wake of the refugee movements to Europe from 2015 onward. They were in turn conjured up as public scandals and cited as arguments to promote both the social and political acceptance and the appropriateness of an increasing data interoperability and an expansion of the scope of existing European database systems as well as of the construction of new ones. In a second step, they outline the shape of this new development phase of sociotechnical assemblage of identification and control of an embodied identity of migration.

"Vulnerability and Flexible Population Filtering: Lessons Learned, from the EC Hotspot to the Pandemic," chapter 3 by Evie Papada and Antonis Vradis, explores the growing relevance of vulnerability in relation to state policies aiming to control mobility. At a first instance, the authors look at vulnerability assessments as a sovereign practice of filtering and border enforcement. Following the EU-Turkish statement which came to force March 2016, migrants crossing from the Turkish coast onto the Greek Aegean islands are subject to a set of administrative procedures that assess the country responsible for processing their asylum claim. While from the perspective of EU asylum law the designation "vulnerable asylum seeker" is meant to provide additional safeguards to those undergoing an asylum process, they point to a shift in practice, whereby vulnerability designations now occupy an increasingly important role in the administrative decision to grant access to the asylum process. Second, Papada and Vradis shift the gaze to the ongoing pandemic and examine the implications of a moment when the two vulnerabilities, that of the individual and that of the population, are measured against each other as well as the technologies and materialities they produce. In the process, the chapter critically interrogates both the authority that assigns vulnerability but also vulnerability as a generalized system of thought that exceeds the most vulnerable and becomes a majoritarian understanding that encompasses the social body as a whole. The study is based on two years of ethnographic fieldwork on the island of Lesvos and in Athens, Greece.

In chapter 4, "Reconfiguring Removal: Commercial Purpose Creeps in Biometric EU Databases," Martin Lemberg-Pedersen and Oliver Halpern examine how a data frenzy permeates current European and global border policymaking and practices pursued by states and humanitarian and commercial for-profit actors. It argues that accompanying the extraction and storage of data on mobility, consumer behavior and biometrics are not only digital border practices that "algorithmitize" complex sociological, psychological, and individual processes and agencies, but also an associated range of ethical and political problems. By combining forced migration studies, border studies, and political science and economy, this chapter therefore examines a particular problem complex central to the union's evolving digital border practices, namely the evolution of four large EU databases that make use of personal, individual biometrics of migrants in digital EU border practices, namely Eurodac, SIS II, VIS, and the soon-to-be Entry/Exit system. First, Lemberg-Pedersen and Halpern trace their construction and function. Second, analyzing EU policy documents, they critically discuss an ongoing purpose creep, whereby the legislation underpinning these four databases is currently being renegotiated in order to utilize biometrics to increase the deportation of migrants from the European Union. Third, they analyze the multi-leveled governance underpinning the re-assembling of the purposes, functions, and interests of these digital border practices, by identifying the market dynamics and lobbyism efforts in order to grasp the extent of the influence of commercial actors on these border politics. Thus, examining these particular digital border practices of the European Union, the chapter seeks to link critical discussions of their political economy with their impact on the lives of people in migration contexts. Toward the end, the authors discuss how this leads to vulnerability for mistrust and data trading, privacy violation, racialization, and technological errors with ever-larger databases, but also how commercial and EU-level discussions fail to acknowledge the resistance and struggle facing these issues.

In the first section's final chapter 5, "Liminality, Asylum, and Arbitrariness in the Greek State's Implementation of the 2016 EU-Turkey Statement," Vasilis Vlassis reads the EU-Turkey Statement published in March 2016 as a radical recalibration of the European Union's asylum and migration policies, re-conceptualizing notions of deservedness, protection, and safety.

Introduced as a "deal" between the European Union and the state of Turkey, the statement delegated a significant part of the European Union's "border control" to neighboring Turkey following the long tradition of "outsourcing" bordering practices to third countries. The exchange for Turkey would be monetary returns, as well as acceleration of the visa liberation roadmap for Turkish citizens, thus rendering the fate of migrants a bargaining chip between the two actors. Among others, the statement also dictated the return of all newly arrived Syrians to Turkey, and the relocation of one Syrian person from Turkey to a European state for every person returned. Published under a dubious legal status, its implementation was left to the capacities of each member state separately. In the case of the Greek state, the implementing law 43765/2016 and its various subsequent amendments brought significant changes in the asylum procedures of the Greek state, including but not limited to altering the core of the asylum interviews and radically reconfiguring the composition of the appeal committees. This chapter discusses the statement as a rupture in the European Union's border, migration, and asylum regime, with a focus in the legal, administrative, and other actions that the Greek state undertook in the course of implementing it. Based on material published by NGOs, legal documents and communications of the Greek state, and research conducted in Athens, Lesvos and Chios in the period 2016–2017, this contribution seeks to understand the "complex temporality of borders" (Little 2015) that unfolded after the publishing of the statement, in the practices of Greek and Frontex border guards, asylum handlers, and police officers. It shows how the border is not a fixed entity but one that can be configured anew through sociotechnical means.

Configuration of Migration Space

The third part of the book investigates the "Configuration of Migration Space." The migration mobile corresponds to the creation of spaces—both cyber spaces and material spaces—that are re-designed to contest and circumvent border controls as well as to facilitate solidarity networks. We here draw on the notion of "mobile commons" (Papadopoulos and Tsianos 2013). Mobile commons are situated within a broader frame of critical mobilities not only of human movement but also objects, capital, information, and material things (Trimikliniotis, Parsanoglou, and Tsianos 2014). The mobile commons are dependent on being commonly produced by all the people in motion who—in the words of Trimikliniotis, Parsanoglou, and Tsianos—"are the only ones who can expand its content and meanings" (p. 53). Transgressing the dichotomy of public/private, "the mobile commons exist to the extent that people use the trails, tracks or rights and continue to generate new ones as they are on the move" (Trimikliniotis, Parsanoglou, and Tsianos 2014, 53).

The point of departure in this section is that the migration spaces constituted though cyber-material practices, such as socio-material alliances between activists, computers, the internet, transmitters and receivers of information, web platforms, and mobile phones (Galis and Neumayer 2016), also make visible migrants' attempts to resist and undo borders. In other words, if borders are everywhere (cf. Balibar 2002), then we should search for unbordering processes everywhere, too. This is what the three chapters in this section do. By configuring new urban spaces or zones, migrants strive to create new conditions of mobility and possibility, not just as ideational concepts, but also in their cyber-materiality (cf. Barad 2003). Cyber-material intertwinings bear political agency that specifically aims at undermining bordering practices. The mobile commons encapsulate the innumerable uncoordinated but cooperative actions of mobile people that contribute to its making. "People on the move create a world of knowledge, of information, of tricks for survival, of mutual care, of social relations, of services exchange, of solidarity and sociability that can be shared, used and where people contribute to sustain and expand it" (Papadopoulos and Tsianos 2013, 190). Moreover, the digital "infrastructures of connectivity" constitute a basic component of the mobile commons. The concept emphasizes the emancipatory aspects in the ever-evolving struggle against and within the border regime and thus also feeds into the third section of this book. In this second part, however, mobile commons as a concept help us encapsulate how migrant space is being configured digitally and physically by the social and political actors, migrants on the move, people in solidarity, etc. The focus here is not on the border regime(s) but on the ever-evolving migration space configured within the border regime or in response to this.

The three chapters included in this section offer different perspectives and analyses on how local authorities regulate and manage migration and which role information and communications technology (ICT) and digital technologies have for migrants' everyday lives. The focus here is on everyday practices and how information, knowledge, and relations are developed and maintained through digital means. In chapter 6, "Asylum Seekers Experiencing Forced Immobility as Offline and Online Actors," author Claudia Lintner investigates local political, socio-legal, and territorial regimes and asks in which way they frame and control refugee mobility and discursively problematize it. Her paper focuses on Wi-Fi hotspots in the city of Bolzano as particular public spaces representing urban changes and supporting or not the coexistence of people with different backgrounds in the city through the continuous negotiation of diversity and difference. It is further argued that the way public spaces are framed and controlled influences and shapes refugees' everyday lives as offline and online actors. Accordingly, there is a concern with boundary maintenance that is designed to keep out people who do not fit into the shared classification constructed by the dominant group. As such, classifications define very clearly what and who is culturally different and who appears disruptive and deviant. Examples of strongly classified public spaces include shopping malls, churches, museums, and universities, where only those who belong and behave are welcome. As such, refugees and asylum seekers are the exemplary non-citizens. Being present, they suffer simultaneously from harmful visibility and harmful invisibility. Against this background, the chapter is based on the following research question: How do local political, socio-legal, and territorial regimes frame and control refugee mobility and discursively problematize it given the presence of refugees in public spaces? And how does this shape refugees' everyday lives as offline and online actors?

In chapter 7, "Navigating the Resources of the Migrant Digital Space," Luca Rossi suggests that in order to provide a more comprehensive representation of migrants' digital space it is necessary to develop better mapping strategies for such a space. Providing an exhaustive mapping of the digital spaces that play a role into migrants' digital practices is a complex task. Migrants' digital practices, and by extension the digital space they define, are characterized by ephemerality, goal-oriented nature, heterogeneity, and often hiddenness. As a result, most of the existing research on migrants that is supported by a large amount of digital data often relies on data produced by and about major online actors: large NGOs, agencies, and official or well-established civil society groups. While this approach has undoubtedly proven to be useful, it leaves a lot of digital territory unexplored. For this reason, DIGINAUTS adopted a different approach to its digital data collection. Starting from a set of seed-resources identified through interviews and online ethnography, DIGINAUTS built a non-representative sample of online resources with a specific focus on what has been identified as relevant from the perspective of a migrant subject. Rossi suggests that content produced by and around minor, informal actors is quantitatively more abundant than what is produced by and around major actors and qualitatively complementary. The chapter offers an attempt to create better mapping strategies by exploring the Facebook component of the aforementioned dataset, in the context of the 2015 migration crisis in Europe. The dataset contains the entire (anonymized) content of 179 Facebook pages (geographically localized in Germany, Greece, Sweden, or Denmark) counting 75,043 posts and 2,118,810 comments for the period between December 2010 and June 2018.

The final chapter in this section, "'Fast Trusting': Practices of Trust During Irregularized Journeys to and Through Europe" by Nina Grønlykke Mollerup and Marie Sandberg, probes the notion of trust as not only an essential for human and societal interaction but as a socio-material practice that needs to be established repeatedly over time. Irregularized migrants' journeys are characterized by fast and insecure decision-making about which route to take, which smugglers to travel with, and more, and these decisions are a matter of life and death. For irregularized migrants navigating extreme danger, uncertainty, and changing environments, trust as a long-term commitment presents itself as exceptionally difficult to establish. The authors therefore investigate the notion of fast trusting by focusing on the trust practices of irregularized migrants and solidarity workers who help them during their journeys. Based on ethnographic fieldwork with previous irregularized migrants and solidarity workers carried out in the Danish-Swedish borderlands, in 2018 and 2019, they show that there are at least four different, yet related, trust practices enacted in the various ways irregularized migrants move through the European border regime. Mollerup and Sandberg identify these as relay trust, positional trust, institutional trust, and desperate trust. As they unfold these heterogeneous trust practices, they engage theoretically with a socio-material understanding of materiality and performativity as well as recent studies within anthropology of uncertainty concerned with the implications of crisis, borders, and precarity. Analyzing the complex stories about irregularized border-crossing journeys, they argue that trust is practiced not merely through interpersonal relations, but also through socio-material connections established between social media platforms, digital devices, smartphones, solidarity networks, narratives, and information flyers, what we term hybrid alliance building. This means that practices of trust establish themselves not only in the interfaces between humans but also in the entangled relations between humans, materialities, and technology.

Reconfiguring the Border Regime(s) and Emancipation of Space

The fourth part, "Reconfiguring the Border Regime(s) and Emancipation of Space," looks at how borders are contested and reconfigured through migrants' digital practices and how this in turn can lead to emancipation of space. When we initiated our work on the DIGINAUTS project, we were inspired by Hakim Bey's notion of TAZ—temporary autonomous zones (2003). For Bey, TAZ is a "free zone," space, room, or route that is created to enable individual or collective agency. In an idealist description, TAZ can be an actual physical location/space or a virtual location. In particular, such spaces are described as "Temporary" in contrast to a permanent institutionalized formation. "The TAZ is . . . a guerrilla operation which liberates an area (of land, of time, of imagination) and then dissolves itself to re-form elsewhere/elsewhen, before the State can crush it" (Bey 2003, 101), and "Autonomous" as for being "[b]eyond state control or other regulatory agencies" (Bey 2003, 101). TAZs are actual locations that include virtual locations:

> The TAZ has a temporary but actual location in time and a temporary but actual location in space. Nevertheless, it must also have "location" in the Web, and this location is of a different sort, not actual but virtual, not immediate but instantaneous. . . . We must consider the Web primarily as a support system, capable of carrying information from one TAZ to another. . . . Such spaces have either been neglected on the part of the State or have somehow escaped notice by the mapmakers. (Bey 2003, 101)

TAZ refers to spaces that are temporarily disconnected from an omnipresent state (Galis and Summerton 2018). The TAZ can enable flows and movements of individuals or groups: core ideas of explicitly facilitating mobility or passageways. In our context, the configuration of TAZs corresponds to the creation of spaces—both digital spaces and material spaces—that are re-configured to contest and circumvent border controls as well as to facilitate solidarity networks and mobility. Therefore, the notion of TAZ also assists us in approaching the digital world primarily as a support system, capable of carrying information from one TAZ to another. The idea of TAZ speaks directly to our notion of the migration mobile. In this book, we use the broader notion of migration space. The migration space captures the alternative infrastructure(s) we see developing through high-tech and low-tech digital practices.

Traditionally within science and technology studies (Star 1990; Bowker and Star 2000), infrastructures are largely viewed as highly standardized and highly structured entities that are typically characterized by institutional stability, long lifetimes, and clear mechanisms for maintaining at least some measure of control over the system. When we situate the idea of the migration mobile as constitutive parts of this, the conventional image of infrastructures collapses. The migration mobile that we describe involves unregulated cyber-material alternatives within a heavily technologized and surveilled environment: the border. In that sense, the migration mobile allows us to see the formation of alternative infrastructures. Not the classic view on infrastructures: they are fluid, not stable. They are beyond state control, not institutionalized, mobile, self-organized means of resistance. Here we also acknowledge the fact that migrants are vulnerable to problems of non-access and dependency upon traditional infrastructures, notably electric power and surveillance risks. The chapters of this section show a number of ways in which migrants use digital resources to enable, facilitate, or sustain migrants' individual or collective agency in configuring their journeys and migratory space. Following Bey, we argue that these spaces or zones can be viewed as temporary autonomous zones, TAZs—that is, fluid ad-hoc spaces, often beyond state surveillance, that enable flows and movements. What also follows from this position is that the construction of irregularized and illegalized migrants is refuted. Both by people on the move and by people in solidarity.

The three chapters we include in this part in different ways focus on acts of resistance and on how digital platforms, collectives, and strategies are used to provide counter-information in terms of navigation, networking, and solidarity. Where the majority of the existing literature has focused on the route to Europe and various destinations in Europe, some of the contributions in this part pay attention to the strengthening of the deportation regime, and this development is challenged through both digital and analogue practices and technologies. The chapters look at use of ICTs ranging from GPS signals to social media platforms.

In "Counter-Narrating the Mediterranean Border Regime and Reclaiming Rights: Refugee Voices in Libya and Across the Sea," the book's chapter 9 by Sara Creta and Chiara Denaro, the two authors argue that new technologies and new forms of connectivity are enhancing the creation of digital publics where the paradoxically precarious, speechless emissaries and humanitarian subjects assume new forms of resistance practice using digital tools. By advancing a more nuanced concept of "acts of citizenship" (Isin and Nielsen 2013) and by focusing on a social justice–driven approach to digital practices (Leurs and Smets 2018), this chapter investigates the human rights–oriented digital practices of those who seek to mobilize to contest the European Union's border regime of externalization and expose border practices or violations that are affecting their lives. Drawing inspiration from research conducted with people on the move surviving in Libya (both in detention centers and in urban settings), the chapter investigates how digital spaces become contested spaces of protest and rights claiming. While people on the move seek to circumvent power structures to become visible in an increasingly violent border regime enhanced by the European Union to control movement, their data could instead be unfairly used against their knowledge. In light of the increasingly market-oriented nature of humanitarian communication including the United Nations and its agencies, this chapter first attempts to suggest the need to engage with data politics in a way that considers both the politics in data as well as the politics of data. Second, it highlights the agendas and interests that advance the implementation of these technologies. Third, it focuses on prioritizing justice concerns on terms that go beyond techno-legal solutions, and positioning those who are most impacted by developments at the forefront of discussions.

Leandros Fischer and Martin Bak Jørgensen in chapter 10, "Autonomy of Migration in the Age of Deportation: Migrants' Practices Against Deportation," investigate migrant strategies especially toward and against deportation. In several European countries today, we can identify a paradigm

shift from the focus on migrants' integration to their securitization and deportation. In Denmark, the government recently changed the name of social
benefits available for refugees from an "integration benefit" to a "return benefit" and has generally stepped up deportations, and we see an expansion of
the category of deportable populations. This politicization of immigration in
Denmark has caused enormous insecurity among migrants. Similar tendencies can be observed in Germany, where the end of *Willkommenskultur* has
been met with an increase of deportations to Afghanistan and the Balkans.
They argue that this means that potential deportees and undocumented
migrants increasingly have to develop survival strategies for if and when
they are deported. Likewise, they show how migrants, here in the case of
rejected asylum seekers, refute the categorization of "rejected" and "deportable" and ultimately the illegalization of their status and presence. Migrants
are starting to share information and strategies online on how to return to
Turkey and the Middle East. In the case of Denmark, we see a still increasing number of people disappearing from the authorities and going to other
European countries living as irregular migrants or trying to apply for asylum
through the loopholes in the Dublin agreement. We see, for instance, a larger
number of rejected asylum seekers from Scandinavia applying for church
asylum in Germany, Iraqi Kurds going to Italy, Afghanis going to France, and
Palestinians going to Belgium due to networks, or new policy practices. The
chapter explores how these decisions are shaped though digital practices and
how these decisions in turn shape digital practices. The work here is explorative and based on a questioning of the existing literature in order to develop
a better understanding of the role of ICT for deportable populations. The
chapter offers some initial findings of online ethnography and ethnographic
fieldwork in northern Denmark and Hamburg on how migrants individually
and collectively use ICTs to both resist deportation but also develop strategies
for survival. The chapter also engages in a theoretical conceptualization of
reverse mobility, which offers a supplement and/or challenge to the dominant
understanding of rather linear migration flows.

   Chapter 11, "Migration and Counter-Information Practices: Enhancing
Mobility While Subverting the Mainstream Media" by Vasiliki Makrygianni
and Vasilis Galis, focuses on the emancipation of space. ICTs are of vital
importance for the preparation of the migratory trip as they are strongly linked
to the decision of departure and facilitate aspects of organization. There is a
growing number of self-organized digital collectives created and used by
migrants and people in solidarity in order to provide counter-information
in terms of navigation, networking, and solidarity. In this chapter, they discuss how counter-information digital platforms become a lens and a tool
for shared decision-making, information spreading, and navigation among
migrants and solidarians. Various platforms that act as spaces of solidarity

have been created by Net communities that provide (counter-)information, challenge both discursively and materially the idea of borders and actively facilitate the freedom of movement. Crucially, the ways in which migrants and people in solidarity appropriate and repurpose these platforms, rather than simply use them, have received less attention. Thus, this chapter simultaneously examines how migrants are using ICT and how their varied usage affects not only the migration journey but also the digital platforms themselves. The analysis is based on empirical material collected through ethnographic interviews conducted mainly in Greece in the period 2016 to 2018, as well as digital data collected using Application Programming Interface interfaces and web-scraping techniques. The ambition is to generate a heterogeneous set of data, produced within context-specific platforms, that can be further explored and combined with qualitative data from the interviews. The chapter moves beyond the methodological state of the art in combining quantitative and qualitative methods and online/offline data gathering to more effectively research the complex, cross-platform nature of migrants' ICT use and counter-information.

CONCLUSION

The Migration Mobile offers an account of the very different technologies implicated in border crossing and migration management. Through analyses of empirical cases drawing from the European border regimes, the book investigates how technologies employed by states and EU border agencies configure the border regimes; how migration spaces are configured by political actors through uses and re-uses of low-and high-tech technologies; and finally, how the border regimes and "the border industrial complex" are contested and reconfigured by the use of ICT by migrants and solidarity networks.

REFERENCES

Agustín, Ó. G., and M. B. Jørgensen. 2019. *Solidarity and the "Refugee Crisis" in Europe*. Cham: Springer.

Alencar, A. 2020. "Mobile communication and refugees: An analytical review of academic literature." *Sociology Compass* 14 (8): e12802.

Antonakaki, M., B. Kasparek, and G. Maniatis. 2016. "Counting heads and channelling bodies: The hotspot centre Vial in Chios, Greece." *Transit Migration* 2.

Awad, I., and J. Tossell. 2021. "Is the smartphone always a smart choice? Against the utilitarian view of the 'connected migrant.'" *Information, Communication & Society* 24 (4): 611–26.

Baldassar, L., M. Nedelcu, L. Merla, and R. Wilding. 2016. "ICT-based co-presence in transnational families and communities: Challenging the premise of face-to-face proximity in sustaining relationships." *Global Networks* 16 (2): 133–44.

Balibar, E. 2002. "World borders, political borders." *PMLA/Publications of the Modern Language Association of America* 117 (1): 68–78.

Barad, K. 2003. "Posthumanist performativity: Toward an understanding of how matter comes to matter." *Signs: Journal of Women in Culture and Society* 28 (3): 801–31.

Bey, H. 2003. *TAZ: The Temporary Autonomous Zone, Ontological Anarchy, Poetic Terrorism*. Williamsburg, NY: Autonomedia.

Borkert, N., K. E. Fisher, and E. Yafi. 2018. "The best, the worst and hardest to find: How people, mobiles, and social media connect migrants in(to) Europe." *Social Media + Society*. Advance Online Publication: 10.1177/2056305118764428.

Boseley, M. "'Like a horror movie': 19-year-old shares Ukraine escape on TikTok," *The Guardian*, March 11, 2022, https://www.theguardian.com/world/2022/mar/11/diana-totok-ukraine-escape-tiktok. Accessed March 14, 2022.

Bowker, G. C., and S. L. Star. 2000. *Sorting Things Out: Classification and Its Consequences*. Cambridge, MA: MIT Press.

Browne, S. 2015. *Dark Matters*. Durham, NC: Duke University Press.

Cabot, H. 2010. *On the Doorstep of Europe: Asylum and Citizenship in Greece*. Philadelphia: University of Pennsylvania Press.

Casas-Cortes, M., S. Cobarrubias, N. De Genova, G. Garelli, G. Grappi, C. Heller, and I. Peano. 2015. "New keywords: migration and borders." *Cultural Studies* 29 (1): 55–87.

Chayka, K. "Watching the world's "first TikTok war." *The New Yorker*, March 3, 2022, https://www.newyorker.com/culture/infinite-scroll/watching-the-worlds-first-tiktok-war. Accessed March 14, 2022.

Croeser, S. 2014. *Global Justice and the Politics of Information: The Struggle Over Knowledge* (Volume 52). New York: Routledge.

Darling, J., and H. Bauder. 2019. "Introduction–Sanctuary cities and urban struggles: Rescaling migration, citizenship, and rights." In *Sanctuary Cities and Urban Struggles*, 1–22. Manchester, UK: Manchester University Press.

De Genova, N., ed. 2017. *The Borders of "Europe": Autonomy of Migration, Tactics of Bordering*. Durham, NC: Duke University Press.

Dijstelbloem, H. 2021. *Borders as Infrastructure: The Technopolitics of Border Control*. Cambridge, MA: MIT Press.

Dijstelbloem, H., A. Meijer, and M. Besters. 2011. "The migration machine." In *Migration and the New Technological Borders of Europe*, 1–21. London: Palgrave Macmillan.

Ehn, B., O. Löfgren, and R. Wilk. 2016. *Exploring Everyday-Life: Strategies for Ethnography and Cultural Analysis*. Lanham, MD: Rowman & Littlefield Publishers.

Fischer, L., and M. B. Jørgensen. 2021. "Impossible research? – Ethical challenges in the (digital) study of deportable populations within the European border regime." In *Research Methodologies and Ethical Challenges in Digital Migration Studies— Caring for (Big) Data?*, edited by M. Sandberg et al. London: Palgrave MacMillan.

Flick, U. 2018. *An Introduction to Qualitative Research*. Thousand Oaks, CA: Sage Publications Limited.

Galis, V. 2021. "The redundant researcher: fieldwork, solidarity and migration." In *Research Methodologies and Ethical Challenges in Digital Migration Studies— Caring for (Big) Data?*, edited by M. Sandberg et al. London: Palgrave Macmillan.

Galis, V., and C. Neumayer. 2016. "Laying claim to social media by activists: a cyber-material detournement." *Social media+ society* 2 (3): 2056305116664360.

Galis, V., and J. Summerton. 2018. "We are all foreigners in an analogue world: cyber-material alliances in contesting immigration control in Stockholm's metro system." *Social Movement Studies* 17 (3): 299–317.

Galis, V., S. Tzokas, and A. Tympas. 2016. "Bodies folded in migrant crypts: Dis/ ability and the material culture of border-crossing." *Societies* 6 (2): 10.

Gerhards, J., H. Lengfeld, Z. S. Ignácz, F. K. Kley, and M. Priem. 2019. *European Solidarity in Times of Crisis: Insights from a Thirteen-Country Survey*. New York: Routledge.

Gillespie, M., L. Ampofo, M. Cheesman, B. Faith, E. Iliadou, A. Issa, S. Osseiran, and D. Skleparis. 2016. *Mapping Refugee Media Journeys: Smartphones and Social Media Networks*. Research report. Milton Keynes, UK: The Open University.

Isin, E. F., and G. M. Nielsen, eds. 2013. *Acts of Citizenship*. London: Zed Books Ltd.

Jakes, L. "For Ukraine's refugees, Europe opens doors that were shut to others." *New York Times*, February 26, 2022, https://www.nytimes.com/2022/02/26/us/politics/ ukraine-europe-refugees.html. Accessed March 14, 2022.

Konotey-Ahulu, O. "Ukraine crisis highlights Europe's history of treating some refugees differently." Bloomberg, March 10, 2022, https://www.bloomberg.com /news/articles/2022-03-10/refugees-of-color-fleeing-ukraine-are-being-met-with -discrimination-delay. Accessed March 14, 2022.

Krause, U. 2017. "Researching forced migration: critical reflections on research eth- ics during fieldwork." *Refugee Studies Centre. Working Paper Series* (123).

Lahusen, C., and M. T. Grasso. 2018. *Solidarity in Europe: Citizens' Responses in Times of Crisis*. Berlin: Springer Nature.

Law, J., and A. Mol. 2001. "Situating technoscience: an inquiry into spatialities." *Environment and Planning D: Society and Space* 19 (5): 609–21.

Leurs, K., and K. Smets. 2018. "Five questions for digital migration studies: Learning from digital connectivity and forced migration in(to) Europe." *Social Media + Society* 4 (1): 2056305118764425.

Lyon, D. 2013. "The border is everywhere: ID cards, surveillance and the other." In *Global Surveillance and Policing*, edited by Elia Zureik and Mark Salter, 78–94. London: Willan.

Mezzadra, S., and B. Neilson. 2012. "Borderscapes of differential inclusion: Subjectivity and struggles on the threshold of justice's excess." In *The Borders of Justice*, edited by É. Balibar, S. Mezzadra, and R. Samāddāra, 181–204. Philadelphia, PA: Temple University Press.

Mezzadra, S., and B. Neilson. 2013. *Border as Method, or, the Multiplication of Labor*. Durham, NC: Duke University Press.

Millner, N. 2011. "From 'refugee' to 'migrant' in Calais solidarity activism: Re-staging undocumented migration for a future politics of asylum." *Political Geography* 30 (6): 320–28.

Moser, I., and J. Law. 2006. "Fluids or flows? Information and qualculation in medical practice." *Information Technology & People* 19 (1): 55–73.

Papadopoulos, D., and V. S. Tsianos. 2013. "After citizenship: autonomy of migration, organisational ontology and mobile commons." *Citizenship Studies* 17 (2): 178–96.

Parmar, A. 2020. "Arresting (non) citizenship: The policing migration nexus of nationality, race and criminalization." *Theoretical Criminology* 24 (1): 28–49.

Pittaway, E., L. Bartolomei, and R. Hugman. 2010. "'Stop stealing our stories': The ethics of research with vulnerable groups." *Journal of Human Rights Practice* 2 (2): 229–51.

Ponzanesi, S., and K. Leurs. 2014. "On digital crossings in Europe." *Crossings: Journal of Migration & Culture* 5 (1): 3–22.

Rodríguez, C., B. Ferron, and K. Shamas. 2014. "Four challenges in the field of alternative, radical and citizens' media research." *Media, Culture & Society* 36 (2): 150–66.

Rozakou, K. 2016. "Crafting the volunteer: Voluntary associations and the reformation of sociality." *Journal of Modern Greek Studies* 34 (1): 79–102.

Sánchez-Querubín, N., and R. Rogers. 2018. "Connected routes: Migration studies with digital devices and platforms." *Social Media + Society* 4 (1): 2056305118764427.

Sandberg, M., L. Rossi, M. B. Jørgensen, and V. Galis. 2021. *Research Methodologies and Ethical Challenges in Digital Migration Studies—Caring for (Big) Data*. London: Palgrave MacMillan.

Squire, V. 2010. "Politicizing mobility." In *The Contested Politics of Mobility*, 49–50. New York: Routledge.

Star, S. L. 1990. "Power, technology and the phenomenology of conventions: on being allergic to onions." *The Sociological Review* 38 (1): 26–56.

Stierl, M. 2020. "Do no harm? The impact of policy on migration scholarship." *Environment and Planning C: Politics and Space* 2399654420965567.

Trimikliniotis, N., D. Parsanoglou, and V. Tsianos. 2014. *Mobile Commons, Migrant Digitalities and the Right to the City*. Cham: Springer.

Tsianos, V., and S. Karakayali. 2010. "Transnational migration and the emergence of the European border regime: an ethnographic analysis." *European Journal of Social Theory* 13 (3): 373–87.

van der Ploeg, I., and I. Sprenkels. 2011. "Migration and the machine-readable body: Identification and biometrics." In *Migration and the New Technological Borders of Europe*, edited by H. Dijstelbloem and A. Meijer, 68–104. London: Palgrave Macmillan.

van Liempt, I. C., and J. Zijlstra. 2017. "Smart(phone) travelling: understanding the use and impact of mobile technology on irregular migration journeys." *International Journal of Migration and Border Studies* 3 (2–3): 174–91.

Wissink, M., F. Düvell, and A. van Eerdewijk. 2013. "Dynamic migration intentions and the impact of socio-institutional environments: A transit migration hub in Turkey." *Journal of Ethnic and Migration Studies* 39 (7): 1087–105.

Zapata-Barrero, R., and E. Yalaz. 2020. "Qualitative migration research ethics: a roadmap for migration scholars." *Qualitative Research Journal* 20 (3): 269–79.

Zaru, D. "Europe's unified welcome of Ukrainian refugees exposes 'double standard' for nonwhite asylum seekers: Experts." March 8, 2022, ABC News, https://abcnews.go.com/International/europes-unified-ukrainian-refugees-exposes-double-standard-nonwhite/story?id=83251970. Accessed March 14, 2022.

PART II

Configuration of the Border Regime(s)

Chapter 2

The Embodied Identity of Migration and Border Biometrics

Brigitta Kuster and Vassilis S. Tsianos[1]

INTRODUCTION

This chapter is about the recourse to the body on borders and will endeavor to outline some of the particular questions posed by such an ontology of the body based on control politics and its further processing as a data-based identity in the context of European migration policy. In the first part of the text, we will cite three specific cases: These came about as a result of refugee movements into Europe from 2015 onward, and have—as we will show, not rationally justified—stoked up controversies and subsequently been deployed as arguments to make the case both for social and political acceptance and for the desirability of increasing data interoperability and expanding the scope of European large-scale information technology (IT) systems. We are neither interested in these "cases" per se, nor the stories associated with them—not even in the sense of a connecting link between person and documentation or biometric data processing—but rather their "fabula."

With Mieke Bal's work on narratology (2018), which distinguishes between "fabula," "story," and "text," and locates the analysis of narrativity in cultural contexts in their complex interplay, a fabula can be understood as a social memory trace. After reading a text, to which the story provides access, it remains with the reader. A fabula thus connects to the social imagination; it is not created by an individual case or story, but rather by the narrative order of a series of events. Michel de Certeau has spoken of a fable as symbolizing a given society, and that when it speaks, it refers simultaneously to orality and fiction (de Certeau 1992, 3f). The fabula, however, is by no means to be understood in terms of a reputation (good or bad) or as a rumor; rather, it is that which persists beyond textuality or datafication. Within the context of the cases we will examine, the fabula is the social memory of border control. It asks what remains of the body, what voice it raises under the conditions of its biometric capture at the border. In the second part, we will summarize our proposed concept of embodied identity of migration. This concept allows us to conceive of a conflicted social body in which the fabula of transit migration and the fabula of migration control meet.

Hussein K., Bilal C., and Franco A.

When Eurodac launched its activities in January 2003, its aim, on one hand, was to prevent multiple asylum applications or, in other words, double identities, and on the other, to control so-called secondary migration to Europe. It was in this second sphere of action's catchment area (i.e., of "digital deportability" [cf. Tsianos and Kuster 2016b; Papadopoulos, Stephenson, and Tsianos 2008]), or the radical restriction of the possibility of reaching points of arrival that do not comply with asylum law regulation, that the incidents surrounding Hussein K. were to unfold.[2] Hussein K. entered Germany via Greece at the end of 2015 in order to apply for asylum in Freiburg im Breisgau. His case was to become a public controversy after he committed a sexual offense and a murder in Germany. Over the course of the ensuing investigations, it emerged that the German authorities were completely unaware that this asylum seeker from Afghanistan, who had been registered since 2013, had already a criminal record and had been convicted as a criminal in Greece.

However, the European registration systems for criminals (SIS, Interpol) and refugees (Eurodac)—in particular the Greek implementation of Eurodac—were to become the foci of public criticism. Hussein K. had been regularly registered in Eurodac, the European Union fingerprint database for identifying asylum seekers and irregular border-crossers, as someone who had applied for asylum in Tyros, Greece, on January 8, 2013. However, in 2015, it was standard practice in Germany not to transfer registered asylum seekers back to Greece as per the Dublin III Regulation—on account of the 2011 rulings of the European Court of Human Rights and the Court of Justice of the European Union regarding systemic deficiencies in the Greek asylum system. Thus, technically speaking, the Eurodac database had nothing to do with this case; Hussein K. had by no means fallen through the cracks in the registration process. So why then was Eurodac to become the focus of such public attention?[3]

"Maria L's Murder Case. Hussein K's path across Europe" ran the headline in the magazine *Focus* on December 15, 2016: "How can such a thing happen? How was it possible that a refugee could travel across Europe, is sentenced to ten years in prison for a violent act in Greece on the way, and yet two-and-a-half years later allegedly rapes and murders 19-year-old Maria L. in Freiburg?" In the *vox populi* across the media, indignation spread about the uselessness of limited information on the embodied identity of migration, from a security perspective. This came about through collecting biometric data tied to specific purposes and restricted access due to their recording in a database separated from other state personal registration systems (not least for data protection reasons, that is, to protect privacy and safeguard the right of the individual). The German weekly magazine *Der Spiegel* finally clarified the facts around the topic that had so aroused public opinion:

> In any case, data concerning Hussein's legal record had not appeared anywhere outside Greece. After he violated parole, the Greek prosecutor raised the alert about him, but only on a national level. He did not, however, instruct Greek police to have an international search warrant issued for Hussein K., although it seemed obvious that K. had fled the country. (*Der Spiegel* 51/2016, 31)

With the Hussein K. incident, the long-standing clamor for interoperability between existing European databases VIS, SIS, Eurodac, Interpol, etc., suddenly became comprehensible, if one follows the technological determinism that underlies the rationale for this identification policy: Had the databases been interlinked, it was often argued, Hussein K. would have already been arrested once he applied for asylum and the crime could thus have been prevented. As with Pre-crime, better known from the 2002 film *Minority Report*, directed by Spielberg, interoperable databases would seem to hold the promise of robust prevention. From this perspective, interoperability shows itself to be a tried-and-tested means of state-driven coercion, even if it considerably restricts personal rights and the rights of self-determination as well as privacy protection. Were interoperability to function, the embodied identity of migration would come dangerously close to criminal anthropological theories about a *delinquente nato*, for example, as developed by Cesare Lombroso in the nineteenth century or by Francis Galton, the "inventor" of biometric identification with a fingerprint.[4] Closely aligned to the discourse on criminality, migration, in times of the war on terror, has been reframed in such a way that striking historical resonances to the nineteenth century reappear and can equally be detected in terms of dissecting abstractions and biometric visualizations of the body (cf. Amoore and Hall 2009, 454).[5] While migration has always served as a convenient point of reference for diffuse fears and unspecific threats, migrants have constantly been perceived and portrayed as illegitimate (especially over the course of illegalization) and potentially criminal; otherwise they are treated as victims, particularly in the wake of 9/11 in the context of the discourse on international migration, as a discursive connection, referred to in the literature as the "migration-security nexus."[6] It denotes a steadily growing linkage between migratory and security issues. Security issues are thereby increasingly treated as transcending nationally bound societies. For example, a June 8, 2017, Council of the European Union document expresses the "conviction" that "Member States of the European Union can only provide security and protection for their people through a common effort, as only together do they have the relevant means and information, in particular as regards identifying those persons who enter the Area of Security, Freedom and Justice threatening common European values."[7] The document further states that "recent terrorist attacks and other criminal acts showed that the use of fraudulent identity information repeatedly played a key role in the perpetrators' *modus operandi*."

Bilal C., a young Algerian, has operated within the realm of threads that such a kind of danger defense tries to shed light on with its spotlight. He has been in the Federal Republic of Germany since the summer of 2015 and has been in custody in Aachen since April 2016. Arrested for pick-pocketing and social security fraud, the Federal Prosecutor's Office in Karlsruhe now accuses him of having conducted reconnaissance on the Balkan route for the attackers on the Bataclan concert hall in Paris on November 13, 2015, in cahoots with another accomplice. He allegedly researched access routes in advance—from Budapest via Austria and Germany to Brussels or via Patras to Bari and through Switzerland and France to Brussels—and transmitted detailed route descriptions via Facebook, or practical tips for accommodation and photos of border crossings to one of the attackers, the Belgian Abdelhamid Abaaoud, nicknamed Omar, considered the leader of the terrorist commando cell. According to an article in *Die Welt* on November 13, 2016: "Analysis of cell phones and social networks revealed that Bilal C. had indeed traveled through the Balkan states and Austria on his way to Germany in July 2015 as the alleged Syrian 'Jdjrad Samas.' En route, he kept setting up new Facebook accounts and communicated via encrypted chat programs probably with Abaaoud in Syria."[8]

In a *Deutschlandfunk* broadcast of February 2, 2017, the English term "scout" was used to characterize Bilal C. Moreover, the investigative group set up by the German Federal Criminal Police Office immediately in the aftermath in order to probe these incidents was called "scout." We are struck by how Bilal C.'s reconnaissance and investigative practices in many ways resembles how a migration researcher operates. Conversely, however, as a whole this episode equally amounts to the nightmare of every critical liberal migration scholar who criticizes the migration-security nexus as counter-factually overemphasizing security aspects and regulatory policies in migration control. Among the specters haunting a migration researcher's bad dreams are, of course, the perfect implementation of interoperability being the apotheosis of the migration-security nexus at the level of data collection. And amid this migration researcher's horror scenarios, the surveillance-state approach to so-called mixed flows of transnational mobility would realize its full potential.

Indeed, at present, through access modalities, data traces of mobile bodies and the relevant databases are increasingly becoming institutionally linked to criminality, thus reinforcing a migration policy oriented toward risk profiles. Hence, the so-called nexus goes well beyond discursive connections of migration, flight, and terror. This can be keenly witnessed not only in the history of increasing interoperability of European databases, but also in law enforcement agencies' ever-expanding access rights to data related to migration and flight. As in the previous example of Hussein K., in the case of Bilal C., the commotion over which articulates the equation of terror and flight, the insight into an incomplete and not yet sufficiently operative interoperability came *post factum*. And indeed, it is undeniable that the capacity for interoperability consists in increasing the probability of a match (i.e., an equation). Obviously, this equally increases the likelihood of false matches. Interoperability's purpose, however, is that it promises a proactive effect, and even suggests prevention: It is supposed to ensure that something—in this instance the match between flight and terrorism—does not take place, at least according to the dominant sociotechnical discourse. In this curiously paradoxical effort to prevent crime and further develop criminological thinking through a retrospective linking of hitherto unrelated influencing variables, the specter of the "dangerous person," as in the figure of the German neologism *Gefährder* (potentially dangerous individual or threat) emerges as a kind of ghostly projection, whose contours emerge over the course of the increasingly dense intermingling of migration and terrorism. This intermingling and superimposing of matters related to migration, security, and counter-terrorism, in turn, is ensured by the growing interoperability of databases that follow different objectives. In Germany, for example, as of 2004, *Gefährder* have been defined as "those for whom facts justify the assumption that they could commit significant criminal acts."[9] Data on *Gefährder* are regularly compared with data from foreign authorities. We want to emphasize that this type of a risk and offender profile cannot be understood without taking into account historical linkages between race, racism, and migration control.

If we understand Bilal C. as someone who explored migration issues with regard to the migration-security nexus, we articulate the fact that it was not Bilal C. who invented the connection between terrorism and flight/migration, but rather the control centers and the long history of criminology. Migration comes first. Movement precedes its control. And researchers generally come last. Ultimately, research and knowledge production in the sense of state building and securing are also connected by a non-blameless history. This equally holds true for border studies, even if they are meant to represent critical thinking. The Islamic State, in turn, should certainly be understood as a fascistoid war machine; it exploited the existing superimposition of refugees and terrorists, deliberately targeting anti-Islamic racism to radicalize Muslims throughout Europe as well, in the sense of the terror militias. This political calculus, based on the European stigmatization of refugees as terrorists, is in line with Islamic State's long-announced strategy to radicalize Muslims across Europe by exacerbating conflicts between white Europeans and second-and umpteenth-generation migrants and by inflaming racist tensions.

"Challenges and practices for establishing the identity of third-country nationals in migration procedures," as the title of a study published by the EU Commission in 2017[10] states, is obviously a complex as well as contingent matter, not only because migrants are often unable and/or unwilling to provide valid proof of identity,[11] but rather because countries where immigration occurs often do not have a clear legal or operational definition of "identity," which they can apply in migration procedures and biometric data collection processes for migrants. Hence, the report just cited identifies a considerable diversity of methods across individual EU member states not only for establishing and documenting identity,[12] but also with regard to measures ranging from fingerprinting and taking photographs to documenting biographical information, even personal interviews, language biometric evaluations, the collection of bio-data such as gender, age, and, most recently, the reading of data carriers.[13] If one examines those processes deployed for dealing with identity at the border, the essential difference between what counts as documenting identity (in the sense of ascertaining somebody's identity) and what is called establishing identity (in the sense of securing its validity) becomes strikingly evident. While dimensions of cultural technology can be determined in those practices deployed in documenting an identity, establishing identity points to the legally codified and institutionally specified inscription of a previously observed identity in state registries. Hence, as part of the securing process, previously collected biographic or biometric information is assigned a name or, as in the case of Eurodac, a record and identification number. The process of documenting a person, however, proves to be far more volatile, unsteady, and precarious. It vacillates between documentation and verification. Verification, for example, that a person is indeed who he or she claims to be can be established through the presentation of an identity document or through the live capture of his or her biometric data. In the latter case, it is a matter of the initial reading, extraction, and recording of identity-related information from a person's body, referred to as "identity enrollment" at the border or during the asylum procedure, for example, via codified measures and procedures executed by a police records department. Another key difference over the course of identity management arises between identification and verification; authentication or verification involves checking whether a person is who he or she claims to be. Also known as positive recognition, this requires a one-to-one match (i.e., an unambiguous comparison of the captured live data with the registered data of one and the same person). In stark contrast to this process are those procedures executed by Eurodac. They correspond to identification by a so-called one-to-many (1:n) matching of fingerprint templates; considered as negative recognition, their objective is to prevent one person using multiple identities.

A focus study published in 2017 and written by Julian Tangermann on the challenges and practices of establishing identity during the migration process in a German context[14] cites the case of Franco A. This specific case was to give rise to widespread public discussion on the quality or shortcomings of documenting identity in the asylum process. Franco A. was a right-wing extremist and an openly anti-Semitic soldier in the German armed forces who, under the name of David Benjamin, posed as a Syrian refugee and was granted subsidiary protection over the course of his asylum procedure. After his fingerprints were recorded and stored, he was registered at a first reception facility for refugees in Giessen in the federal state Hesse in late December 2015 and subsequently applied for asylum in Zirndorf, Bavaria, in January 2016. Franco A.'s identity fraud was neither discovered at the time of registration, nor when his biometric data were recorded, nor at his "asylum interview" in November 2016. Ultimately, a provisional arrest by Austrian police at Vienna airport—the result of bizarre wheeling and dealing involving weapons and right-wing propaganda material—was to ensnare Franco A. Subsequent investigations by the German Federal Criminal Police Office, eventually revealed, not least on the basis of fingerprint data, that this man was none other than a twenty-eight-year-old first lieutenant in the German Armed Forces with the Franco-German *Jägerbatallion* 291 stationed in Illkirch, France.[15] In light of this incident, the German Federal Ministry of the Interior ordered an inspection in which two thousand asylum decisions with a similar profile had to be re-examined. Although no other case with a similar procedural error was discovered, the implementation of the planned technical improvements for establishing identities was then escalated; these included the automated cross-checking of photos that had been initially created and stored by the Federal Office for Migration and Refugees, or the analysis of cell phone data.[16]

Even with the dissemination of this particular fabula concerning European borders, however, no direct linkage exists between the case itself and the primarily technologically oriented expansion of the means used in identity management.[17] One could argue that clearly no *technical* failure occurred in this particular instance. Rather, the decisive factor relates to a much older aspect of identification practices, namely very basic *social interaction*. It is reported that Franco A. stunningly succeeded in convincing the asylum office staff that he, as a French-speaking Syrian, should have his interview conducted in French. The political capital, however, that Franco A. managed to accrue as a right-wing radical worked out well; he is now hailed as a whistle-blower among right-wing circles. The basis for his heroic deed remains simple, however, for it involves the contingency of securing migrant identity.[18]

EMBODIED IDENTITY OF MIGRATION

Since 2010, we have been following how Eurodac functions and examining its practices: We not only visited the headquarters of this European administration, but also talked to transit migrants on their way to Europe—at its external border or within internal European border conflict zones, where the crisis engendered by Schengen has manifested itself repeatedly on a short-term basis: Evros 2009, Igoumenitsa/Brindisi 2011/2012, Vienna 2012/2013, Lesvos and Chios 2014–2016, and Ventimiglia 2018, to name a few of the numerous sites and periods that were central to our research. Despite a trial of strength in an undoubtedly controversial relationship between transit migrants and those agents who control and regulate their mobility and autonomy, it was paramount from the outset of our research that we conceptualize how the practices of control and migration interact. We thus not only focused our interest into examining Eurodac's biometric database in terms of its technical functioning and political rationale. For us, the question of conceptually locating transit migrants was key in looking at the processing of identity in the form of fingerprint templates and their circulation under the particular conditions and constraints for the purpose of migration regulation and control, or for the definition and fixation of an identity of migration.[19] Our aim was to be able to conceive of material-semiotic and sociotechnical entities in the context of Eurodac, where forms of knowledge, social practices, and infrastructures converge and potentially clash. In order to address this complex and conflictual intertwining of technology, social relations, and politics, we speak of a sociotechnical assemblage in relation to Eurodac. In doing so, we grapple with the co-presence of technical action within contexts of social interaction (i.e., technical processes and human practices from the perspective of the distributed agencies of activities by different actors and agents within the context of hybrid action; Rammert 2006). In contrast to

Rammert's notion of "constellation," however, all the heterogeneous elements retain their multiplicity in the sociotechnical assemblage. Hence, they form a common vector without ceasing to modify each other, thereby reducing their diversity. It is only in this way that we can conceptualize the autonomous actor status of transit migrants in its protagonism, without losing sight of how they stand together with the agents of control, or oppose them in a sharpened conflict of interests. Here, we refer to the concept of "surveillance assemblage" as formulated by Kevin D. Haggerty and Richard V. Ericson. According to these authors, a "surveillance assemblage" operates by abstracting human bodies from their territorial situations and splitting them off into a series of separate streams (Haggerty and Ericson 2000, 606). Here, however, the concept of surveillance generalizes the spatial setting of a prison, that is, it relates the governance of individuals to confining a body in a more or less total institution. This disciplinary-political genealogy of surveillance can hardly be applied to a migration control setting at the border. For border control invariably involves a movement of either inclusion or exclusion. Spatially speaking, the border is not a milieu, but rather a revolving door. At the border only two possibilities exist: Come in! or Stay out! Hello or goodbye—as a third and increasingly practiced imperative here: *fygé*, hit the road, abscond. In most cases, the data flows generated by such a bifurcatory revolving door as an abstraction and separation of human bodies only have an impact whenever we speak of secondary migration on European territory. The separated data flows thus address the uncertain verifiability of migrants *after* their identification at the European Union's external borders. Geographically speaking and in relation to the Schengen Zone, this border proves to be almost ubiquitous. It establishes a migrant condition that we call "digital deportability."

Hence, in Eurodac's day-to-day operations, biometric technology and digital database architecture are not applied, but rather brought into action within the process of a common European asylum system and the Europeanization of border security policies, as well as anti-terror and internal security policies in order to both produce and fix, maintain, authenticate, sort, and secure what can be conceived as the embodied identity of migration in Europe. As we view matters, such a co-constitutive interplay of human and nonhuman actors and things, of technical and sociopolitical issues in border conflicts, concerns not least that dual constellation between the autonomy of migration[20] and state control, into which we intervened with the notion of the information and control continuum in order to show that what we have observed empirically "in the field" does not correspond to random episodes of border events, but rather that border conflicts are contingent, and above all endemic (cf. Tsianos and Kuster 2012). This is because within a particular sociotechnical assemblage of European migration and border control those control practices are invariably reactive; they occur subsequently to the multiplicity and to the unpredictability inherent in the mobility of transit migrants. "Migration comes first. Movement comes before its control" (Kuster and Tsianos 2016a, 54). However, analytically, autonomy cannot be separated from control. This notion of the information and control continuum thus aims to show that the practices, tactics, and forms of knowledge of transit migrants do not stand outside the current sociotechnical assemblage of European migration and border control in which their embodied identity of migration is created and contested. Migrants thus find themselves in that contested continuity that the fiction of identity is meant to catch up with. Hence, we speak of migration being a co-constitutive and self-reflexive part of the information and control continuum. It is critical at all times to simultaneously keep track of the technologies of information and control and the practices, tactics, and forms of knowledge of the border. For example, it must be taken into account that border-crossing practices are often strongly *narrativized* and function via myths, error, and rumors, which then find themselves reprocessed as border controversies in the media, as in the three border fabulas recounted earlier about Hussein K., Bilal C., and Franco A.

This information and control continuum, however, extends not only between cross-border movements of migration, their autonomies, and the sociotechnical operations of control, but also, on one hand, between moments of bifurcatory experience and the signifying force of the border, and, on the other, the dissipating effects of data flows aimed at identification, and emanating from them to a border's next temporal-spatial incision. With the embodied identity of migration, we thus address the field of *collisions* and *adhesions* that span transit migrants' practices, conceived as autonomous, and the identity anchored in their bodies, ascribed to them by control systems. The location of identity within this information and control continuum of the sociotechnical assemblage of European migration and border control cannot be decided on one side or the other—panoptic realism versus empiricism of the autonomous subjects of transit migration—if one does not want to reduce migration to a system antagonism, and to determine the border as a site for enmity (cf. Mbembe 2017). In order to grapple with the whole field in which the identity of migration is not only contested, but also produced and made plausible, in which all political and social constructions, intractabilities, and volatilities of a body's mobile spatiality can be inscribed, as well as erased,[21] we have devised the notion of migration's embodied identity. Of course, as we ourselves have repeatedly argued, it is true that migrants now embody the border by carrying this mobile barrier around with them in the form of their fingerprints (Tsianos and Kuster 2016b; Kuster and Tsianos 2013).[22] Their "own" body thus becomes a password, a cipher enabling or preventing access, as Gilles Deleuze (1993) described it in his well-known text on the dividualizing societies of control. Yet it is equally true that the embodied identity of migration seeks to pin down the persistence and dynamics of bodies, things, and concerns of transit migration to Europe, fixing them by means of subsequent acts of governmental validation, as well as inscription and identification in the field of legal claims (cf. Kuster 2020).

But how, in fact, does a State inscribe a body? Craig Robertson has spoken of particular documentative technologies and procedures that are able to identify, valorize, and confirm "an administratively useful identity" (Robertson 2009, 337). This can only be accomplished, Robertson argues, through a verification regime that produces identity as a stable object crucial to the modern state's governance practices (Robertson 2009, 329).[23] Such state-controlled technologies and practices are still defining and in the formative phase today, and not least in Hollywood. They constitute, however, far less imaginary horizons through dream machines or executive acts of state violence via "paper empires," as Ann Laura Stoler (2002), for example, discussed for the late imperial nineteenth-century archives. Rather, documented identities are now produced on European frontiers in networked and intelligent database systems and run by agencies. And as the evolution of EU-LISA shows, database systems are evolving from simple index databases toward increased relationality and nominality by growing capacity for interoperability through integrated data management architectures. Interoperability is not simply a matter of increased compatibility, but is in itself an assemblage, as the term refers to the ability of independent, heterogeneous systems to work together as seamlessly as possible in order to exchange information in an efficient and usable manner. Moreover, and we consider this particularly important, the data managed in the present case and that enable the usability of the exchange, postulate absolute identification through the body: The body is liable for the inscribed identity. Hence, we speak of a new tendency toward body ontology, understood as a digitally managed metric of an immigrant *bios (βίος)*. Here, a singular and individuated body is reduced to traces identifiable by it, to be read, in turn, by machines, as Irma van der Ploeg (2005) has highlighted. Recording migrant volatility as an algorithmic trace, identity is to become a mathematical certainty in order to thus inscribe the ephemeral location of identity in migration *as* and *in* the corpora of administration in the context of Schengen's sociotechnical assemblage of European migration and border control.[24]

Initially, we used the term "embodied identity of migration" almost counter-intuitively, for embodiment, especially in the humanities, is usually employed as an experience-centered term and assumes a subjective perception of the body. In transit migration to Europe, however, not only do permanent transition and change, as emphasized by social constructivism,[25] play a role, but also mutations and bodily forces of gravity, as well as their standstill or freezing, not infrequently violently enforced in order to concoct the weight of evidence, whereby biometric data serve as authenticators (i.e., as authenticating instances of a truth with regard to the body). Indeed, border studies as a discipline fall short when it comes to articulating the relations between symbolic and physical, geographical, territorial, and relational dimensions of bordering processes, as Claudia Bruns (2020a) points out; she thus refers to the desideratum of a body history from a feminist perspective particularly within this field of study. Specifically, with embodied identity of migration, however, it is not merely a matter of coercion or dis/identification; it is not only about inscriptions of subjectivation or differential iteration, but rather about simulations and prognoses with different materializing scaling effects. These range from fingerprint records to national citizenship or from subject to profile, from route reconstruction to risk prevention, anticipatory and recursive, forward-tracing and back-tracing.

Eurodac, along with its co-producing data machines at the service of its sociotechnical assemblage, represents an attempt to reduce the embodied identity of migration to its difference as a machine-readable ontology of the body (by means of fingerprints), and thus to establish a "location of identity" within this information and control continuum. However, the corporeality of migration and the nonspecific flight of the flesh's desire cannot be understood within a paradigm of mobility versus control, but only as multiplicity in the literal sense, and not as multiplicity of subject positions, but rather as multiplicity of differential connections.[26] The embodied identity of migration denotes the location of identity, which must necessarily be thought of as differential because its site, namely the body itself, is differential. Under the signal of a stronger mandate for EU-LISA, the interoperability of all existing European databases, as well as the development and management of new large-scale IT systems, the possibilities for establishing and securing embodied identity are proliferating exponentially. We are thus dealing with a current differentiation, proliferation, and multiplication of identifications.[27] Hence, we are in the realm of actualizing a virtual identity that is differential, infinite, ex post, and anticipatory. Gilles Deleuze, however, distinguishes between a "differenciation," which qualifies, specifies, divides, organizes, and operates in the realm of actuality, and a "differentiation," which "determines the virtual content of the Idea as a problem" (Deleuze 2001, 209). In our case, the problem that arises is the embodied identity of migration. Deleuze doubles difference because he wants to conceive of actuality as a process of the virtual, as its differentiation, and not as its counterpart. If, in 2030, Josef K. were to be matched as the holder of a stolen passport through iris recognition in EU-LISA, then, one could argue, in the Deleuzian sense, that detecting his identity fraud would comply with a divergent line that would correspond without any similarity to the virtual multiplicity of Josef K.'s embodiments.

The three border fabulas described in this text derive their mediatic prominence and controversial aspect from failures in the regulatory dimension of European border control. The particular border fabula, however, with which we want to wrap up this article, symbolizes the violence of state identification practices on Europe's borders.[28] This first-person account came to our attention while writing this text; it emerged from networks that have grown over the years, in which we try to interact with the formation of the European Union's external border in both a research-based and activist way. Linked with its emergence was the demand that we take it upon ourselves to respond in a research-politically and activistically adequate way to flag practices that blatantly violate human rights, European law, and international law. Accordingly, it is a *fabula* in Mieke Bal's sense of the term, which, as a "mobile undercommons of migration" (Kuster 2017), spreads the word and embodies a voice of what has been silenced when the state crimes in question have become the norm: pushbacks[29] at the European Union's external borders. We drew our writing to a close in early April 2020.

On September 26, 2016, Khalil Mosa, a Syrian refugee, who had been granted refugee status in Germany, traveled to the main bus terminus in Didymoticho, a small town on the Greek-Turkish border, where he was checked by the Greek police. After confiscating all his papers and his cell phone, they brought him to a police station where he was detained for four days. Throughout his detention, the police subjected him repeatedly to violence, beatings, and whippings. On the fourth day, together with thirty-five other persons of different nationalities, he was taken illegally in a rubber dinghy across the Evros river, which forms the Greek-Turkish border, to Turkey. On arrival, the Turkish border police checked him, and along with the whole group he was taken to a camp. There they registered Khalil Mosa, issuing him with a certificate stating that he had entered Turkey illegally from Greece. Upon release, he traveled to Istanbul in the hope of being able to report the loss of his official German papers to the German Consulate, thus enabling him to return in the near future to Germany following the issue of replacement documentation. Given he could not get an appointment, however, he decided to go as far as the German Embassy in Ankara. He was received there on March 10, 2017, whereupon he was asked to submit a report from the Greek police by December 31, 2017, at the latest, in which they confirmed the confiscation of his German passport and the subsequent pushback. Lacking the wherewithal to survive in Ankara, he hastily returned to Istanbul, where he could stay with a cousin and start working clandestinely in a tailor's shop. On April 23, 2018, Khalil Mosa turned up at the German Embassy in Athens. Yet again, he was asked to show documentation concerning his illegal deportation from Greece to Turkey in the autumn of 2016, despite the fact that he had obviously returned illegally to Greece, again via the Evros region. On

May 22, 2018, Khalil Mosa received a fax from the German Embassy in Ankara rejecting his application for a travel visa to Germany on the grounds that he had failed to submit the necessary documents. Ever since, he has been living in the Thermopyles refugee camp near the Greek town of Lamia. On December 10, 2019, Christiane Schlötzer reported on Khalil Mosa's peregrination in the *Süddeutsche Zeitung* under the heading *Grenzwertig* (on the limit). According to the article, the Greek asylum authorities decided on October 4 that Khalil Mosa had no right to asylum in Greece because he had already been granted refugee status in Germany. In autumn 2020, we learned from Khalil Mosa's supporters in Thessaloniki that he had finally received permission to return to Germany. To date, however, he has neither received an apology from any state organ, nor any indemnity.

REFERENCES

Amoore, Louise. 2006. "Biometric borders: Governing mobilities in the war on terror." Political Geography 25: 336–51.

Amoore, Louise, and Alexandra Hall. 2009. "Taking people apart: digitized dissection and the body at the border." *Environment and Planning D: Society and Space* 27: 444–64.

Bal, Kirstie. 2005. "Organization, surveillance and the body: Towards a politics of resistance." *Organization* 12 (1): 89–108.

Bal, Mieke. 2018. *Narratology: Introduction to the Theory of Narrative*. Fourth Edition. Toronto: University of Toronto Press.

Bray, Abigail, and Claire Colebrook. 1998. "The haunted flesh: Corporeal feminism and the politics of (dis)embodiment." *Signs* 24 (1): 35–67.

Brouwer, Evelien. 2019. "Interoperability of databases and interstate trust: A perilous combination for fundamental Rights." VerfBlog, May 25, 2019. https://verfassungsblog.de/interoperability-of-databases-and-interstate-trust-a-perilous-combination-for-fundamental-rights.

Browne, Simone. 2015. *Dark Matters. On the Surveillance of Blackness*. Durham, NC: Duke University Press.

Bruns, Claudia. 2020a. "Gendering border studies? Schnittstellen zwischen Border und Gender Studies." In *Grenzforschung, Handbuch für Wissenschaft und Studium*, edited by Dominik Gerst, Maria Klessmann, and Hannes Krämer, volume 3, 338–58. Baden-Baden: Nomos.

Bruns, Claudia. 2020b. *Europas Grenzen: Karten, Körper, Kollektive seit der Antike*. Vienna/Cologne/Weimar: Böhlau.

De Certeau, Michel. 1992. *The Mystic Fable. Volume One. The Sixteenth and Seventeenth Centuries*. Translated by Michael B. Smith. Chicago: The University of Chicago Press.

De Genova, Nicholas, ed. 2017. *The Borders of Europe. Autonomy of Migration, Tactics of Bordering*. Durham, NC: Duke University Press.

Deleuze, Gilles. 1993. "Postskriptum über die Kontrollgesellschaft." In *Unterhandlungen 1972–1990*, 254–62. Frankfurt a. M.: Suhrkamp.

Deleuze, Gilles. 2001. *Difference and Repetition*. London: Continuum.

Dongus, Ariana. 2019. "Galton's utopia—Data accumulation in biometric capitalism." *spheres*. http://spheres-journal.org/galtons-utopia-data-accumulation-in-biometric-capitalism/.

Fanon, Frantz. 1952. *Peau noir, masques blancs*. Paris: Editions du Seuil.

Grosz, Elizabeth. 1987. "Notes towards a corporeal feminism." *Australian Feminist Studies* 2 (5): 1–16.

Grosz, Elizabeth. 1994. *Volatile Bodies: Toward a Corporeal Feminism*. Bloomington: Indiana University Press.

Haggerty, Kevin D., and Richard V. Ericson. 2000. "The surveillant assemblage." *British Journal of Sociology* 51 (4): 605–22.

Horn, David. 2003. *The Criminal Body: Lombroso and the Anatomy of Deviance*. New York: Routledge.

Knorr-Cetina, Karin. 1989. "Spielarten des Konstruktivismus: Einige Notizen und Anmerkungen." *Soziale Welt* 40 (1/2): 86–96.

Kuster, Brigitta, and Vassilis S. Tsianos. 2021. "EU-LISA zwischen Lobbyismus und *venture sciences*. Konturen eines neuen Forschungsfeldes der empirischen Migrations-und Grenzregimeforschung." *Zeitschrift für Migrationsforschung* 1 (2): 203–29.

Kuster, Brigitta. 2017. "Europas Grenzen und die mobile undercommons." *Texte zur Kunst* 105 "Wir sind ihr/They are us": 118–25.

Kuster, Brigitta. 2018. *Grenze filmen. Eine kulturwissenschaftliche Analyse audiovisueller Produktionen an den Grenzen Europas*. Bielefeld: transcript.

Kuster, Brigitta, and Vassilis S. Tsianos. 2013. "Erase them! Eurodac und die digitale Deportabilität." *transversal journal* 03. "flee erase territoralize." http://eipcp.net/transversal/0313/kuster-tsianos/de.

Kuster, Brigitta, and Vassilis S. Tsianos. 2014. "Eurodac und die IT Agentur: Zur Digitalisierung der europäischen Grenze." *Bürgerrechte und Polizei CILIP* 105 (May): 61–68.

Kuster, Brigitta, and Vassilis S. Tsianos. 2016a. "How to Liquefy a Body on the Move: Eurodac and the Making of the European Digital Border." In *EU Borders and Shifting Internal Security, Technology, Externalization and Accountability*, edited by Raphael Bossong and Helena Carrapico, 45–63. Cham: Springer International Publishing Switzerland.

Kuster, Brigitta, and Vassilis S. Tsianos. 2016b. "Hotspot Lesbos." Aus den Augen, aus dem Sinn. https://www.boell.de/de/2016/08/03/hotspot-lesbos.

Kuster, Brigitta et al. 2021. "No, no Fingerprint! We need to move from the camp! Über Bewegungsfreiheit, informationelle Selbstbestimmung, nobodies against the state und posthuman rights." In *Wie kommen die Rechte des Menschen in die Welt?*, edited by Matthias Schaffrick and Sigrid Köhler. Heidelberg: Universitätsverlag Winter.

Mbembe, Achille. 2017. *Politik der Feindschaft*. Berlin: Suhrkamp.

Mezzadra, Sandro, and Brett Neilson. 2013. *Border as Method, or, the Multiplication of Labor*. Durham, NC: Duke University Press.
Nyers, Peter. 2015. "Migrant citizenships and autonomous mobilities." *Migration, Mobility & Displacement* 1 (1): 23–39.
Papadopoulos, Dimitris, Niamh Stephenson, and Vassilis S. Tsianos. 2008. *Escape Routes: Control and Subversion in the 21st Century*. Ann Arbor, MI: Pluto Press.
Papadopoulos, Dimitris, and Vassilis S. Tsianos. 2013. "After citizenship: Autonomy of migration, organisational ontology and mobile commons." *Citizenship Studies* 17 (2): 178–96.
Rammert, Werner. 2006. "Technik in Aktion: Verteiltes Handeln in soziotechnischen Konstellationen." In *Technographie. Zur Mikrosoziologie der Technik*, edited by Werner Rammert and Cornelius Schubert, 163–95. Frankfurt a. M.: Campus.
Robertson, Craig. 2009. "A documentary regime of verification." *Cultural Studies* 23 (3): 329–54.
Schütz, Alfred, and Thomas Luckmann. 2003. *Strukturen der Lebenswelt*. Konstanz: UTB.
Sekula, Allan. 2003. "Der Körper und das Archiv." D*iskurse der Fotografie. Fotokritik am Ende des fotografischen Zeitalters*, edited by Herta Wolf, volume 2, 269–334. Frankfurt a. M.: Suhrkamp.
Spillers, Hortense J. 1987. "Mama's baby, papa's maybe: An American grammar book." *Diacritics* 17 (2): 64–81.
Stephenson, Niamh, und Dimitris Papadopoulos. 2006. *Analysing Everyday Experience: Social Research and Political Change*. London: Palgrave Macmillan.
Stoler, Ann Laura. 2002. "Colonial Archives and the Arts of Governance." *Archival Science* 2 (98): 100–01.
Tangermann, Julian. 2017. "Identitätssicherung und-feststellung im Migrationsprozess. Herausforderungen und Praktiken im deutschen Kontext." *Fokusstudie der deutschen nationalen Kontaktstelle für das Europäische Migrationsnetzwerk* (EMN), http://www.bamf.de/SharedDocs/Anlagen/DE/Publikationen/EMN/Studien/wp76-emn-identitaetssicherung-feststellung.pdf?__blob=publicationFile.
Tazzioli, Martina. 2014. *Spaces of Governmentality: Autonomous Migration and the Arab Uprisings*. New York: Rowman & Littlefield.
Thacker, Eugene. 2004. *Biomedia*. Minneapolis: University of Minnesota Press.
Trimikliniots, Nicos, Dimitris Parsanoglou, and Vassilis S. Tsianos. 2015. *Mobile Commons, Digital Materialities and the Right to the City. Migrant Digitalities & Social Movements in three Arrival Cities–Athens, Istanbul, Nicosia*. London: Palgrave-Pivot Series Mobility and Politics (MPP).
Tsianos, Vassilis, and Brigitta Kuster. 2012. "Thematic Report 'Border Crossings' (WP 4)." Deliverable No. 6, Transnational Digital Networks, Migration and Gender. http://www.mignetproject.eu/wp-content/uploads/2012/10/MIGNET_Deliverable_6_Thematic_report_Border_crossings.pdf.
Tsianos, Vassilis S., and Brigitta Kuster. 2016a. "Eurodac in Times of Bigness: The Power of Big Data within the Emerging European IT Agency." *Journal of Borderlands Studies* 31 (2): 235–49.

Tsianos, Vassilis S., and Brigitta Kuster. 2016b. "Black Box Eurodac! Eine Akteur-Netzwerk-theoretische Untersuchung der digitalen Deportabilität." In *An der Grenze: Die biotechnologische Überwachung von Migration*, edited by Torsten Heinemann and Martin G. Weiß, 183–204. Frankfurt a. M.: Campus.
van der Ploeg, Irma. 2005. *The Machine-Readable Body. Essays on Biometrics and the Informatization of the Body*. Düren: Shaker Publishing.
Walters, Williams. 2010. "Migration and security." In *The Routledge Handbook of New Security Studies*, 217–28. London: Routledge.

NOTES

1. Our special thanks go to John Barrett who has contributed much more to this text than an excellent and careful proofreading.

2. With the term "digital deportability," we are indicating the expansion of deportability (i.e., the totality of social conditions within the context of illegalization) and of mobility risks—money, endurance, distance and duration of travel, as well as life itself—as a result of technologies of digital identification. Data fluidity provides a slippery space in which the condition of deportability is latently ubiquitous and strikes ad hoc.

3. For a more detailed discussion on the development and expansion of the scope and application of EURODAC, see Kuster and Tsianos 2021 or Brouwer 2019.

4. See Sekula 2003 or Horn 2003. For a comparison between Galton or the construction of suspicious and risky subjects through biometric devices and regimes of the colonial and industrial era of early European nation-states and the "war on terror" in the early 2000s, see for instance Dongus 2019.

5. In this text, Louise Amoore and Alexandra Hall engage with the history of the production of visual knowledge about the body that reduces it to its identifiable traces. The critique they develop aims to think beyond the paradigm of privacy, which is usually directed against too much intrusion into the personal sphere.

6. See Walters 2010.

7. "Council Conclusions on the way forward to improve information exchange and ensure the interoperability of EU information systems" 10151/17, https://data .consilium.europa.eu/doc/document/ST-10151-2017-INIT/en/pdf (July 4, 2019).

8. The quote has been translated from the German by the authors. At least nine of the Paris and Brussels bombers are said to have used the routes explored. Some of them used smuggler boats to cross from Turkey into Greece. Some carried forged Syrian passports, whereas others had no identification documents at all.

9. This definition, established in 2004 by the Working Group of the Heads of the State Criminal Police Offices and the Federal Criminal Police Office, is taken from the Federal Government's response to a minor inquiry. Cf. legal definition of the term "Gefährder" file number WD 3 - 3000 - 046/17 of February 27, 2017, https://www .bundestag.de/blob/503066/.../wd-3-046-17-pdf-data.pdf. The term is a neologism for "dangerous persons" who pose a threat to public security.

10. See "EMN Synthesis Report for the EMN Focused Study 2017: Challenges and practices for establishing the identity of third country nationals in migration procedures," December 2017 - Final (Version 2), https://ec.europa.eu/home-affairs/sites/homeaffairs/files/00_eu_synthesis_report_identity_study_final_en.pdf (July 4, 2019).

11. It can be very difficult and almost impossible for refugees to obtain papers from their countries of origin that enable them to be identified. Documents also get lost or stolen along the way. Moreover, some migrants decide to destroy their IDs out of fear that being identified in Europe will lead to faster deportation, hence the term *harraga*, for example, which in Arabic stands for those who burn their papers in order to elope. Cf. in more detail Kuster (2018, 260f).

12. The year 2016 was not characterized by increased reflection by the European Commission on improving existing and future EU information management systems with a view to managing the external borders and ensuring internal security in the European Union, but instead saw forced debates on the crucial importance of secure travel and identity documents to prevent abuse and threats to internal security and, wherever necessary, to establish a person's identity beyond reasonable doubt. See, for example, Communication from the Commission to the European Parliament and the Council on the Action Plan for a more effective European approach to travel document fraud, COM(2016) 790 final, December 8, 2016, https://eur-lex.europa.eu/legal-content/DE/TXT/PDF/?uri=CELEX:52016DC0790&from=DE (July 4, 2019).

13. Of course, the respective locations and authorities involved also play a role. For example, although identity management in hotspots is carried out by the respective national police authorities, they are supported in this by Frontex (and not, for example, by EASO). Frontex, for example, conducts what is known as "nationality screening" and assists with fingerprinting. "Identification and registration is carried out by Frontex Joint Screening Teams and Fingerprinting Officers, while Joint Debriefing Teams are responsible for interviewing migrants and collecting information on smuggling routes and networks." Translations quoted from "EMN Focused Study 2017, Challenges and practices for establishing applicants' identity in the migration process. Common Template of EMN Focused Study 2017," Final Version: April 5, 2017, https://ec.europa.eu/home-affairs/sites/homeaffairs/files/00_id_study_specifications_final_en.pdf (October 6, 2018); see also Kuster and Tsianos (2016b).

14. Tangermann, Julian (2017), "Identity Assurance and Establishment in the Migration Process. Challenges and Practices in the German Context," Focus Study of the German National Contact Point for the European Migration Network (EMN), http://www.bamf.de/SharedDocs/Anlagen/DE/Publikationen/EMN/Studien/wp76-emn-identitaetssicherung-feststellung.pdf?__blob=publicationFile (July 4, 2019).

15. See also Florian Flade (2017), "Das unfassbare Doppelleben des Oberleutnants Franco A." In: *Die Welt*, April 27, 2017, https://www.welt.de/politik/deutschland/article164061584/Das-unfassbare-Doppelleben-des-Oberleutnants-Franco-A.html; Federal Office for Migration and Refugees press release (issue 017/2017), "Franco A. - Untersuchungen abgeschlossen" of May 31, 2017, https://www.bamf.de/SharedDocs/Pressemitteilungen/DE/2017/20170531-017-pm-statement-cordt-innenausschuss.html; Reimann, Anna (2017), "Wie leicht kann man sich ins Asylverfahren einschleichen?" *Spiegel Online*, May 17, 2017, online: http://www

.spiegel.de/politik/deutschland/fall-franco-a-bei-der-bundeswehr-wie-weit-geht-das
-bamf-versagen-a-1148098.html, cf. Matthias Bartsch, Jörg Diehl, Matthias Gebauer,
Martin Knobbe, and Wolf Wiedmann-Schmidt (2017), "Der hessische Syrer," *Der
Spiegel*, 18/2017, 55.

16. See Tangermann 2017.

17. Regarding a possible connection of a right-wing extremist motive for the crime
and identity fraud, whereby Franco A. intended to use his fingerprints as actants of a
false witness, the order of the Federal Supreme Court of August 22, 2019, para. 14, p.
19, states: "In this context, however, it remains open whether the defendant originally
or at any rate after his arrest in Vienna still intended to commit the crime under the
legend of the Syrian asylum seeker 'D.'. Since further investigations have not yielded
any new findings in this regard, the assumption that the defendant intended to leave
the weapon with his fingerprints—also stored under the false identity as 'D.'—in the
vicinity of the crime scene and thus wanted to provide a clue to the alleged asylum
seeker is contradicted in particular by the fact that due to the taking of his fingerprints
after his arrest in Vienna, these were now also clearly linked to his personal data and
the defendant was presumably aware of this" (quote translated from the German
by the authors). Following the dismissal of a terror charge by the Frankfurt Higher
Regional Court in June 2018, the Attorney General's Office took the case to the
Federal Supreme Court. After lengthy additional investigations, the indictment was
finally admitted by a decision of the Federal Supreme Court in November 2019 and
the case was referred back to the Frankfurt Higher Regional Court.

18. What applies to the European population also applies to the category of migrant
identity, which, strictly speaking, even represents an *aporia* if mobility is given priority over its control. It is precisely here that the primacy of difference over the fiction
of unequivocalness applies.

19. Needless to say, specific technical features, which are too rarely made relevant
to migration studies and mostly committed to the humanities and cultural studies, also
play a central role; these include the ten-fingerprint set, the Automated Fingerprint
Identification System developed by the Steria company, the use of special live scan-
ners to capture and transmit fingerprints electronically as opposed to earlier methods
that used ink, sensor technology, the standardized ANSI/NIST formatted files containing (flat and rolled) electronic fingerprints and alphanumeric data, the biometric
matcher, and a software solution implemented in the current EURODAC system and
owned by "3MCogent" Inc. See, for example, the public tender for the framework
contract for the maintenance and operation of EURODAC: https://www.eulisa.europa
.eu/Procurement/Tenders/LISA2016RP02%20EURODAC%20MWO/Annex%20I
%20Eurodac%20MWO-Executive%20Summary.pdf (July 4, 2019).

20. See: Papadopoulos, Stephenson, and Tsianos 2008; Mezzadra and Neilson
2013; Papadopoulos and Tsianos 2013; Tazzioli 2014; Nyers 2015; Trimikliniots,
Parsanoglou, and Tsianos 2015; De Genova 2017; Kuster 2018.

21. There are different variants of deletion, such as the cancelation of an identity (=
de-identification) or the deletion of an asylum seeker's data after ten years, of persons
apprehended illegally while crossing the European Union's external borders after two
years (data protection), or when obtaining a European citizenship.

22. Louise Amoore (2006) refers to this as "biometric boundaries."

23. In his historical study on the emergence of the passport in the United States, Robertson focuses more on identification practices and the documentation of an individual identity than, as is usually the case, on border control, state formation, and bureaucracy as surveillance. To be sure, there are always interactions between imagined state bodies or allegorical collective bodies and the real bodies that are thereby produced, that is, materialized (cf. Bruns 2020b).

24. In comparison, Robertson, referring to the introduction of the passport in the United States, speaks of the recovery of a "slipped certainty by moving from local and personal social relations to centralized bureaucratic hierarchies" (Robertson 2009, 337). In this sense, he refers to "the threat to an individual's claim to self-representation" as "the discrepancy between the literacy evident through the signing of one's name and the literacy associated with the documentary formulation of a personal and a legal identity" (Robertson 2009, 339).

25. See, for example, Schütz and Luckmann 2003 and Knorr-Cetina 1989.

26. Of interest in this context is the reference Simone Browne makes, drawing on Saidiya Hartman's book *Lose Your Mother* (2006), regarding scarring and branding in the wake of the Middle Passage deportation and enslavement. Some enslaved people used these violent inscriptions on their bodies to rekindle kinship ties or social connections to enslaved companions. Browne interprets this practice as a revelation of the limit of dehumanization through branding (Browne 2015, 102).

27. Kirstie Ball also points to research on the workings of surveillance operations that has shown that it is openings in the spatio-temporal gaps between observers and observed that enable resistance. This is very much in line with our observations about the concern of EURODAC matchings called "wrong hits," which are due to the temporal and spatial gaps regarding the assumed correspondence between the movements of migrants and the movements of the data. Cf. Kuster and Tsianos 2016a.

28. Aggelidis, Dimitris (2018), "Mou piran ta Xartia mou," Efimerida ton Syntakton 12.2.2018, https://www.efsyn.gr/ellada/dikaiomata/140103_moy-piran-ta-hartia -me-pigan-sto-potami-kai-me-perasan-apenanti; for a shallow humanitarian version of the case that completely misses the functioning of the Dublin Regulation, cf. also Christiane Schlötzer, "Grenzwertig," in *Süddeutsche Zeitung*, No. 286, December 11, 2019, p. 3. At this point, we would like to thank Georgios and Sigrid Tsiakalos for their solidarity and care.

29. Pushback is the process of pushing back near the border foreign persons without the appropriate residence permit for the country of destination. In the European Union, the principle of *non-refoulement* applies in this regard, a principle of international law under the Geneva Refugee Convention Article 33 and Article 3 of the European Convention on Human Rights.

Chapter 3

Vulnerability and Flexible Population Filtering

Lessons Learned, from the European Commission Hotspot to the Pandemic

Evie Papada and Antonis Vradis

INTRODUCTION

In the aftermath of the European "crisis," policies championing the imperative to protect the most vulnerable refugees have turned vulnerability into a defining marker of asylum policy (Smith and Waite 2018). Even more recently, in the midst of the currently ongoing global pandemic, vulnerability has taken center stage in shaping policy responses; yet this time round, it is vulnerable populations, not individuals, that seem to drive these. In this chapter, we first place vulnerability at the center of the European Commission's (EC's) hotspot approach for managing migration. We do so in order to address the centrality of the concept in affecting the filtering of migrant populations in and beyond the European Union's territorial margins. Here, we look at the European Union's hotspot approach[1] and the EU-Turkey statement[2] in concert, as the new architecture of the border regime. Beyond a focus on deterrence and detention as key spatial strategies in the regulation of migrant mobility, we look instead at immigration controls at borders and the ensuing practices of filtering and caring associated with the humanitarian border (Walters 2011). In this first part of the chapter, we draw a relationship between EU reliance on asylum as a tool for migration management and the function of categorical vulnerability as a benchmark of international protection. While the designation "vulnerable applicant" was meant to facilitate the allocation of welfare benefits and provide additional safeguards to those undergoing the asylum process, we point to a shift in practice, whereby vulnerability has occupied an increasingly important role in the administrative decision to grant access to the asylum process on the Aegean islands of Lesvos. Then we demonstrate how vulnerability came to be assessed at the hotspot in Lesvos and became a weapon both in the hands of the authorities but also for asylum applicants.

In the second part of the chapter, we proceed to explore the notion of vulnerability beyond the migrant mobility context, bringing it into the current pandemic conjuncture. Here, we explain how this notion of the vulnerable body has permeated the European body politic and therefore show, retrospectively, how crucial the vulnerability exercise has been for EC policy—not only for the migrant populations originally affected by this, but now virtually for the continent's entire population.

CONTEXTUALIZING VULNERABILITY IN THE EU BORDER REGIME

The idea that borders are not rigid lines that separate territorial and sovereign jurisdictions but rather a sociotechnical apparatus or regime that continually reshapes the geographical contours of traditional borderlands is now commonplace among critical border scholars. This holds particularly in the case of the European Union's migration and border control regime, which in the past couple of decades has morphed into an assemblage of agencies, actors, processes of standardization, and harmonization focusing on the management of asylum and its external borders. As a result, scholars have brought attention to the creation of an internal mobility regime, exemplified by the Dublin and Eurodac regulations, aiming at containing migrants at the territorial margins, and an external one, through carrier sanctions, readmission agreements, and development policies (Lavenex 2006; Białasiewicz 2012; Collyer 2012). Underpinning these processes is the coexistence of multiple logics of control. For instance, scholars have pointed to the importance of discourses of security (Bigo et al. 2014; Huysmans 2000) and humanitarianism (Cuttita 2018; Little and Vaughan-Williams 2017). We bring attention to vulnerability as an additional rationale of governance under the current transformation of the EU border regime. The emergence of camps and new infrastructures of migration control such as hotspots, as well as the legislative processes that have taken off since Europe's 2015 asylum crisis, has accentuated the importance of legal material spaces (Hess and Kasparek 2019, 8). The Aegean islands become the incubator of these new processes and practices which extend further into the continent.

Vulnerability conveys onto policy interventions, particularly in relation to the ways in which it undergirds care and control practices and differentiations between "vulnerable" victims and dangerous "wrongdoers" (Brown 2014; Brown et al. 2017). Similar concerns have been raised by critical disability scholars where categorical and emotive understandings of vulnerability are squarely applied to those living with impairments for purposes of administrative control (Burghardt 2013). This reductive understanding of vulnerability makes the concept malleable and easily adaptable as part of strategies that seek to govern behaviors and resources for citizens and non-citizens alike.

MANAGING MIGRATION THROUGH
ASYLUM AND VULNERABILITY

Asylum had long been woven into the European Union's efforts to manage migration, its regulation now transpiring from within an ensemble of actors, regulations, and discourses rather than dominant state powers (see Figure 3.1). Concomitantly, the figure of the asylum seeker is depoliticized, squeezed into moral frames of deserving or undeserving migrants, treated as objects of humanitarian compassion (Geiger and Pecoud 2010; Gammeltoft-Hansen 2014; Williams 2016). Asylum is deployed as a management strategy specifically through the dimension of externalization (Hyndman and Mountz 2008) by incorporating Turkey into the EU list of "safe third countries" for asylum seekers in general and "first country of asylum" for Syrians in particular. This is exemplified in the "one in, one out" equation which underwrites the EU-Turkey statement: for every Syrian readmitted to Turkey from the Greek Aegean islands, a vulnerable Syrian who resides in Turkey gets to be resettled into an EU country. Those who chose to continue their journey to Greece after March 2016 were faced with the threat of imminent deportation, unless

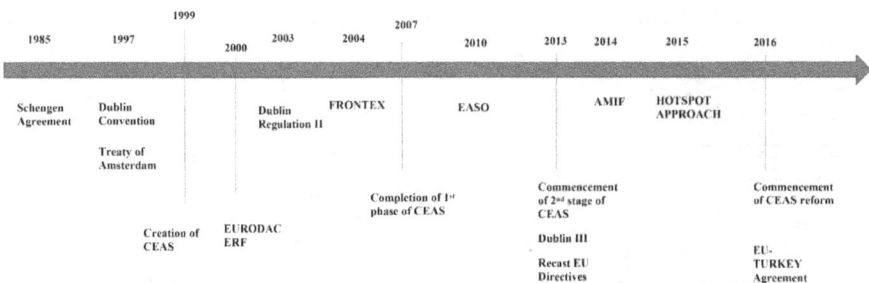

Figure 3.1. The development of the common European asylum system. *Source*: Authors.

they were found to belong to a vulnerable group or were subject to relocation under the Dublin Regulation. Their exclusion from entering the asylum
process in Greece was in clear breach of international refugee law and the
principle of non-refoulment (McDuff 2019); it has nonetheless been sustained
through a political stunt that holds Turkey as operating efficient and fair asylum procedures and therefore being a safe third country.[3]

In particular, following Turkey's representation as a safe third country
of asylum for Syrian applicants, asylum procedures were shaped around
the requirement to affect expulsions to Turkey. In practice, it compelled
immigration authorities at the Greek hotspots, officially known as reception
and identification centers (RICs), to select whether an asylum claim will be
examined on the Eastern Aegean islands or in Turkey. For such a nomina-
tion to occur, certain adjustments to the asylum procedures had to be made.
These came through the introduction of L4375 in April 2016 a few weeks
following the announcement of the EU-Turkey statement. The legitimization
of returns under the EU-Turkey agreement had been practically supported
by the creation of additional administrative layers and procedural tracks.
L4375 provided that the applications of those landing in the Greek hotspots
would be handled under the so-called fast-track border procedures,[4] designed
particularly for the European Union's external borders. The scope, steps to
be followed, and temporal limitations that underwrite such procedures are
stricter than those used in regular asylum procedures in the mainland and vary
from country to country.[5] In the case of the hotspot islands, fast-track border
procedures are aimed at speeding up the asylum process (as it is understood
that the majority of applications have little merit) and operationalizing the
EU-Turkey Agreement, by checking the admissibility of the application.
This means that only the asylum cases of people who are most likely to be
rejected are processed; the principal focus is on assessing whether their asylum procedure can take place elsewhere through the admissibility procedures.
It affected Syrian nationals in particular, as they now faced the proposition
that they will find protection in Turkey, and those nationalities that scored
low on the EU average recognition rate. Fast-track border procedures need to
be understood as yet another "legal fiction to keep those physically present
unadmitted" (Goodwin 2007, 207). Because applicants are not allowed to
enter the territory despite their physical presence, they are placed in detention
within the RICs.

Exempt from the admissibility (and fast-track border) procedures were
those designated as vulnerable. Article 14(8) L4375/2016 identified the following vulnerability categories: unaccompanied children, persons suffering
from disability or incurable illness, pregnant women or new mothers, single
parents with minor children, the elderly, victims of torture or other serious
forms of psychological harm, victims of sexual violence or exploitation,

victims of human trafficking, and persons suffering from post-traumatic stress disorder, in particular survivors and relatives of victims of shipwrecks. In addition, the vulnerable benefit from priority registration of their asylum claim and for housing and they are allowed to move freely within Greek territory (meaning they are exempt from geographical restrictions). The obligation for the Greek authorities to identify vulnerable persons originates in EU Asylum Directive 2013/32/EU and the Reception Conditions Directive 2013/33/EU which L4375/2016 transposes into Greek legislation. The identification of vulnerability is meant to provide applicants with special procedural guarantees: it underscores the provision or the enhancement of entitlement for those who are in need. In asylum law, the enhancement of entitlements is understood to be directly linked to the process of establishing a truth claim; it is about safeguarding the best possible conditions under which the refugee determination process can occur. Fast-track border procedures simply do not provide the best possible conditions, hence the vulnerable are exempt from those. As Hancox and Costello (2016) argue, however, while the designation of vulnerability affords some the entitlement to beneficiary treatment, it casts others as "abusive asylum subjects" in the context of continually stricter and more restrictive asylum procedures such as the fast-track ones.

Our analysis of the use of vulnerability in the Greek fast-track border procedures points to two further findings. First, L4375/2016 stipulated that applicants should be screened for vulnerabilities at the RICs, by way of a medical/psychosocial examination, upon the first three days of their arrival. Given the exemptions afforded to those identified as vulnerable with regards to the asylum procedure and geographical restrictions, vulnerability assessments become consequential to the outcome of the asylum process. Following our informant, a legal professional at the time working in the protection unit of the UN High Commissioner for Refugees (UNHCR) in Lesvos:

> I must say that vulnerability plays a dominant role on the islands. It's a screening tool, well for me it's very "managerial," it has taken a completely different form from what we knew vulnerability to be years ago, in terms of what it means that someone is vulnerable in the asylum procedure and how you will do the RSD assessment of this—now it has become a lot more managerial. (Lesvos, May 2018)

Second, vulnerability does not only provide some with entitlements (as opposed to everyone) but it can also be used to legitimize fast-track border procedures. Historically, the question of asylum seeker vulnerability had been closely linked to Greece's control capacity as a net receiver of asylum seekers as a country but also to the creation of a credible asylum system given its potential as a migration management tool (Kasparek 2016). Specifically, the importance of Greece being a safe space for all, particularly the vulnerable, had been underlined in 2011 following a damning decision of the EU Court of Human Rights regarding its treatment of asylum seekers.[6] At the time, the decision had led to many countries being unable to return asylum seekers to Greece through the Dublin Regulation, much to the dismay of conservative countries in the north. Similarly, the changes brought about to the integrity of the asylum procedures at the border through L4375 prompted asylum authorities to find the means by which to ensure that the integrity of the asylum procedures is not questioned. According to a UNHCR protection officer employed on the island of Leros at the time: "Politically, they had to ensure that Greece appeared as a safe space with good reception conditions, in order to implement the Agreement. Vulnerability assessments provide exactly this reassurance that authorities respect human rights and standards" (Skype, October 2018). Notwithstanding these efforts, vulnerability assessments continued to be a politically contentious issue, particularly in relation to the high numbers of vulnerability identification and the impact this could potentially have on the implementation of the agreement.

Vulnerability as a Weapon

This section illustrates how vulnerability came to be assessed at the hotspot of Lesvos and became a weapon for the authorities, as well as a weapon for the asylum applicant. The hotspot administration was now tasked with the implementation of the fast-track border procedures and operationalizing the vulnerability assessments. Surrounding the hotspot, a diverse network of individuals including humanitarian personnel, volunteers, and legal aid actors attempt to influence processes, sometimes as supporting and other times as antagonistic agents (see also Kalir and Wissink 2016). During our discussions, the latter argued that the assessment of vulnerability within the border asylum process was arbitrary and constituted a state of exception, not only because "petty sovereigns" (Butler 2004, 57), in this case immigration caseworkers and RIC staff, practiced asylum law arbitrability, but also due to the emergency character of the fast-track border procedures which defied even minimum procedural standards. These arguments resonate with findings in other border spaces, where sovereign jurisdiction intervenes in an irregular manner. For instance, in their study of migrant waiting zones in airports, Mailet et al. (2018, 143) suggest that states "mediate jurisdiction and legal protection" offering alternative modes of legal inclusion "which exclude migrants and asylum seekers from regular legal processes, thereby changing their legal status." In the context of the hotspot, vulnerability assessments can be described as sovereign acts of territorial in/exclusion, aiding the implementation of a process of asylum externalization at the European Union's borders.

To begin with, the obligation to identify vulnerability is reflected in the way procedures are organized under the hotspot approach. Its assessment is anchored within a series of administrative procedures including the identification, registration, nationality screening, admissibility check, and asylum application, conjuring up a vulnerability assessment chain. Authorities (in this case the Greek Coast Guard or Frontex) are legally obliged to identify vulnerable cases during landing/disembarkation, the registration procedure (Greek police and Frontex) which includes a medical screening (dedicated psychosocial unit of KEELPNO) and/or at the interview stage, be it for the admissibility or the eligibility of the asylum claim principally handled by EASO immigration caseworkers. According to our respondents in the medical unit at the hotspot, referrals of vulnerable individuals from Coast Guard or Frontex are rare. The bulk is therefore identified further down the chain. At the registration processes, medical personnel are given by law three days to detect vulnerabilities. Here the views were split. Several argued that most vulnerability categories described in L4375 were visible and registered while others maintained that in most cases it has been practically impossible to detect vulnerabilities within this timeframe. As one of the social workers explained:

> We only find out that minors are here unaccompanied days later, not to speak of post-traumatic stress disorder (PTSD). It is impossible to identify trauma in such a short timeframe. Age assessment for unaccompanied minors requires a hospital appointment. In practice, most undergo a quick medical screening where only very visible vulnerabilities such as pregnancies or visible mental disorders can be found—there is hardly ever interpretation in place. (Lesvos, July 2018)

From then on, an applicant's health card stating their vulnerability needs to travel to the office of the Regional Asylum Service in order to be uploaded into the database. Informants speak of serious problems in the practical day-to-day cooperation between the different authorities, resulting from rigid procedural routines that characterize internal police work. Accordingly, all communication between the police and asylum service takes the form of written requests, which are physically passed on from individual to individual, leading to many with registered vulnerabilities appearing at admissibility interviews from which they should have been exempt. Following an informant, a social worker who was employed in Moria during the former vulnerability assessment process, argued: "Let's assume that there is a medical team in place and that a person walks away with a medical card stating his or her vulnerability. From then on, it is down to sheer luck whether that information reaches the regional asylum service" (Lesvos, June 2018).

Despite the practical problems and reliance on visible characteristics, out of the 23,212 first instance decisions taken under the fast-track border procedures in 2017, 15,788 were admissible for reasons of vulnerability. In June of that year, the EC announced measures to define more precisely medical vulnerability in order to avoid what they termed overidentification.[7] The Hellenic Centre for Diseases Control and Prevention (known as KEELPNO) took on the medical support contract at the hotspot and began a consultation with the remaining service-providing actors (humanitarian organizations, nongovernmental organizations, and legal advisers) in order to come up with a more precise, medical definition of vulnerability for the assessment process. Many viewed KEELPNO's appointment as politically motivated, and the organization was regularly described as the right arm of the government, with a clear political mandate to reduce the number of vulnerable designations.

The system introduced by KEELPNO reset the five vulnerability categories (L4375/2016) into a graduating scale of medical importance based on the ICD 10 international medical classification system. Importantly, it replaced the yes or no answer to vulnerability with A and B (Figure 3.2), corresponding to an assessment of medium and high vulnerability, respectively. The strictly medical interpretation of the categories set in a legal document amounted in the eyes of legal and humanitarian actors on the islands to a policy change, because it severely narrowed vulnerability's dimensions. Some concrete examples were cases of people who had suffered sexual violence or torture but had no physical residuals, in which KEELPNO staff would have to rely on testimonies in order to verify their claim. The same goes for cases of unaccompanied minors in which minor medical conditions generally overtook in importance the social and environmental conditions that made their lives vulnerable at the hotspot. Again, the new system encouraged the identification of visible vulnerabilities.

Category A or "*medium vulnerability*" category is meant to include vulnerable individuals for which a "*significant vulnerability could develop without preventative support measures*" and for which "*frequent monitoring of vulnerability status is recommended*"

Category B or "*high vulnerability*" category includes vulnerable individuals for which "*significant vulnerability is evident. Follow up assessment and development of a care plan is recommended. Reference should be made to the immediate need of support*"

Figure 3.2. KEELPNO vulnerability categories A and B. *Source:* Authors.

VULNERABILITIES AND THE OMISSION OF ITS
SOCIAL DIMENSIONS OF VULNERABILITY

The release of the new vulnerability form was followed by an immediate decision to refrain from uploading medium vulnerabilities into the online databases. In other words, for the purpose of asylum procedures, a medium vulnerability amounted to no vulnerability because it remained unrecorded. The practice lasted until the second half of 2018 when the vulnerability template was revised, including a third category which distinguished between vulnerable applicants, vulnerable applicants with special reception needs, and finally non-vulnerable applicants with no special reception needs. Vulnerability templates must be read as technologies of classification that can be traced in other aspects of the asylum process such as nationality, ethnicity, gender, and age; above all, it is now an indispensable part of bureaucratic apparatuses that "inflect the terror, unpredictability, and also indeterminacy of state regulatory power" (Cabot 2012, 16). The move to medicalize vulnerability identification shows attempts toward increasing the legibility over asylum seekers by repurposing its meaning and function, an indispensable materiality of border surveillance.

The third manner in which vulnerability has been used as a weapon at the hands of the authorities relates to the way it has been deployed during the admissibility stage of the procedures. This is the moment of encounter between immigration caseworkers, mostly EASO personnel, and asylum applicants. First, the admissibility interview examines whether Turkey is a safe country for applicants. This means that applicants are discouraged from discussing incidents in their country of origin that relate to their asylum claim and may reveal a vulnerability as defined in L4375. Often interview questions aimed at addressing the existence of vulnerabilities were disguised as concerns about applicants' general health—"how do you feel today?" or "can you perform your daily tasks?" were perceived as irrelevant by legal aid personnel. Other questions in the interview script reinforced the medical dimension of vulnerability. For instance, emphasis was placed on whether the individual is taking any medication and where they got the medication from, and a request was made for documents that prove the medical problems these medications are trying to address. Following my informant, a legal aid adviser working for an asylum rights campaigning organization: "The individual is vulnerable because they are a torture victim even if it had happened 30 years ago. The law does not prescribe that you should consider whether she cries at night or suffers persecution syndrome" (Skype, January 2019).

When applicants claimed they were vulnerable or a vulnerability indicator appeared, often EASO caseworkers would invite the opinion of an external vulnerability expert. The latter was not present at the interview; instead, caseworkers dialed in vulnerability experts and orally transferred questions to the applicant. Besides going against procedural standards, legal aid personnel condemned the inhospitable interviewing environment as a space that is not conducive to discussing traumatic events. This is particularly important when considering that in practice, the obligation of the authorities to identify those vulnerable becomes an obligation for the applicant to prove their vulnerability. Another informant, a legal actor advising asylum seekers in Lesvos at the time, said:

> the individual applicant is forced to walk into a system of which they have no power, no understanding and no true guard or champion to fight for them. The state has all the power, controls everything and as I say it's their turf. So, this is a very unequal and uneven playfield that they [asylum seekers] have in order to explain a very personal thing. (Lesvos, June 2018)

Finally, informants spoke about tactics of direct manipulation, such as efforts to delegitimize applicants' narratives by deliberately mixing questions and cause emotional confusion, that derail discussions of harm in the country of origin to types of harm they may be experiencing in Moria (in order to claim that the origin of vulnerability precedes their arrival and therefore Turkey might indeed be a better option for them). The sheer difficulty in convincing EASO caseworkers about an existing vulnerability has led several legal aid organizations to employ their own medical experts who were able to provide written vulnerability reports, carefully matching the legal language in which vulnerability was presented. Legal advisers spoke of the lengths to which they had to go to turn vulnerability from a weapon in the hands of the interviewer to one in the hands of the refugee.

Vulnerability assessments appear thus alongside other technologies of control used by state authorities to foster migrant identification and exclusion from territory (Nyers 2003; Pickering and Weber 2006; McDowell and Wonders 2009). Indeed, the operationalization of vulnerability under the gaze of the Hellenic Police becomes yet another enforcement ritual, but also one characterized by manipulation and an intermingling of formal and informal practices. As immigration caseworkers and legal advisers battle over the meaning and interpretation of vulnerability categories, there opens a space of what Susan Coutin has termed "maneuvering within a set of conditions" (2000, 173), whereby authorities are continually required to adapt their strategies in order to effect the selective filtering of population that the EU-Turkey Agreement implies.

VULNERABLE TIMES

What now follows is an attempt to contextualize the working of the concept of vulnerability, both in its operationalization in the EU migration policy and in the current, pandemic (and post-pandemic) conjuncture. To do so, we should probably begin with an attempt to understand what an invocation to vulnerability in the context of immigration controls might imply. The moment when we utter the word "vulnerable" is the moment when we decide there shall be a point in the future when these "vulnerable" shall be no more: there shall be a moment when this temporal assignment may be revoked. This is the curious nature of assigning vulnerability: the very moment when a universal right is invoked—that of asylum and refuge in face of plight, as we saw in the previous sections—is the same moment when that very universality is revoked; a moment when the slippery slope of coding, categorizing, filtering, and dividing populations begins. Crucially, the birth of that moment rests in the instance when authority assigns the status of the vulnerable to her who invokes it. And even though the process is meant to denote a personalized trajectory, an individual invocation to authority, the only way in which authority can make this invocation legible is through rendering populations docile in the eye of authority. This is, in other words, a logistical exercise at heart.

In her concluding remarks in *The Deadly Life of Logistics* (2014), Deborah Cowen shows how mobility has been the primordial antidote to death; commencing from National Geographic's production *Great Migrations*, she shows how movement has always been lying as a foundational element of life across species—as the show's motto itself proclaims: "move or die" (2014, 197).

The moment when the individual becomes a population is the moment when the authorities' *fantasy* of what this population comprises takes precedence. Cowen uses the UPS "love logistics" campaign in the United States "to highlight the infrastructures, production techniques, the synchronicity and the efficiency that constitute the corporate *fantasy*" of logistics (2014, 203, emphasis her own). It is entirely possible to extend this notion of a "fantasy" into other realms, beyond the corporate: the humanitarian lens/gaze on the migrant population comes to mind here. The "fantasy" herein lies in the false conviction that it is possible to trace, categorize, and decide on the vulnerable population as if it is, indeed, such a *singular* and *homogeneous* entity; an uncomplicated, invariable sum of individuals whose *unique* life *trajectories and vulnerabilities* can be made to fit the predetermined process of assigning vulnerability status according to predetermined criteria.

In its very essence, the question comes down to those exact two keywords: the *unique* and the *pre-determined*. It boils down to rendering what had unquestionably been *unique* and *personal* (better even: unique *because* it is personal): authority-legible.

This "authority-legible" extends far beyond our classic understanding of the state as an entity that "sees" (and therefore shapes) the world around us, if in a different way (Scott 1998). First, the authoritarian complex of immigration controls includes, but at the same time far exceeds, the confines of the status apparatus—and it instead includes an entire array of third sector, private, and individual actors; it is a state of mind, not just a state. Second, rendering the status of people-as-populations authority-legible is a process that commences from this "securitisation of mobility" (Cowan 2014, 217) that may concern the very "securitisation" of migrant mobility that intensified in, and following the "long summer of migration" of 2015, and that now appears, a short five years later, to be creeping into the most intimate of our everyday life aspects, and not just for migrants.

In this way, the security technologies and the legal arsenal deployed in face of the 2015 crisis of migrant reception have been vastly superseded and succeeded by the technologies and the legal arsenal deployed during the—still ongoing, at the time of writing—COVID-19 pandemic: when a few years ago (Vradis et al. 2018), we wrote that the traditional, paper-bound passport was becoming something of a relic, in all its materiality and absurdly long lifespan for our twitchingly fast-changing world, it would have been difficult for us to imagine what was to replace it—but replaced it would become, whatever document there was to be. The technology was there and so were the political will and the constant maneuvering around the migrant reception crisis. What was missing up into then was only the spark. Now that we have that, too, the governmental apparatus is alight: the so-called green passports introduced (yet again!) by the EC take their cue from the asylum applications of and since the 2015 era: any assigned status to the "document" bearer is always revocable and temporary; it depends: always. It depends on intrastate agreements; it depends on what, domestically, states and authorities deem to be an acceptable (or better even, manageable) level of risk when it comes to the movement of populations; it depends on the weighing of the pros and cons of such movement, some weighing that will in turn depend on ever-shifting variables. Variables of prediction that in turn rest on patterns of analysis that seek to make the sum of individual life trajectories, vulnerabilities, and circumstances legible. But patterns concern populations, not individuals. This logic, the logic of preemptively dealing with a conceived threat, permeates the response of the EC (and state authorities, for that matter) to the two aforementioned crises: the crisis of migrant reception (since 2015) and the crisis of managing COVID-19 (since 2020). We say the crisis of migrant reception, not migration, and the "crisis of managing" instead of simply "the crisis of

COVID-19." Neither is a misnomer: they point, precisely, at the integral role of state management in our present predicament.

In the concluding pages of *The Deadly Life of Logistics*, Deb Cowan makes a heroic attempt to examine whether, and in what way, it might be possible for our understanding of logistical spaces to be entangled with an encounter of queer theory; how we may be able to unstraighten, in other words, the vastly horizontal lines that draw out the universality that is the logistical plain. "Heroic," because any attempt to queer logistics runs directly contrary to the very idea at the heart of what the logistical logic really is—straight, plain lines that come to meet clearly drawn out points of convergence; a seemingly insurmountable contradiction in terms. And yet, this logistical logic, much like the organized violence of empire sketched out by Linebaug and Redkicker (2001, in Cowen 2014, 227), points at a potential for connection *precisely* through the all-encompassing, universal application of force that comes through the authorities' management of both crises: in both cases, in other words, the potential for different populations to mingle, to connect, to see one another, and to conspire lies, precisely as it does paradoxically, upon the fact that they are treated as a singular population in the very first place: a singular population that is vulnerable as a body—as a body, in terms of its homogeneity (one whole consisting of interconnected parts) and its docility (one will-less body that follows, passively, the orders of the nous).

In describing the role of vulnerability, as we saw earlier on, one of our informants working in the Lesvos UNHCR protection unit would call the process "managerial": the denotation is an interesting one, not only because it may point at the crude, technocratic logic underpinning the operation, but further it highlights the intention to manage (rather than to resolve) what might appear to be an unresolvable matter. Of course, what is fairly easy to discern here is that such "unresolvable" cases rarely exist, and that the managerial logic points, instead, to a long-term process of containing, limiting, diffusing, spreading, or else handling a population—some handling that could very much resemble that of us handling something material, perhaps a liquid. This is where the striking similarity between the two logics of population control—both, coincidentally, introduced by the EC, only five years apart—becomes the most apparent. In both cases, the invocation of the vulnerable is claimed to be the driving force: an extraordinary ordinance (whether in the form of a vulnerability assessment leading to a temporary residue, or the proof of vaccination that is meant to protect against the vulnerable social body). In the one case, an individual may escape the fate of a confined population, should they manage to convince the powers-that-be that they are vulnerable *enough* to require protection. In the other case, an individual may escape the fate of a confined population, should they manage to convince the powers-that-be that they are harmless, or invulnerable *enough* to warrant protection for the now vulnerable social body. The obvious example here is of course the proof of vaccination requirement now imposed on anyone from travelers to revelers, at airports and ports, but also football stadiums, concert halls, bars, and cafés the world over. On the one hand, of course, the latter appears as a complete inversion of the logic of the former: here it is the social body that is vulnerable and the individual is the one that may potentially cause harm. On the other hand, in the case of vulnerability assessments of incoming migrants, it is the individual migrant that is vulnerable and the social body is the one that stands in the position to potentially alienate/refrain from harm. Is this truly, then, a reversal of the vulnerability logic, a logic turned on its head? We would argue that it is not so. First of all, the migrant vulnerability assessments came on the back of a much wider net of regulations, laws, and state practices that conceived of these incoming populations as a potential threat that had to be neutralized: a threat that had to therefore be identified, classified, categorized, coded, contained, and channeled in ways that would leave the wider social body intact; in ways that would protect the conceivably vulnerable social body from the virulent-like threat of migration. And so, the individual vulnerability assessments do not only mark a transition from population to individual; they also comprise, in their essence, a process where two vulnerabilities (that of the individual, and the one of the population) are measured against one another. Score above the social body's vulnerability threshold, goes this logic, and your reward is to become part of it—needless to say, not an integral or fully recognized, unconditional part, but rather a part that is always conditioned by opaque and ever-changing rules and regulations. Cue, now, to the vulnerability of the social body in light of the threat posed by the conceivably virulent individual body. Once again, the conceivably virulent individual body is only admitted to society once it can prove it poses little threat to the latter. Once, but not once and for all: there is no longer an integral social body to return to, only a sum of individuals always-conditionally allowed passage, based on opaque and ever-changing rules and regulations.

The vulnerable, rather than a marginal, secondary figure in human life course and history has always marked the outer margins of a society—it quite literally frames the context in which it operates, by being in these very margins. From the Muselmann in the Nazi concentration camps to the vulnerable migrant in the camps of the present, Giorgio Agamben has correctly identified this liminal form of life as emblematic of (each) era. In the COVID-19 predicament, Agamben focuses on the fluidity of the status of the vaccinated: an always-revocable (or better even: an always re-affirmable) status of inclusion into the social body that frees authorities even from the very burden to evaluate the rightness of the individual's claim to innocuous and healthy status—and instead positions the onerous task of self-certification to the individual themselves.

A circle is, in many ways, now complete: the potentially vulnerable migrant must convince the authorities that they pose less of a threat to the one felt by the hosting social body and therefore, by rule of the calculation of risk, they should be provided not with safe passage, but with unsafe settlement. The potentially threat-carrying individual, on the other hand, must again convince authorities that they pose less of a threat to them; in both cases, this is little other than a continuous calculation of risk, with a constantly undetermined, never-ending outcome.

BY WAY OF A CONCLUSION

The very existence and use of the notion of the "vulnerable" in coming to describe certain individuals and populations points, indirectly yet clearly, to two things. First, there must exist, by definition, another, invulnerable individual or part of the population (importantly, a synonym of the term being "immune"). These invulnerables are the measure against which the vulnerable are evaluated. Second, it points at an authority that comes to decide who falls under the vulnerable or the invulnerable category, and what rights are assigned to each. The very existence of a process of assigning these rights, finally, points at their potential future invocation: the authority gives, and the authority takes away.

David Cayley speaks of Ivan Ilich's description of a "watershed moment" in contemporary life, a holistic "age of systems" where there is, in essence, no "outside" and where the past system wherein individuals pursued their own well-being is no more. Instead, we see the rise of "an immune system which constantly recalibrates its porous boundary with the surrounding system" (2020). The terms "constant" and "porous" are of equal importance in helping us understand the prevalence of vulnerability as a system of thought that exceeds the most vulnerable and becomes a majoritarian understanding that encompasses the social body as a whole. Tellingly, in epidemiology "prevalence" denotes the proportion of a population affected by a medical condition (either a disease or a risk factor). The current age of the pandemic sees the two (disease and risk factor) conflate into one another: the risk (of harm) has come to equal the actual (harm); the possible has become the actual fact.

When we were conducting our fieldwork in Lesvos, at the peak of the migrant reception crisis a few years back, we had come to highlight the EC's Hotspot Approach both as a pillar of the new architecture of population governance that was being formulated before our very eyes, but also as a potential watershed moment, not entirely unlike the ones Caley speaks of in relation to health and population. For the first time, the authorities gave themselves a carte blanche to decide not only what constitutes an emergency, but also what is the appropriate response across a range of registers (from health to security) and scales (from population to the individual). What we see unrolling in the face of the management crisis of COVID-19 is in a sense a continuation and an expansion of the testing field that played out in Lesvos, and a solid reminder of what happens when the experimental field thrusts into the mainstream.

REFERENCES

Bialasiewicz, L. 2012. "Off-shoring and out-sourcing the borders of Europe: Libya and EU border work in the Mediterranean." *Geopolitics* 17 (4): 843–66.

Bigo, D., K. Côté-Boucher, F. Infantino, and M. Salter. 2014. "The (in)securitisation practices of the three universes of EU border control: Military/Navy-border guards/police-database analysts." *Security Dialogue* 45 (3): 209–25.

Butler, J. 2003. "Violence, mourning, politics." *Studies in Gender and Sexuality* 4 (1): 9–37.

Cabot, H. 2012. "The governance of things: Documenting limbo in the Greek Asylum Procedure." *Political and Legal Anthropology Review* 11–29.

Cayley, D. 2020. "Questions about the current pandemic from the point of view of Ivan Illich." https://www.quodlibet.it/david-cayley-questions-about-the-current -pandemic-from-the-point.

Collyer, M. 2012. "Deportation and the micropolitics of exclusion: The rise of removals from the UK to Sri Lanka." *Geopolitics: The Geopolitics of Migration and Mobility* 17 (2): 276–92.

Coutin, S. B. 2000. *Legalizing Moves: Salvadoran Immigrants' Struggle for U.S. Residency*. Ann Arbor, MI: University of Michigan Press.

Cowen, D. 2014. *The Deadly Life of Logistics: Mapping Violence in Global Trade*. Minneapolis: University of Minnesota Press.

Cuttitta, P. 2018. "Repoliticization through search and rescue? Humanitarian NGOs and migration management in the Central Mediterranean." *Geopolitics: Bordering the Middle East* 23 (3): 632–60.

Gammeltoft-Hansen, T., and N. Nyberg Sorensen. 2013. "The rise of the private border guard: Accountability and responsibility in the migration control industry." In *The Migration Industry and the Commercialization of International Migration*, edited by T. Gammeltoft-Hansen and N. Nyberg Sorensen, 146–69. London: Routledge.

Hancox, E., and C. Costello. 2016. "The Recast Asylum Procedures Directive 2013/32/EU: caught between the stereotypes of the abusive asylum seeker and the vulnerable refugee." In *Reforming the European Asylum System. The New European Refugee Law*, edited by Vincent Chetail, 365–445. New York: BRILL.

Huysmans, J. 2000. "The European Union and the securitization of migration." *Journal of Common Market Studies* 38 (5): 751–57.

Hyndman, J., and A. Mountz. 2008. "Another brick in the wall? Neo-refoulement and the externalization of asylum by Australia and Europe." *Government and Opposition* 43 (3): 249–69.

Kalir, B., and L. Wissink. 2016. "The deportation continuum: Convergences between state agents and NGO workers in the Dutch deportation field." *Citizenship Studies* 20 (1): 34–49.

Kasparek, B. 2016. "Complementing Schengen: The Dublin System and the European Border and Migration Regime." In *Migration Policy and Practice. Migration, Diasporas and Citizenship*, edited by H. Bauder and C. Matheis, 59–78. New York: Palgrave Macmillan.

Lavenex, S. 2006. "Shifting up and out: The foreign policy of European immigration control." *West European Politics: Immigration Policy in Europe: The Politics of Control* 29 (2): 329–50.

Little, A., and N. Vaughan-Williams. 2017. "Stopping boats, saving lives, securing subjects: Humanitarian borders in Europe and Australia." *European Journal of International Relations* 23 (3): 533–56.

Maillet, P., A. Mountz, and K. Williams. 2017. "Researching migration and enforcement in obscured places: Practical, ethical and methodological challenges to fieldwork." *Social & Cultural Geography: Geographical Research with 'Vulnerable Groups': Re-examining Methodological and Ethical Process* 18 (7): 927–50.

McDowell, Meghan G., and Nancy A. Wonders. 2009. "Keeping migrants in their place: Technologies of control and racialized public space in Arizona." *Social Justice* 36 (2[116]): 54–72.

McDuff, E. 2019. "Courting asylum: How asylum claimants in Greece are using judicial power to combat neo-refoulement and the EU-Turkey Safe Third Country Agreement." *Flux: International Relations Review* 9 (2): 70–73.

Médecins Sans Frontières (MSF). 2017. *International Activity Report 2017*. Geneva.

Nyers, P. 2003. "Abject cosmopolitanism: The politics of protection in the anti-deportation movement." *Third World Quarterly* 24 (6): 1069–93.

Painter, J., E. Papada, A. Papoutsi, and A. Vradis. 2017. "Hotspot politics? or, when the EU state gets real." *Political Geography* 60: 259.

Pickering, S., and L. Weber. 2006. *Borders, Mobility and Technologies of Control.* Dordrecht: Springer Netherlands.

Scott, J. 1998. *Seeing like a State: How Certain Schemes to Improve the Human Condition Have Failed.* New Haven: Yale University Press.

Vradis, A., E. Papada, J. Painter, and A. Papoutsi. 2018. *New Borders: Hotspots and the European Migration Regime.* London: Pluto Press.

NOTES

1. Introduced in the European Agenda on Migration in May 2015, the hotspot was presented as an integrated approach to tackle the unruly movement on Europe's

borders and its knock-on effects on the European Union. Once a geographical area is declared a hotspot, the European Asylum Support Office (EASO), Frontex, Europol, and Eurojust come in to assist member states to swiftly identify, register, and fingerprint incoming migrants (European Commission 2015).

2. The EU-Turkey Agreement or "Deal" is a political agreement between the European Commission and Turkey. It rests on a mechanism of exchange, whereby for every Syrian that enters through the Greek Aegean islands, another one is returned to Turkey. In addition, the agreement stipulates that all those who enter the Greek Aegean islands are served with an automatic rejection and deportation order on the basis that Turkey constitutes a safe country for them to seek asylum. In return, Turkey has been promised humanitarian aid to cope with the increasing number of refugees within its territory as well as more favorable terms for Turkish citizens who wish to travel and reside in the European Union. For more details please visit https://www .consilium.europa.eu/en/press/press-releases/2016/03/18/eu-turkey-statement/.

3. The ability of Turkey to protect asylum seekers has been questioned by the Greek Asylum service.

4. Fast-track border procedures were exceptional procedures introduced by L4375/2016 and ran until December 2019, when they were incorporated into the new asylum law L4636/2019 and became more permanent in character. See also Greek Council for Refugees: https://asylumineurope.org/reports/country/greece/ asylum-procedure/procedures/fast-track-border-procedure-eastern-aegean/https:// asylumineurope.org/reports/country/greece/asylum-procedure/procedures/fast-track -border-procedure-eastern-aegean/.

5. There is again a huge variation in the transposition and implementation of this approach while there is a substantially lower recognition rate in member states for applications processed within border, accelerated and admissibility procedures compared to regular asylum procedures (ECRE 2016).

6. ECtHR M.S.S v. Belgium & Greece and joined Cases C-411/10 and C-493/10 N.S. v. Secretary of State for the Home Department ruling of the Court of Justice of the EU (CJEU). The Courts had ultimately decided that the individuals from Afghanistan belonged to a particular vulnerable group (the asylum seekers group) on grounds of their uncertain legal status. This led, for a long time, to the suspension of Dublin removals to Greece.

7. The EC's report on the implementation of the EU-Turkey Agreement in March 2017 states that EASO and RIC authorities are working together to define vulnerability categories and develop a standard medical template. https://ec.europa .eu/home-affairs/sites/homeaffairs/files/what-we-do/policies/european-agenda-migration/20170302_progress_on_the_implementation_of_the_joint_action_plan_ en.pdf. This should be read in conjunction with allegations made by Human Rights Watch regarding unduly pressure posed by the EC representatives in Greece onto the Greek Asylum service to lessen the number of those identified as vulnerable. The full press release can be found at https://www.hrw.org/news/2017/06/01/eu/greece -pressure-minimize-numbers-migrants-identified-vulnerable. In parallel, Médecins

Sans Frontières (MSF) published a report condemning plans to restrict the number of those identified as vulnerable and creating the possibility for vulnerable people to go through the admissibility procedure. In addition, the report stated high levels of unreported vulnerability, experiences of violence, and high levels of mental health trauma (MSF 2017).

Chapter 4

Reconfiguring Removal

Commercial Purpose Creeps in Biometric EU Databases

Martin Lemberg-Pedersen and Oliver Joel Halpern

INTRODUCTION

A data frenzy permeates current policymaking on border control practices pursued by both states and humanitarian and commercial for-profit actors. Biometric information is now part of the stable of digital border practices facilitating removal, including deportation, which raises a range of ethical and political problems. By removal, we mean a wide (and widening) range of actors, spaces, and practices that are increasingly geared toward facilitating the expulsion of unwanted migrants (Peutz 2006). In this way, our gaze falls on a constellation that is much larger than the one which is explicitly and directly defined by the act of deportation. Moreover, because the term "deportation" has been strategically devalued by states who are at pains to return migrants "voluntarily" (Kalir et al. 2021; Halpern 2021), using a different word bypasses the problem of having to defend whether a particular act of removal constitutes deportation. Combining forced migration studies, border studies, and political economy, this chapter examines the case of the European Union's evolving digitization of removal practices through the evolution of four large EU databases using personal, individual biometrics of migrants in digital EU border practices. These are the Eurodac, the Schengen Information System (SIS II), the Visa Information System and the soon-to-be Entry/Exit System (EES).

These databases invoke obvious and acute data harms, such as mismatches, posed to individual migrants upon whom these strategies are imposed, as well as larger concerns about data trading or security breaches that risk the release of sensitive personal information. However, we contend that a deeper and more disturbing trend grows from the data-craving (Lemberg-Pedersen and Haioty 2020) nexus of actors who promote the uptake of biometric technologies across removal practices. This chapter suggests that these practices are contributing to the strengthening of ties between industry and politics, with vested industries being given the opportunity to present themselves as both experts and actors within a field where they first construct and define the migrant "problem" and then present their own technologies as pertinent solutions. In this way, governmental transparency is being eroded by a rapidly growing political economy of border control technology.

In order to show this, we first trace the construction and function of the four EU databases. Second, analyzing EU policy documents, we critically discuss the renegotiation of the legislation underpinning these four databases as an ongoing purpose creep, toward generalized surveillance using biometrics to increase the deportation of so-called third-country migrants from EU territory. Third, we analyze the political economic processes underpinning this development, which leads to discussions of political economy, market dynamics, and lobbyism efforts and the influence of the biometrics and surveillance sector on these border politics. Toward the end we discuss how this leads to vulnerability, mistrust and data trading, privacy violation, racialization, and technological errors with ever-larger databases, but also how commercial and EU-level discussions fail to acknowledge the resistance and struggle facing these issues.

Methodologically, we conducted this inquiry by constructing a database of private contracts for border control–related activities, which we sourced from the websites of EU agencies and funding programs of Frontex, EU-Lisa, Framework Programme 7 (FP7), and Horizon 2020 (Lemberg-Pedersen and Halpern 2021). The contracts were selected if they directly related to removal and deportation practices. We also gathered information from the Transparency Register about meetings between representatives from, respectively, the European Commission and selected companies active on the market for EU border control in order to examine their engagement with policymakers. This information was then combined with open source data from reports, technical studies, and cost assessments identified through the EU-portal Cordis, which has also been used to generate information about research projects under FP7 and Horizon 2020 and their participants. Other sources include lobbyfacts.eu, Corporate Europe Observatory, and Transparency International's Integrity Watch. Being heavily reliant on piecemeal information and constrained by the enormous input of time required to "follow the trail" from one incomplete source to another, we were always aware that the data we collected only represented a fraction of the full picture. Due to the shadowy nature of the politico-industrial collaboration producing border control, it was difficult to estimate, for example, what percentage of the total pool of existing contracts were actually registered by us during our investigation. Nonetheless, this method of data collection allowed us to convert the confusing patchwork of publicly available primary source material into a workable and informative database.

EUROPEAN DEPORTATION CONTINUUMS AND CORRIDORS

The matrices of political subjectivities in deportation politics are often characterized by messiness and cross-cutting interests. This applies to the many national, transnational, public, and private actors involved in deportation politics, but also how people who move through deportation structures can employ a number of diverging strategies, such as negotiations with border guards, acceptance or subterfuge of surveillance systems, irregular existence, dissenting or collaborating with grassroots, or monitoring bodies.

According to Kalir and Wissink (2016), some studies define a deportation regime as constituted by street-level public bureaucrats, on the one hand, and nongovernmental organizations (NGOs) and civil-society actors, on the other. However, the two authors argue that the analytical framework of "deportation continuums" is well suited for examining such constellations of power. These are defined by a focus on the interactions of multiple stakeholders involved in the continuous crafting of political subjectivities, competing imaginaries of citizenship, and alternative visions of deportation (Kalir and Wissink 2016). This concept thus aids us in explaining the dynamics, such as institutional barriers and turf wars, as well as public-private engagements and contractual relations.

Compatible with this conceptualization, Drotbohm and Hasselberg (2015) have suggested that a framework of "deportation corridors," where deportation is understood not as the singular event of physical removal enforced by a state but, rather, as a process spanning multiple spaces, scales, temporalities, actors, and interests. Their concept, in turn, builds on Nyer's (2003) work on "transnational corridors of expulsion" and Peutz's (2006) call for "an anthropology of removal" to study daily performances of deportation. As such, it can include practices such as pre-return detention, return counseling by non-state actors, diplomatic readmission agreements and technological infrastructures such as biometric databases, as well as social life (or death) after deportation. Taken together, the concepts of deportation continuums and corridors allow us to direct a critical gaze toward how deportation practices require funds, personnel, technological equipment, and infrastructures.

Deportation governance takes place through processes of multi-leveled governance. However, beyond the state and NGO actors emphasized by Kalir and Wissink (2016), the political economy of this continuum must also include the range of commercial for-profit sectors and companies competing on markets for border control (Lemberg-Pedersen 2022). On these markets, deportation data is therefore fashioned through ensembles of technologies, actors, logics, and interests wider than state-centered regimes.

The EU databases have been developed according to which types of individuals are registered; irregular migrants found in member states can be registered into SIS, asylum seekers are registered in Eurodac, and those entering on a legal visa are registered in the Visa Information System (VIS). The four EU information systems combine biometric identification technology with computerized data processing, that is, diffuse borders that cannot be geographically localized, but instead rely on both physical and virtual locations as well as institutions of control and surveillance connected through digital data networks (Tsianos and Kuster 2016; Amoore 2006; Amoore, Marmura, and Salter 2008; Guild, Carrera, and Geyer 2008).

Biometric technologies are widely used because they are supposed to be cheaper, faster, less prone to errors, and easier to share than human verification. Most of the EU systems under scrutiny here function for identification purposes; that is, where biometric data is stored in a computer system in order to identify a person who is otherwise not identifiable, for instance because they do not have ID or travel documents (known as one-to-many matches); rather than for the purposes of verification, where biometric data is used to verify an already-known identity (one-to-one matches). The most common way to register those crossing European Union's external borders is by entering their alphanumeric (e.g., name, gender, age) or biometric data (e.g., fingerprints, iris scans, palm prints). As such, biometric data is particularly sensitive as it is unique for those registering.

The technologies underpinning EU databases are produced and supplied by companies active on the market for deportation. These exercise a growing presence in policymaking through lobbyism efforts and private rule-setting when trying to influence institutions and persons involved in tenders for deportation contracts to deliver services and infrastructure (Lemberg-Pedersen et al. 2020; cf. Baird 2018; Jones et al. 2020). The markets for deportation functions are also shaped and induced by states or transnational political institutions such as the European Union. Here, the European Commission's recast proposals, designed to reconfigure the regulations of the European Union's border-control databases, are an apt case in point. By integrating or expanding the use of biometric information in databases such as Eurodac, the

SIS II and the VIS, and then linking this data to the purpose of returns, these technological infrastructures have been refashioned considerably from their original purpose. The following section details these processes in more depth.

RECASTS AND RECONFIGURATIONS OF EU BORDER CONTROL DATABASES

In 2015 and 2016, the Commission conducted a review of the SIS II, calling the second-generation database a "genuine operational success," describing how, in 2015, "national competent authorities checked persons and objects against data held in SIS on nearly 2.9 billion occasions and exchanged over 1.8 million pieces of supplementary information" (European Commission 2016). However, despite the alleged success of SIS II, in December 2016, the Commission tabled three legislative proposals recasting the database's functions and purposes, concerning the use of SIS for the return of migrants (COM(2016) 881 final); the establishment, operation, and use of SIS for border checks (COM(2016) 882 final); and police and judicial cooperation on criminal matters (COM(2016) 883 final). The 2016 recast proposals for the database included Commission arguments that deepened police and juridical cooperation between member states was urgently needed (European Commission 2016b, 2).

In the second of the three SIS proposals, the Commission wrote of

> [a]n effective EU returns policy contributing to and enhancing the EU system to detect and prevent the re-entry of third-country nationals following their return. This proposal would help reducing incentives to irregular migration to the EU, one of the main objectives of the European Agenda on Migration (European Commission 2016b, 5). Three new uses of the database were suggested; increased border management, increased police and juridical cooperation and increased returns of TCNs from EU territory, all of which required expanded interoperability and standardization. (European Parliament 2017b)

The enforcement of return decisions issued to irregularly staying immigrants was to be improved by "introducing a new alert category for return decisions . . . and functions for creating, updating and deleting alerts on return," a step that was framed as contributing to the implementation and monitoring of the Returns Directive (2008/115/EC) (European Commission 2016a, 11). The new category was then to be differentiated into alerts for the purpose of return and an alert in relation to return decisions issued to illegally staying third-country nationals (Council of the EU 2018). Then-Commissioner for Migration, Home Affairs and Citizenships, Dimitris Avramopoulos, justified the measures as necessary in order to "close information gaps" and "improve information exchange" so that in the future "no critical information should ever be lost on potential terrorist suspects or irregular migrants crossing our external borders" (European Commission 2016c). Accordingly, larger swaths of data should be collected and more searches would be made mandatory. Moreover, the biometric data should also be made multi-modal, that is, based on diverse typologies, such as fingerprints, facial images, photographs, and palm prints. Crucially, by making it mandatory to enter alerts on non-compliance on return decisions and entry bans, and the storing and sharing of this information in the new SIS III, the ambition was to evolve the SIS system into an instrument for monitoring third country nationals (TCNs) subject to return decisions (European Parliament 2018b). Currently, the project Access to SIS II (A2SISII) is exploring ways to connect Frontex to the SIS II database, in line with the Frontex 2019 Regulation (Lemberg-Pedersen and Halpern 2021).

For Eurodac, the Commission also tabled a new proposal in 2016 containing seventeen measures widening the kinds, categories, and storage of data in the system. This included expanding the scope of the database to include return purposes, so that member states could search for, store, transmit, and compare data belonging to "illegally staying" third-country nationals or stateless persons who were not applicants for international protection, making them identifiable for return operations (European Commission 2016c, 12). As this measure transformed the database's original functionality of a repository for fingerprints of asylum seekers, it effectively expanded the purpose of Eurodac, so that it no longer served the purpose of ensuring member states' effective implementation of the Dublin III Regulation (EC 2016c, 11). The recast proposal also introduced more biometric identifiers into the system, reconfiguring the database from one solely using fingerprint data to one including also facial recognition (European Commission 2016c, 12–13).

The Commission justified this expansion of the data collected by saying that they would facilitate interoperability with new surveillance technologies such as facial recognition to be integrated in a centralized system underpinning the governance of migrants across the EU databases (European Commission 2016c, 4). In the 2016 recast proposal, the data retention period was extended from eighteen months to five years, the age of registration was lowered significantly from fourteen to six years, and the use of facial recognition technology was introduced. Moreover, it opened up for the possibility that also third-country authorities could access Eurodac in order to transfer personal data for such purposes. The Commission portrays such exchanges of highly sensitive biometric data as solving a problem of asylum applicants refusing to have their fingerprints taken, and such identification processes are seen as crucial for the European Union's stated goal of drastically upscaling returns from the European Union. However, this argument confuses the issue of enforceability of data systems with the widening of parameters identifying the population to be registered. Further, it does not address the potential data harms arising from EU interoperability with third countries, nor the ethical dimension of registering younger children, and rolling out more technologies for such purposes.

The VIS, according to the Commission's 2018 recast proposal making VIS interoperable with the other large-scale systems through a European Search Portal and EU-Lisa's Biometric Matching System (BMS), would then prevent security risks and irregular migration to the European Union (European Commission 2018). This interoperability was to make it easier to transfer categories of data. For instance, the Commission suggested to store also information collected via the aforementioned lowering of the fingerprinting age (from fourteen years to six years), and on longer-stay visas and residence permits issued by member states. If realized, this would add an additional twenty-two million entries to VIS's current fifty-two million visa applicants (Statewatch 2018).

The formal development of the EES followed a 2008 feasibility study conducted for the Commission by the consultancy company Unisys (2008). The EES was then announced by the Commission in 2013 (European Commission 2013), further developed in a communication to the Parliament and Council and then established in 2017 via Regulation 2017/2226, as part of the so-called Smart Borders package of legislative proposals. It was framed as modernizing the Schengen Area's external borders, and it was expected to be rolled out in 2020. It has, however, faced delays, partly due to the COVID-19 pandemic, but also due to lacking technological infrastructure among many member states.

The original EES package proposed to record the time/place of entry and exit for TCNs entering the Schengen Area, information that none of the other databases record. In registering and tracking people's travel histories, the EES was also envisioned as complementing alerts already recorded in SIS. The EES is to be applied to TCNs who are admitted for a short-stay visa to the territory of the Schengen member states or whose entry for a short stay has been refused. The explicit aim is to facilitate the mobility of visa-holding travelers, while intensifying the identification of TCNs not fulfilling their visa requirements, who are to be deported. In the system envisioned, all member states will have National Uniform Interfaces on their territory. Also, the EES is to be interconnected and interoperable with the VIS database via a Secure Communication Channel established between them, as well as between the EES Central System and the national interfaces (EU-Lisa 2017; European Parliament 2017b). The plans also include the development of a web service through which maritime transport carriers and airplane companies can determine whether TCNs holding a Schengen short-stay visa have already used the number of authorized entries. As a result of this, private companies, too, will be tasked with the daily management of EU exit infrastructure. This represents a further extension of carriers' liability.

This section has shown some of the details of this pervasive reconfiguration of the EU databases toward return. The following section expands on this by examining relations between EU agencies and actors on the market for border control. By drawing the links between these processes, this chapter argues that the contractual relations underpinning the drive for upscaling removal operations represent an incursion of the private sphere into the political, which corresponds to an increasingly intransparent system of governance within the European Union.

Actors, Dynamics, and Lobbyism on the EU Markets for Deportation Data Infrastructures

The fast-paced evolution of the interoperable EU border systems means that the establishment of new infrastructures and the upgrading of these have become a central and permanent priority in EU border policymaking. Moreover, the flurry of new systems, such as the SIS to SIS II, Eurodac, the BMS, VIS, and now EES, also serve as simplifying arguments for one another (cf. Jeandesboz 2016). Trading on the lock-in effect generated by the need for interoperability, each system is used to justify the continuous evolution of the others, leading to circular arguments for the technical feasibility and functional interoperability of the large-scale systems. When it comes to commercial interventions in the multi-leveled EU border governance, the flurry of systems and upgrades also leads to a corresponding flurry of border contracts. Here, one particular EU agency assumes a central role.

The EU's Agency for the Operational Management of Large-Scale IT Systems in the Area of Freedom, Security and Justice (EU-Lisa) was established as the agency responsible for the European Dactyloscopy Database (Eurodac), the SIS, the VIS, and the future EES. EU-Lisa manages data via its BMS, which is a search engine that systematizes biometric data through technologies measuring, analyzing, and processing digital representations of unique biological data traits for the purpose of identification and verification (Ajana 2013). BMS had been constructed through a 2006 contract from the Directorate General: Justice Freecom and Security. It was budgeted at €157 million, and awarded to a Bridge consortium, consisting of Sagem Défénsé Sécurité (part of Safran), Accenture and Daon, as well as Bull and Uniqkey (Daon 2008).

A 2010 market analysis estimated that products for biometric fingerprint technologies would reach a market volume of around fifteen billion dollars in 2015 (Tsianos and Kuster 2016). By 2019, the global biometric market was estimated to grow from thirty-three billion dollars to $65.3 billion by 2024 (Market and Markets 2019). The company Accenture won contracts for both the SIS II, alongside its partners ATOS Belgium and Hewlett-Packard Belgium—one worth, for instance, €2.8 million in 2018. That same year, Accenture also won a contract for the VIS, alongside Safran and Hewlett Packard Belgium in the Bridge Consortium, worth €54.8 million (Lemberg-Pedersen et al. 2020).

In general, there is great opaqueness regarding interaction between the companies and EU institutions, and when it comes to how such actors lobby the Commission on the phrasing and wording of communications and legislative drafts and acts. The greater the lack of transparency, the higher likelihood of informal interventions in the drafting of policies, funding priorities, and legislations (cf. Baird 2018). The lobbying efforts may take several forms. A widespread strategy is described by the lobbying organization Aerospace and Defence Industries Association of Europe (ASD), one of the biggest European lobby organizations for the security and military industry: Companies wishing to be "proactive and strive to generate new procurement opportunities" should engage with representatives from their member state who are placed in the Programme Committee of the funding instruments desired by the company (ASD 2016, 10). To this end, companies employ both in-house lobbyists as described earlier, or external lobbyists, who can arrange meetings with the relevant Directorate Generals or higher-level Commission representatives, or approach Members in the European Parliament (MEPs). External lobbyists, like communications bureaus, may also orchestrate larger media campaigns in targeted European cities and financial centers on behalf of their client companies. Both kinds of lobbyists also collaborate or facilitate networks through the intergroups of the European Parliament, or via more informal extra-parliamentary groups. Intergroups are forums of MEPs assembled in order to promote specific topics or themes through informal exchanges and facilitated contact with extra-parliamentary actors, such as companies, communications bureaus, or interest groups. Between 2014 and 2019, there were twenty-eight such groups. The Sky and Space Intergroup is particularly relevant as a hub for security and defense lobbyism. It brings together MEPs with institutional actors like EU-Lisa or Frontex, but also large defense, information and communication technology (ICT), and military contractors like Airbus, Safran, and Leonardo. From 2009 to 2014, the Sky and Space Intergroup Secretariat of two or three persons was even provided by the ASD (Corporate Europe Observatory 2011).

If we turn to the lobbyism efforts of companies involved in the reconfiguration of the EU databases toward deportation, then Atos, Thales, Indra, and Safran are illustrative. First, Atos is a French ICT and biometrics technology company, founded in 1982. In 2018, the company boasted revenues of $11.3 billion and had 122,000 employees (Forbes 2019c). Atos entered the market for border infrastructures very early, as it was responsible for the development of the first-generation SIS I. Since 2014, it has also been involved in consortiums for the SIS II system as well as the upcoming EES. Its technology supply includes integrated maritime surveillance systems which, they claim, are responsible for saving migrants' lives through their use by the Spanish coastal patrols and border guards in the Mediterranean (Atos 2017). Its former chief executive officer, Thierry Breton, has gone on to become France's representative at the EU Commission, as commissioner for Internal Markets (European Commission 2019b). Second, Thales is a French security and defense company founded in 2000 that specializes in biometrics, radar systems, and space technology. In 2018, it had a revenue of €15.8 billion and over eighty thousand employees (Thales 2019). Since 2012, Thales has been developing drone technology for use by Frontex (Akkerman 2019). With Thales's acquisition of Gemalto—a company specializing in biometrics which had itself already incorporated 3M's Identity Management business— they have shown a clear interest in developing their company down this line. Thales have registered six lobbyists in Brussels, with a budget of around three hundred thousand euros, and answering to the Senior Vice President for EU, NATO and EU relations, Marc Cathelineau. Alongside these, both 3M and Gemalto also registered lobbyists. Thus, from 2014 and until its take-over by Gemalto, 3M registered five lobbyists. Its lobbying budget was between six hundred thousand euros and €699,000. Gemalto registered only one lobbyist, who from 2014 had three meetings with representatives from the European Commission. Combined, the lobbying efforts of 3M and Gemalto on identity management have been instrumental in building Thales's market position within this area. Third, Indra is a Spanish ICT and consultancy aiming at becoming specialists in border security, particularly regarding biometrics for integrated border systems. In 2018, they achieved revenues of €3.1 billion and employed forty-three thousand people (Indra 2019). Indra registered six lobbyists in Brussels, with a budget between nine hundred thousand euros and one million euros. Safran is a French aerospace and defense company which created revenues of €21.5 billion in 2018, and reported employing ninety-one thousand people (Safran 2019a). It was created in 2005 by merging two previous companies, Snecma and Sagem SA; via this heritage, it claims to be the oldest aircraft manufacturing company in the world (Safran 2019b). Through its subsidiary company, Morpho, Safran has won a number of important border contracts in the ICT and biometrics sector, such as the VIS system. The company Safran has held nine meetings with representatives from the European Commission since 2014. They have seven lobbyists for these tasks, of which Marie de Saint-Cheron, senior vice president in

European and Multilateral Affairs, is the person with the main responsibility. Their lobby budget is estimated to be around €495,000.

Besides the opaque interactions between lobbyists and EU institutions, also more overt nexus points are organized by agencies, such as EU-Lisa, for instance its roundtables. During these, representatives from EU institutions, industry actors, and foreign agencies are regularly invited as experts within the field. From the first roundtable in 2014 until mid-2019, EU-Lisa has hosted ten such roundtables. At the roundtables, it is possible for industrial actors to liaise with government representatives and communicate their preferences and suggested solutions to the development of information technology systems. Roundtables, as well as conferences, are important sites for the industry in order to influence the policies and choices of technological solutions underpinning the large-scale information systems. For instance, in 2016, under the heading "Interoperable IT systems for Europe: Towards greater standardisation and better efficiency," EU-Lisa once again invited industry to a roundtable. Invitees included three representatives from the agency itself, one from Europol, and seven from the industry (EU-Lisa 2016b). The roundtables have several effects. On the one hand, if the same company is invited to several roundtables, their chances to influence EU-Lisa decisions on technological solutions become proportionately higher. On the other hand, this strategy also requires companies to constantly develop high-tech solutions, even before problems corresponding to the technological capacities exist. As such, they both influence the political agenda so it corresponds to the already developed solutions, but they are also challenged to respond to sudden, and potentially infeasible, political wishes.

EU-Lisa has served as an accelerator for the technical and commercial vision of interoperable EU borders upon which political proposals for recast have been modeled. Following 2016 to 2018, EU-Lisa began issuing more contract tenders for the evolution of the SIS II, VIS, Eurodac, and EES databases. This has helped accelerate a commercial market for the data infrastructure underpinning future EU deportation technologies, and several consortiums launched bids on these tenders. In June 2020, EU-Lisa awarded a consortium consisting of Idemia and Sopra Steria a €302.6 million contract of four-year duration, for the development, delivery, and maintenance of a new shared BMS to serve as a key infrastructure for the EES. These examples serve to demonstrate the way in which private companies who pose as both consultancies and service providers generate markets for their products and services which fundamentally change the landscape of governance through the dialectic relationships they foster with elected governmental actors.

CONCLUSION

This chapter has detailed how several large-scale EU information systems have been reconfigured along a purpose creep toward accelerated returns. Several concerns have, however, been raised in this respect. The Commission has tabled many expansions and linkages, such as increased data retention periods, lowering age of biometric registration, multi-modalities, or the inclusion of commercial companies in searches across the systems, during the renegotiations of Eurodac, VIS and SIS, ECRIS-TCN, and the launch of EES. The reasons for these invasive measures, and their potential to cause data harms and violations of privacy, have been neither adequately justified nor motivated, and the proportionality and accountability of these vast data mining operations in relation to the rights of people on the move remain underdetermined. Instead, the overall rationale of interoperability is invoked at the risk of being used to conflate distinct phenomena like migration management, internal security, and the combat against terrorism. According to the European Data Protection Supervisor (EDPS), this has the implication that interoperability involves new forms of data processing which are "not covered by existing legal bases," leading the supervisor to strongly recommend that "their impact on the fundamental rights to privacy and data protection needs to be carefully assessed" (EDPS 2017, 6–7).

The political drive toward constructing border infrastructures with interoperable information systems has involved actors from the ICT, defense, and biometrics sectors of member states from before the 1990s. These have been hired to consult on, design, develop, maintain, and evolve the information systems, including their biometric functions, and these strategies are pursued in different ways and by interest groups reflecting different commercial, public institutional, and national interests. Various lobbying strategies and forums are deployed by actors on the market for EU border control, and policies therefore evolve through a plethora of luncheons, talks, meetings, workshops, seminars, and conferences; all events where norms and knowledges are negotiated and adjusted.

These important policy settings remain, for the most part, opaque and inaccessible to the general public, as does the realization that many of the norms embedded in data infrastructures for border control are constituted through certain constrained epistemic communities, with certain assumptions, rules, and standards. While chief executive officers from commercial providers of ICT and border control technology have often been invited by the European Commission, Frontex, or EU-Lisa to participate in official expert groups, inclusion of NGOs focusing on human rights or data privacy has only taken place to a very limited degree. Our tracing of EU-Lisa workshops and framework contracts illustrates that commercial interests have been a mainstay throughout the development of the interoperable EU border systems. Commercial interests in border control technology continuously seek to place themselves in, and are increasingly also invited into, the machine room of EU multi-leveled governance. Such activities from corporate interest groups illustrate that the market for these technologies is extremely lucrative and growing. Accordingly, so are the activities of commercial actors proactively pursuing contracts and market shares, with both political and commercial actors hiding behind the teleological rhetoric of interoperability to fast-track profit-inducing measures at the expense of governmental transparency and migrant safety. It is remarkable that despite the observable and decade-long tendency for corporate involvement in multi-leveled EU governance, and the fact that lobbyism has historically impacted EU policymaking in troublesome ways, these kinds of activities remain virtually unaddressed when it comes to naming the challenges to be addressed by European migration policymakers.

These markets are characterized by a pervasive craving for data about deportable populations which are depicted as risky Others. And the trajectory of deportation data is one that traverses continuums of technological and financial tools shaped by wider ensembles of actors, logics, and interests outside state-centered logics and regimes. Biometric databases linked to deportation politics, such as Eurodac, SIS, VIS, and EES, therefore represent the material and functional underpinnings of the virtual data flows accompanying the stages of expulsion. The construction of such deportation data represents interventions where the flux of life is *datafied*, that is, translated into computerized data used for identification and verification purposes in accordance with the targets determined as risks in the deportation databases (Lemberg-Pedersen 2022). Technologies for measurement, identification, and imaging have enhanced the capacity of various actors in deportation continuums to monitor and govern bodies at the refugee/technology interface. This poses urgent questions about how the normalization of data craving in deportation politics reinforces structural harms on already vulnerable people.

REFERENCES

Aeronautics, Space, Defence and Security Industries in Europe (ASD). 2016. "News from Brussels." *Quarterly Newsletter*, May 2016.

Akkerman, M. 2019. *The Business of Building Walls*. Amsterdam: Stop Wapenhandel.

Amoore, L. 2006. "Biometric borders: Governing mobilities in the war on terror." *Political Geography* 25: 336–51.

Amoore, L., S. Marmura, and M. B. Salter. 2008. "Smart borders and mobilities: Spaces, zones, enclosures." *Surveillance & Society* 5 (2): 96–101.

Atos. 2017. "Controlling borders as global threats evolve." https://atos.net/en/blog/controlling-borders-global-threats-evolve.

Baird, T. 2018. "Interest groups and strategic constructivism: business actors and border security policies in the European Union." *Journal of Ethnic and Migration Studies* 44 (1): 118–36.

Corporate Europe Observatory. 2011. *Lobbying Warfare. The arms industry's role in building a military Europe*. Brussels: Corporate Europe Observatory.

Council of the European Union. 2018. "Schengen Information System: Council adopts new rules to strengthen security in the EU." https://www.consilium.europa.eu/en/press/press-releases/2018/11/19/schengen-information-system-council-adopts-new-rules-to-strengthen-security-in-the-eu/.

Daon. 2008. "Press release. Daon. European Union—Biometric Matching System." http://www.nws-sa.com/biometrics/EU_Matching_CS.pdf.

Drotbohm, H., and I. Hasselberg. 2015. "Deportation, anxiety, justice: new ethnographic perspectives," *Journal of Ethnic and Migration Studies* 41 (4): 551–62.

EU-Lisa. 2016b. "Industry Roundtable report. Interoperable IT systems for Europe: Towards more harmonisation, quality and efficiency." https://www.eulisa.europa.eu/Publications/Reports/Industry%20Roundtable%20Oct%202016.pdf#search=roundtable.

EU-Lisa. 2017. "Executive Summary, Annex I. Call for Tender. Framework contract for the implementation and maintenance in working order of the Entry and Exit System (EES)."

LISA/2017/RP/03. (Restricted Procedure—Article 104 (1) (b) Financial Regulation, Article 127 (2)paragraph 2 Rules of Application)." https://www.eulisa.europa.eu/Procurement/Tenders/LISA2017RP03/Annex%20I%20Executive%20summary.pdf.

European Commission. 2013. "'Smart borders': enhancing mobility and security." https://ec.europa.eu/home-affairs/whatisnew/news/news/2013/20130228_01_en.

European Commission. 2016a. COM(2016) 881 final - 2016/0407 (COD), Brussels.

European Commission. 2016b. COM/2016/0882 final - 2016/0408 (COD), Brussels.

European Commission. 2016c. COM/2016/0272 final - 2016/0132 (COD), Brussels.

European Commission. 2018. Proposal for a Regulation of the European Parliament and of the Council amending Regulation (EC) No 767/2008, regulation (EC) No 810/1009, Regulation (EU) 2017/2226, Regulation (EU) 2016/399, Regulation XX/2018 [Interoperability Regulation], and Decision 2004/512/EC and repealing Council Decision 2008/633/JHA. Brussels, 16.5.2018, COM(018) 302 final.

European Commission. December 21, 2016. "Security Union: Commission proposes to reinforce the Schengen Information System to better fight terrorism and cross-border crime." Press release. Brussels.

European Data Protection Supervisor (EDPS). November 17, 2017. "Reflection paper on the interoperability of information systems in the area of Freedom, Security and Justice, at the EDPS." https://edps.europa.eu/sites/edp/files/publication/17-11-16_opinion_interoperability_en.pdf.

European Parliament. 2017b. "Interoperability between EU information systems for border and security." http://www.europarl.europa.eu/legislative-train/theme-area

-ofjustice-and-fundamentalrights/file-interoperability-between-eu-information-systems-forborders-and-security.

European Parliament. 2018b. Regulation (EU) 2018/1860 of the European Parliament and of the Council of 28 November 2018 on the use of the Schengen Information System for the return of illegally staying third-country nationals, Brussels: journal reference L 312/1.

Guild, E., S. Carrera, and F. Geyer. 2008. "The Commission's New Border Package. Does it take us one step closer to a 'cyber-fortress Europe'?" *Centre for European Policy Studies Policy Brief.* No. 154.

Halpern, O. J. 2021. *Uncertain, Illegible, Incomplete: Exploring Categorisation in Police Bureaucracy of Deportable Migrants from Denmark.* Copenhagen: University of Copenhagen.

Indra. 2019. "About Indra." https://www.indracompany.com/en/indra.

Jeandesboz, J. 2016. "Smartening border security in the European Union: An associational inquiry." *Security & Dialogue* 47 (4): 292–309.

Jones, C., J. Kilpatrick, and M. Gkliati. 2020. "Deportation Union. Rights, accountability, and the EU's push to increased forced removals." https://www.statewatch.org/media/1321/deportation-union.pdf.

Lemberg-Pedersen, M., J. Rübner Hansen, and O. J. Halpern. 2020. *The Political Economy of Entry Governance.* Copenhagen: Aalborg University.

Lemberg-Pedersen, M., and E. Haioty. 2020. "Re-assembling the surveillable refugee body in the era of data-craving." *Citizenship Studies* 24 (5): 607–24.

Lemberg-Pedersen, M., and O. J. Halpern. 2021. *Frontex and Exit Governance: Dataveillance, civil society and markets for border control.* Copenhagen: University of Copenhagen.

Lemberg-Pedersen, M. 2022. "The contours of deportation studies." In *Handbook on Return Migration*, edited by R. King and K. Kuschminder. Cheltenham: Edward Elgar.

Kalir, B., and L. Wissink. 2016. "The deportation continuum: convergences between state agents and NGO workers in the Dutch deportation field." *Citizenship Studies* 20 (1): 34–49.

Market and Markets. 2019. Biometric System Market by Authentication Type (single-Factor: Fingerprint, Iris, Palm Print, Face, Voice; Multi-Factor), Offering (Hardware, Software), Functionality (Contact, Noncontact, Combined), End user, and Region—Global Forecast to 2024. Report.

Nyers, Peter. 2003. "Abject cosmopolitanism: The politics of protection in the anti-deportation movement." *Third World Quarterly* 24 (6): 1069–93.

Safran. 2019a. "Very strong 2018 performance." https://www.safrangroup.com/media/safran-very-strong-2018-performance-further-growth-and-profitabilityimprovement-2019-20190227.

Safran. 2019b. "Company's history." https://www.companieshistory.com/safran/.

Thales. 2019. "Full year results 2018." https://www.thalesgroup.com/en/group/investors/press-release/2018-full-year-results.

Tenders electronic daily. 2020. "Estonia-Tallinn: Framework contract for implementation and maintenance in working order of the biometrics part of the entry exit system and future shared biometrics matching dystem 2020/S 085–20083." https://ted.europa.eu/udl?uri=TED:NOTICE:200083-2020:TEXT:EN:HTML.

Tsianos, V. S., and B. Kuster. 2016. "Eurodac in times of bigness: The power of big data within the emerging European IT agency." *Journal of Borderlands Studies* 31 (2): 235–49.

Chapter 5

Liminality, Asylum, and Arbitrariness in the Greek State's Implementation of the 2016 EU-Turkey Statement

Vasilis Vlassis

INTRODUCTION

The "EU-Turkey Statement" (hereafter the "Statement") was published in March 2016 and was introduced as a critical part of the European Union's response toward the then-ongoing "migrant crisis." Its relatively short text radically recalibrated several aspects of the European Union's "migration machine," namely "the sum of systems that are used in Europe in migration policy and border control . . . a cross border policy apparatus for limiting the movement of aliens and for making choices about the migrants (desirable/ undesirable) who report to the borders" (Dijstelbloem, Meijer, and Brom 2011). As part of the Statement's implementation, new admissibility criteria for asylum claims were introduced, the Turkish state was recruited to enforce strict border controls that would deter migrants from crossing into Greece, the mobility of migrants already present in the Greek islands was significantly restricted, and their living conditions were significantly worsened. As an outcome of the Statement, the fate of migrants became a bargaining chip between the European Union and the state of Turkey (*The Economist* 2016). Finally, thousands of people on the move were now confined on Turkish soil and the governance of those populations was outsourced to the Turkish state.

The Statement was a turning point in the governance of migrant populations. Despite multiple controversies that sparked around it (some of which formulate the core of this chapter), it was effective in engaging the Turkish state in deterring migrants from crossing into the European Union and has even been seen as an example for future policymaking (Delcker 2017). It is a prime example of how policy decisions, once inconceivable as normal practices, become legible once crisis has been proclaimed.

The chapter aims to provide critical analysis of the Statement and the way that it conceptualized the elements of the "migrant crisis" that were perceived to be at the core of the concept by European policymakers, and the way that said perceptions allowed for arguably extra-juridical policymaking. Furthermore, it seeks to present practices through which said policies were materialized and the subsequent reconfiguration of critical elements of the European border regime. Toward those goals, the chapter focuses on instances of the implementation of the Statement by the Greek state, namely its impact on the asylum procedure as it was carried out by the Greek authorities, and how the Greek state dealt with cases of migrants caught up in the temporal margins that the Statement created. These cases, even though they are not exhaustive, are argued to indicate the arbitrariness of practices that characterized the implementation of the Statement in the Greek context, which in turn sheds light on the aspects of the "migrant crisis" that were deemed to be at the core of the crisis, and therefore were prioritized in the European response.

The reality of bordering practices cannot be penetrated through the study of policy papers, joint statements, and operational manuals alone. Ethnographic methods, incorporating accounts of people working in the field, offer a view of bordering as it happens, which often is far from the declared goals and practices. As Wonders puts it, "state policies have little meaning until they are performed by border agents" (Wonders 2006), and border agents, like all human agents, carry with them prejudice and bias and "are informed in their practices by notions of what constitutes border" (Green 2010). From policymaking to actual border work, things differ significantly as work ethics and habits, worldviews of caseworkers, and unspoken institutional constraints all have their part in the way that policies are enforced (Johnson et al. 2011; Vlassis 2021). The material on which the chapter is based was collected during the period 2016 to 2018, as part of a PhD project, and included non-participant observation of border work in the hotspots in the Greek islands of Chios and Lesvos, analysis of policy papers and news articles, as well as interviews with border guards working for the Greek Police and Frontex, people working with migrant support groups and nongovernmental organizations (NGOs), as well as interviews with Greek police officers based in Athens, working in different departments of the Greek police. The chapter is structured as follows: The following section shortly introduces some analytical aspirations around bordering and the concept of crisis that will be used in the analysis, followed by a brief presentation of the main points of the "Statement" and its legal status. Three sections then present the empirical material, followed by a discussion and some concluding remarks.

ANALYTICAL ASPIRATIONS

On Borders and Classifications

Borders are traditionally considered to comprise an empirical-physical phenomenon, well defined, visible on a map as lines demarcating the limits of territorial power of states, and guarded by the state's armed forces (Paasi 2009). Seen as fixed entities, borders may or may not be considered effective in their declared task, which is primarily to assess an individual's status, classify them, and therefore include the desired, exclude the undesired, facilitate those worthy of traveling, and slow down or deter the unworthy. However, instead of discussing borders as fixed entities, branches of border scholarship see borders as a series of bordering practices, open-ended and always in a state of becoming (Kaiser 2012). By avoiding a view of borders as "objects of knowledge . . . already given," instead one may "investigate the processes by which these objects are constituted" (Mezzadra and Neilson 2012).

On a policy level, the spatial divide between "inside" and "outside" that borders produce, and the subsequent mediation, facilitation, or blocking of the mobility of populations, cannot be discussed outside the sociopolitical relations existing within the territory of different states, and also involves relations between them (De Genova 2016). Borders are not merely the boundaries between two states, but are constantly "overdetermined, and, in that sense, sanctioned, reduplicated and relativized by other geopolitical divisions" (Balibar 2002). Thus there is no linear pattern in the transformation of borders. They are "being both multiplied and reduced in their localization and their function, they are being thinned out and doubled" (Balibar 1998). In other words, the intensity of, for example, control at border venues and in procedures, as well as their symbolic value, is subject to radical and unpredicted changes enabled by factors that precede their locality.

Bordering practices produce and function based on classification regimes, enabled through policymaking and border officers' actions on the field. Assigning people or their actions into categories is a ubiquitous part of bordering. Such categories are products of human work and other kinds of organized activity: contingent and conflictual in nature, but at the same time remaining invisible and silenced (Bowker and Star 1999). The categories that are related to border work, such as migrant/refugee, are often present in the public discourse as preexisting properties of individuals, which a well-functioning border detects. However, said categories have been argued to be the outcome of complex assemblages of policies (Mau et al. 2015), various technologies and databases (Van der Ploeg and Sprenkels 2011; Dijstelbloem, Meijer, and Besters 2011), and border officers' labor (Johnson et al. 2011; De Genova 2016). Thus, in a direction parallel to that of examining the constitution of borders as processes, there is great value in tracing the trajectories of said categories and identities.

On Crisis

The focal point of this chapter, namely the Statement, was published as an essential part of the European Union's response to the "migration crisis." What exactly has been at crisis, and how it should be framed, is admittedly a complex task (Agustín and Jørgensen 2019). Opening up beyond the scope of the specific "migrant crisis," the very concept of crisis is an elusive, multi-layered and ambiguous concept, perceived in its utterances as an unpredictable surprise, a historically unique event (Koselleck 2006) that emerges almost ahistorically. While its origins are often rooted in prolonged conflicts, political choices and structural injustice being not only hard to define in unison but also tending to be obscured, crisis renders itself an "immediate present" (Mbembe and Roitman 1995) which demands and necessitates immediate responses (Calhoun 2010) that override previous frameworks, reconstruct preexisting moral codes (Strasser 2016), and intensify control (Strasser 2014). Failure to engage in such actions is seen as moral inefficiency in the new landscape, with the proclamation of crisis enabling trajectories parallel to that of the state of exception (Butler and Athanasiou 2013) in that it creates an extra-political domain of state action and thus becomes an instrument of rule (Agamben 2013). Be that as it may, security and migration policies rarely are performed exclusively under the effect of crisis. Instead, they are driven by a mixture of procedures and approaches infected by the potency of crisis (Jeandesboz and Pallister-Wilkins 2016).

Perhaps counterintuitively, the constant emergence of the term to describe different societal aspects, the large bodies of the world's population that meet basic needs through mechanisms and schemes designed as crisis response mechanisms, and the increasing set of social administration and government measures that are carried out under the context of crisis (Redfield 2005) challenge the uniqueness of each crisis, and instead, it seems as if crisis gains the status of a "defining category of our contemporary situation" (Roitman 2011). Critical states are perhaps better understood as "pervasive contexts rather than singular events" (Vigh 2008), and thus should be critically approached, not necessarily doubting the existence of a critical situation per se, but instead focusing on what is at stake after the crisis has been proclaimed, as well as what has been deemed critical. In other words, we need to put less faith in crisis (Roitman 2011).

THE STATEMENT AND ITS LEGAL STATUS

The text of the Statement consisted of nine points, of which the first three arguably form its core (European Council and Council of the European Union 2016). The first point dictates that, as of the publishing date of the Statement, "all new irregular migrants crossing from Turkey into Greek islands . . . will be returned to Turkey" if their asylum application "has been found unfounded or inadmissible" by the Greek authorities. The second point, often referred to as the 1–1 measure, states that "[f]or every Syrian being returned to Turkey from the Greek islands, another Syrian will be resettled from Turkey to the EU taking into account the UN Vulnerability Criteria." The third point concerns Turkey's part and reads: "Turkey will take any necessary measures to prevent new sea or land routes for illegal migration opening from Turkey to the EU and will cooperate with neighbouring states as well as the EU to this effect." In return for the cooperation of the Turkish state on those three points, the EU member states were to accelerate the visa liberation roadmap for Turkish citizens "with a view to lifting the visa requirements for Turkish citizens." Finally, the Statement foresees the "speed up (of) the disbursement of the initially allocated 3 billion euros under the Facility for Refugees in Turkey and ensures funding of further projects for persons under temporary protection identified with swift input from Turkey before the end of March," as well as the "additional funding for the Facility of an additional 3 billion euro up to the end of 2018," totaling six billion euros.

In many (if not most) instances of public deliberation concerning the Statement, the latter was referred to as a "deal" or "agreement" between the European Union and Turkey (Deutsche Welle 2018; BBC 2016). Notably, the specific terms (deal and agreement) used carry connotations of an orderly understanding between two well-defined and mutually trusting partners. Moreover, they reflect the trade element of the approach that the European Union had by then adopted toward the governance of migration "flows," in sharp contrast to the humanitarian discourse that was paramount during the summer and fall of 2015.

Contrary to that orderly appearance, legal scholars have underlined its dubious status. Cases of migrants affected by the Statement whose cases were taken to the General Court of the European Union have ended with the Court referring to the Statement as "a press release, on the website shared by the European Council and the Council of the European Union," noting "that measure was not adopted by one of the institutions of the EU" and therefore the Court "lacks jurisdiction to hear and determine the actions pursuant to Article 263 TFEU, and, accordingly, dismisses them" (General Court of the European Union 2017). The Court concluded that the Statement is not an EU act and that the Court itself has no jurisdiction to hear and determine cases that concern the Statement. This basically rendered the Statement an extra-juridical act not subjected to any kind of accountability by European institutions. Be that as it may, the Statement has been considered successful by many EU politicians, to the extent it is considered a model to be followed with other states, namely the states of North Africa (Goulard 2016). As discussed later in this chapter, it was not only the Statement that existed on the margins of law but also the practices that came in its wake during its implementation.

Admissibility and Turkey as a Safe Third Country

The concept of the admissibility of an asylum claim has been part of the European asylum system since as early as 2005. It determines whether a state should or should not examine an asylum application based on criteria additional to those of the Dublin Regulation. The 2005 Directive regulating those criteria dictated that inadmissibility of an application for protection may be ordered when the applicant "(a) has been granted international protection by another Member State; (b) comes from a 'first country of asylum'; (c) comes from a 'safe third country'; (d) makes a subsequent application with no new elements; or (e) is dependent on an applicant and makes a separate claim without justification" (Council of the European Union 2005). Different national legal frameworks allowed for different selections of grounds for inadmissibility in member states under the Directive.

Overall, and in practice, there is no exact, timeless, and widely accepted definition of a safe third country (STC). On a practical level, it is perceived as a state through which a person fleeing from their own country of origin has passed, where they could have found protection, but did not do so (Roman, Baird, and Radcliffe 2016). This working definition is based on the grounds of an interpretation of Article 31(1) of the Refugee Convention, stating that asylum seekers who enter the territory of a state "coming directly from a territory where their life or freedom was threatened" shall not be subjected to penalties.

The characterization of Turkey as an STC came at a time when the country was already hosting 2.5 million Syrians (Broomfield 2016) and was accused of illegally pushing Syrian refugees back to Syria (Payton 2016), even shooting refugees at the border (Worley 2016). It has been contested by several NGOs working with refugee support (Amnesty International 2017b; Gogou and Amnesty International 2017; Norwegian Refugee Council, International Rescue Committee, and OXFAM 2017; Spanish Refugee Aid Commission 2017). The European Asylum Support Office (EASO) was appointed with the task of publishing a report on the status of Turkey as a STC (Nielsen 2016). While the examination of the subject falls exactly under the scope of EASO, the report was never published. Further reports on this issue state that the specific report was shelved "upon the judgment of its findings being unsupportive of the priorities of a group of EU Member states and the Commission regarding the implementation of the Statement" (Φωτιάδης 2019). It is worth noting that during the first days after the Statement was published, several refugees and asylum seekers were returned to Turkey under highly questionable circumstances, as documented by Amnesty International and other organizations. The very first instances of people being returned took place on April 4, 2016, when 202 people were returned to Turkey from the islands of Lesvos and Chios. The European Commission announced that none of the returnees sought asylum in Greece, while UN High Commissioner for Refugees (UNHCR) stated that thirteen of the returnees had communicated their wish to seek asylum but their applications were not registered (Amnesty International 2017a).

A New Asylum Procedure

The Greek Asylum Service, being a first-instance authority of the Greek state, was central among the actors tasked with implementing the Statement and begun by determining that asylum seekers whose applications had been rejected could rightfully be returned to Turkey, which would offer them adequate protection (Gkliati 2017). However, the Appeal Committees, being the institution examining the applications in the second degree, overturned 390 out of the first 393 rulings on the grounds of not considering Turkey an STC for Syrians. This was in direct opposition to the spirit of the Statement and more specifically, the characterization of Turkey as an STC (Amnesty International 2017a). This annulment of such an important parameter of the Statement was not warmly received by the European Union. A reported "major upset in Brussels" considered the committees "an enemy of the deal" (Zalan 2016), and resulted in pressure on the Greek state to introduce new legislation.

The Greek state did not fail to deliver, and soon, on June 16, 2016, approved an amendment of the relevant law (4375/2016), establishing a new appeal authority and a new structure for the Appeal Committees (European Commission 2016a). The earlier composition consisted of one government representative, one representative of the UNHCR and a human rights expert selected from a list compiled by the National Commission on Human Rights

(European Council on Refugees and Exiles [ECRE] 2016). The new composition dispensed with the human rights expert, introduced two judges of the Administrative Courts, and retained the UNHCR representative. The whole escapade was criticized by scholars and organizations alike (ECRE 2016; Gkliati 2017; Zalan 2016). An open letter published by members of the old committees pointed out that their institutional replacement was not "due to the rationale of the decisions being incomplete or unjustified, but because it doubted the political planning of the Ministry" (ThePressProject 2016). The outcome in terms of decisions was that the new Appeal Committees, as of December 31, 2017, upheld all inadmissibility decisions of the Greek Asylum (Amnesty International 2017a). It is worth noting that the same law (4375/2016) has caused conditions for asylum seekers to deteriorate in more ways, including but not limited to, restricting free legal assistance for the first-degree examination of their claim as well as refusing their right to be present in person during the examination of the appeal.

The rationale behind considering Turkey an STC lies in the notion of "equivalent protection to that envisaged in the Geneva Convention" (Council of the European Union and European Parliament 2013). This "equivalent protection" offered by Turkey has been noted to be a status of Temporary Protection, by order of the Turkish Council of Ministers, on account of the mass influx of Syrians. This status, as opposed to asylum status, which is offered after a personalized evaluation of a person's condition, is granted collectively, and can also be withdrawn collectively. In addition, it can be problematic in terms of access for stateless persons as well as members of minority ethnicities who were reportedly discriminated against in Turkey (Norwegian Association for Asylum Seekers 2016; Refucomm 2016).

During the same period, the role of EASO was upgraded, both formally as well as in practice. EASO, originally a supportive agent for the Greek Asylum Service's task of handling asylum cases, was now given the capacity to conduct admissibility interviews in the context of the "fast track" procedure applied at the border (ECRE 2016). This involvement of EASO has been criticized as being unclear and exceeding the legal framework of asylum handling (Greek Council for Refugees et al. 2016), as the EU regulation establishing the agency (European Parliament and Council of the European Union 2010) provides no legal basis for such actions. Instead, it clearly states that EASO "shall have no direct or indirect powers concerning the taking of decisions by Member States' asylum authorities on individual applications for international protection" (Preamble §14 and Article 2(6)). Furthermore, the Greek Asylum Service has been repeatedly reported to rely on EASO's records without ever ultimately directly addressing questions to the applicants (European Center for Constitutional and Human Rights [ECCHR] 2018). The same report from ECCHR states that "EASO officers often stuck to a rigid questionnaire without giving the applicant room to elaborate on their personal history of harm or persecution." It concludes that "[i]n sum, the interviews consistently failed to consider the individual experiences and vulnerabilities of the applicants." For their part, EASO has done little toward debunking such claims and have claimed that they "kept no record of its conduct of interviews and ensuing concluding remarks" (ECCHR 2018).

Caught on the Margins

"Today marks a dark day in the history of refugee protection: one in which Europe's leaders attempted to buy themselves out of their international obligations, heedless of the cost in human misery" (Amnesty International 2017b).

The Statement introduced a new temporal categorization for migrants arriving in the European Union, namely those who arrived before and after its publishing date. As the spokesperson from the Greek department of Doctors Without Borders put it, it was "the time when the trolley doors were shut, leaving those behind running to catch up" (Μπερση 2017). The Greek state's determination to not let anything stand in the way of the implementation measures can be seen in the transformation of the Appeal Committees discussed earlier in the chapter. However, the arbitrary and vague nature of the Statement's text enabled more controversy when it came to people who were caught in a "liminal" limbo, concerning their status in relation to their date of arrival. Such was the case of a Syrian citizen whose date of entry was documented by the Police Prefecture of Lesvos as March 19, 2016, only for his asylum application to be rejected on the basis of his fingerprints being registered in the database of Eurodac the twenty-third of the same month, and who thus should be readmitted to Turkey on the basis of the Statement. The Syrian citizen's claims, supported by the NGO Aitima, were to no avail, and were met with a final answer stating that there can be no corrections on the database entry (Aitima 2017).

In the Eurodac Regulation, the "place and date of apprehension" and "date on which the fingerprints were taken" are two separate entry fields (Article 14.2 (b) and (e)), and the regulation also calls for the transmission of the data "no later than 72 hours after the date of apprehension." According to International Organization for Migration, for March 2016, the average number of daily arrivals was 1,885 (International Organization for Migration 2016). UNHCR gives a number of 895 (UNHCR 2016) for Greece, noting that these estimates are based "on the most reliable information available by the authorities." In the context of that period, it is impossible to calculate precise numbers. However, it is safe to assume that daily arrivals exceeded eight hundred. Given that the migrants who asked Αίτημα for help arrived on March 19 and were registered on March 23, a "margin" of more than two thousand persons is the lowest estimation of people affected by this situation alone.

In practice, people being registered a few days after their arrival in the Greek islands was commonplace. Therefore, such implications could be predicted and acted upon. However, as follow-up research including interviews with employees of the Greek Asylum Service, the Greek police, and the Greek Ombudsman showed, that was not the case. The various departments of the Greek police involved in the function and management of the migrant-related databases responded to questions on this case with uncertainty regarding which department is ultimately responsible for decisions on changing entries. Those departments are the Informatics Department, the Asylum Department of the Aliens Sector, and the Forensic Science Division (FSD). The latter is involved due to the forensic "nature" of fingerprint data, and also recruits fingerprint experts who manually (visually) confirm "hits" returned by the automated fingerprint matching procedure.

The Informatics Department responded that the FSD was responsible for any changes in the entries (interview with Informatics Department officer, July 4, 2018), which is in accordance with the FSD's institutional position as the national control authority of the Eurodac system (ΔΕΕ 2015). Requests for a visit with FSD were met with repeated claims of "rigid obligations" and "increased workload," and access to the office of the national unit of Eurodac was repeatedly denied "as it is a space of restricted access, only accessible to authorized persons" (communication with FSD via email, June 2018). A written set of questions to the FSD focused on the procedure of data changes in Eurodac entries, and the case was left partially unanswered and topped with a final refusal for a meeting as "a satisfactory number of the questions have been answered" (communication with FSD via email, August 2018) in previous meetings that addressed different research questions.

Further research on the issue included an interview with a representative of the Greek Ombudsman. Their view of the stance of the Greek police stemmed from a different standpoint beyond the technical potentiality of the change of an entry, and the administrative labyrinth of the Greek police.

> If they [those administering the entries in the database] were to make changes for the first individuals who reported them, then they would have to admit the same for more people. It is a matter of principle not to publicly admit that the specific registrations are mistaken. . . . EL.AS [the Greek police] blamed a technical difficulty, which we consider proverbial and that the difficulty is political. . . . The pressure [upon the Greek state] for the implementation of the Statement is so big that the Greek Police did not want to admit that there are problems in the registers. . . . In both cases, the case was passed to the asylum service, and due to the vulnerability of the individuals there, no longer constituted a conflict.

Both cases that came to us were protected because they came with two different NGOs. People by themselves (Note: not assisted by NGOs) could and easily might have already been returned with the first readmissions. . . . There are no data for the first readmissions. (Interview with Greek Deputy Ombudsman, May 2018, my translation)

This account places the case under the very specific political conjunction of the time. The Greek state had been heavily criticized for its handling of the migration flows, especially for the reluctance of its officials to thoroughly carry out the registration of all incoming migrants (ekathimerini 2015). It could not "afford" doubts to begin circulating about the accuracy of the registration and the legitimacy of the implementation of the Statement. In this context, the refusal to investigate the actual date of arrival of the persons involved, and the overall stance of the Greek police, can be read as a pretense intended to cover up a political agenda that dictated that no cracks can be visible in the solid construction that is the EU's response to the "migrant crisis." The role that registration systems such as Eurodac played in this situation proved to be critical, as it was the technical resort to which Greek institutions would refer to legitimatize their actions (or lack thereof).

DISCUSSION

In migration policymaking, it is not uncommon for conditions to change suddenly and without warning. Griffiths refers to periods of accelerated action, be that political and administrative reorganization or the acceleration of individual cases of deportation, as "frenzied time" (Griffiths 2014) when "time accelerates quickly and rushes out of control." The Statement indexes a period of such frenzied time, as the spokesperson of the Greek department of Doctors Without Borders put it, "the time when the trolley doors were shut, leaving those behind running to catch up" (Μπερση 2017).

It needs to be noted that not all aspects of the Statement were equally enforced. While the sealing of the Greek border, the restructuring of the Appeal committees, and the first reportedly arbitrary deportations following all happened at a rapid pace, other aspects of the Statement, such as the relocation scheme, were implemented much more slowly, if at all. Migrants living in and outside the hotspots were as it often happens stuck in an administrative limbo for extended periods of uncertainty. This "absence of synchronicity" inherent in the "complex temporality of borders" (Little 2015) is indicative of the political priorities that the European Union had set at the time, which in turn sheds light on what was considered "critical" during the "migrant crisis," to be discussed further in the concluding section.

For the Greek state, the implementation of the Statement was a mission. It was never debated in parliamentary hearings (Φωτιάδης 2019) and was instead initiated with the passing of law 4375/2016 followed by various amendments. In what seemed to be a peculiar reward, the European Commission decided "to close infringement procedures against Italy and Greece for non-implementation of the Eurodac regulation" (European Commission 2016b). Among other implementing measures, a geographical restriction was applied to all incoming migrants with open asylum cases, preventing them from leaving the islands to the mainland, which led to the already problematic living conditions of migrants to further deteriorate, resulting in frequent riots (in.gr 2018; Huffpost 2017), and a reported rise in stress, depression, and post-traumatic stress disorder symptoms among the migrant population (Γιατροί Χωρίς Σύνορα 2017).

The introduction of the admissibility evaluation of asylum applications also had a significant, twofold impact. On the one hand, it moved the administrative, social, and humanitarian cost of recognizing and hosting refugees to Turkey. The practice of outsourcing bordering to neighboring countries is not new for the European Union, and has been a practice of the European Union for more than a decade (Gammeltoft-Hansen 2013). On the other hand, it reshaped the concept of asylum within the European context, a focal concept in the discourse around the dichotomies of migrant/refugee and legal/illegal migration. The distinction between deserving refugees versus undeserving (illegal) migrants has been central in representations of migration in the European discourse for years before the "migrant crisis." The naturalization of such identities, and their presentation as mutually exclusive categories, is problematic in (at least) two ways. First, it fails to capture the complexities of migrant journeys and the multiple positions and experiences that irregularized migrants on the move find themselves in (Crawley and Skleparis 2017). Secondly, it ignores the dependence of such categories on legal and socio-cultural constructions, both on a policy level as well as on rank-and-file officers' practice level (Andersson 2014, 361; Heyman 2001; Guild 2004).

Classification systems are products of organized human work and action; they assign persons to categories, and they render the contingencies and the controversies around this work invisible (Bowker and Star 1999). Human mobility comes first, the state's legal apparatus acts on it after. The recognition of a migrant as a refugee is a complex procedure where a person's testimony on their journey's history and family relationships and their exposure to persecution or other threats are juxtaposed with reports of the current situation in their country of origin, institutional guidelines that case workers need to follow, nationality assessments conducted by screeners, database entries, as well as assessment of properties like accent.

Reports of the current situation in the country of origin, travel histories, family relationships, as well as accent, the ability to prove the vulnerability of the individual, etc., are just some of the elements of asylum interviews to be taken into account by case handlers. Examining the admissibility of an asylum claim shifted the case handler's task from assessing whether a person is in danger and in need of international protection to assessing whether they can be safely returned to Turkey. This is vividly illustrated by the words of a lawyer presented in a 2017 report: "[T]he minute an applicant undergoing an admissibility interview utters a word about Syria, they are stopped by the caseworker and told that the interview has nothing to do with Syria, even if in fact it does" (Norwegian Refugee Council, International Rescue Commitee, and OXFAM 2017).

A new form of deservedness became the dominant criterion for the specific form of inclusion that is the recognition of a person's refugee status. Whereas until that point, a person was seen as deserving asylum and protection with regard to the situation of their country of origin, now their deservedness was mediated by the fact that they arrived in the European Union through Turkey. It can be argued that this was a re-merging of the categories of migrant and refugee with the wider category of "irregular migration." The ever-present, perhaps dominant aspect of the debate surrounding the mixed flows, which shaped the moral and ethical tone of the discussion through 2015 and 2016—the distinction between deserving refugees and undeserving migrants or bogus asylum seekers (Triandafyllidou 2018)—was set aside as irrelevant. People, in danger or not, had to stay away from European soil.

In the case of the delayed registration described in this chapter, and its handling by the Greek Asylum Service and the Greek police, the temporal division or rupture that the Statement introduced, and the two subsequent categories of migrants, namely those who arrived before and those after its implementation, are not clear and distinct, due to the textual nature of the Statement and its inherent vagueness. This was exacerbated by the interplay of this vagueness with the reality of bordering practices at the hotspots and in Athens. This interplay creates room for liminality, as the state of being between categories, where "people are tainted with danger, pollution or illegality" (Griffiths 2012).

The resolution of the liminality is achieved by referring to the "data double" of the migrants. Here, this is seen as a migrant's journey being reduced to a database entry, and the predominance of this entry against all other forms of evidence, even evidence that is produced by institutional agents such as the Lesvos police. The Eurodac procedure and the rigidness of its entries are evident in this case and were enabled by the specific position of the Greek state within the European Union and the "migrant crisis." Specifically, a "migrant crisis" in which the momentum of the Statement does not allow for errors to be considered and no less admitted, for fear of similar cases emerging and thus causing "cracks" in the solid and decisive legal artifact that is the Statement. Thus, in this case, we see one instance that corroborates the reoccurring position of many scholars, that sociotechnical systems, especially those of biopolitical control and surveillance, and their use are always embedded in specific social, political, and cultural conditions that shape the acts of their users and subjects (Oudshoorn and Pinch 2003; Woolgar 1990).

CONCLUDING NOTES ON A MIGRANT CRISIS

As discussed earlier in this chapter, crisis can be an ambiguous and elusive concept, and the "migrant crisis" of the mid-to late 2010s was no different. Behind and accompanying its utterance, political agendas and correlations invested the term with different meanings and ethical and moral connotations. Aspects of the "migrant crisis" include but were not limited to a humanitarian crisis, with regard to the loss of life in the Mediterranean and along the migrant route, as well as the suffering of populations on the move in various borderland and makeshift or state-sanctioned camps, a crisis of the European Union, focusing on various political conflicts among member states around policies adopted in the face of the migration phenomena, a crisis of the Dublin convention and Schengen zone, seeing said populations as a threat to the border regime of the European Union, a security crisis, especially after events such as the attacks in Paris in November 2015, directly implying connections between populations on the move and similar attacks (Vlassis 2021). Finally, a crisis of European values suggested the challenging of moral values considered to be part of the European identity, such as solidarity, freedom, and hospitality. Crisis narratives exist beyond the realm of validation and disproof; they are not "false or merely symbolic" (Roitman 2011). Instead, they call for "life deciding alternatives meant to answer questions about what is just or unjust" (Koselleck 2006). How these questions are posed forms new moral obligations, which find their fulfillment at a range of levels, from the higher political level and all the way to rank-and-file officials' practices.

Framing a crisis as an unexpected, unprecedented, and unpredictable event (Calhoun 2010) shrinks "time and space of actions to a 'here and now' of emergency response" (van Reekum 2016). Such representations render invisible and obscure the political backgrounds of crises, while at the same time focusing and capitalizing on human suffering. In the case of the "migrant crisis," the very structure of the Dublin Regulation (Guild 2006; den Heijer, Rijpma, and Spijkerboer 2016; Mitsilegas 2014), and the visa and carrier sanctions, which as part of the Schengen agreement in practice targeted asylum seekers not allowing them to approach Europe in any other way than through smuggling networks (Guiraudon 2018), are perhaps the two main factors that enabled the "migrant crisis," only to remain unaddressed through the period it was unfolding.

"Focus events," events or images that "simply cannot be ignored" (Baumgartner and Jones 1993), like the capsizing of a boat transporting over eight hundred migrants from Libya to Italy and the subsequent death of almost all its passengers on April 19, 2015, and the publishing of the photo of the dead body of a toddler later identified as a Syrian Kurdish child, Alan Kurdi on Bodrum beach in Turkey on September 3, 2015, can be pointed out as constitutive moments that initiated the humanitarian emergency discourse (Agustín and Jørgensen 2019). However, receiving less media attraction, thousands of migrants have lost their lives in the last years in the Mediterranean and other European borderlands (Last et al. 2017; themigrant-files.com n.d.), and human suffering and constant tension have been the norm in the Calais area of France (Reinisch 2015). Arguably, the European border regime has for years been in a state of normalized crisis.

What was truly unprecedented, however, was the loss of control with regards to bordering that ensued not only in the Greek islands but in many other borderlands across Europe, as well as how another "focus event," this time the image of thousands of migrants marching across the continent, cir-culated in European media and "foregrounded a subjective composition of the movements of migrants and refugees characterized by agency and obsti-nacy, by an ability to articulate their demands in an explicitly political way" (Mezzadra and Bojadžijev 2015). This collective march of migrants was seen as an act of debordering establishing the "migrant crisis" as a crisis of control over the European borders, just weeks after the temporary annulment of the Dublin system on behalf of the German state (Kingsley and Oltermann 2016).

It therefore comes as no surprise that the European Union's response was directed toward specific elements of what comprised the crisis. Despite a sporadic rhetoric surrounding the need for a fairer and more elaborate asylum system, relatively few core fundamental changes occurred in that respect. The Dublin Regulation has largely remained intact despite intense criticisms and its commonly accepted failure. The proposal for a new regulation does not seem to entail drastic changes, except a few manipulations, and Frontex's renaming as the European Border and Coast Guard Agency with an increased budget and operational scope cannot be viewed as something new, but rather as a strengthening of the old model of "fortress Europe."

To re-establish a sense of border normality (if there ever was one), the European Union chose to seal its borders with Turkey and place the administration of asylum matters in an arena of exchanges with neighbor-ing countries. Economic and political returns were offered to Turkey and Libya for them to accept further externalization of the European border, and to outsource asylum and border control procedures. In the case of Turkey, this far exceeded the acceleration of litigations that were underway, such as the Readmission Agreement, but called for recalibrations of national laws, and even the reshaping of notions such as "sufficient protection" and "safe third country."

REFERENCES

Agamben, Giorgio. 2013. "The endless crisis as an instrument of power: In conversation with Giorgio Agamben." Versobooks.Com. April 6, 2013. https://www.versobooks.com/blogs/1318-the-endless-crisis-as-an-instrument-of-power-in-conversation-with-giorgio-agamben.
Aitima. 2017. "Asylum seekers on hold: Aspects of the asylum procedure in Greece." http://www.ssrn.com/abstract=2957727.
Amnesty International. 2017a. "A blueprint for despair. Human rights impact of the EU-Turkey deal." https://www.amnesty.org/en/documents/eur25/5664/2017/en/.
Amnesty International. 2017b. "EU-Turkey deal: A shameful stain on the collective conscience of Europe." March 17, 2017. https://www.amnesty.org/en/latest/news/2017/03/eu-turkey-deal-a-shameful-stain-on-the-collective-conscience-of-europe/.
Andersson, Ruben. 2014. *Illegality, Inc.: Clandestine Migration and the Business of Bordering Europe.* Berkeley, CA: University of California Press.
Agustín, Óscar García and Martin Bak Jørgensen. 2019. *Solidarity and the "Refugee Crisis" in Europe.* Cham: Palgrave Macmillan.
Balibar, Etienne. 1998. "The borders of Europe." In *Cosmopolitics: Thinking and Feeling Beyond the Nation,* edited by Pheng Cheah and Bruce Robbins, first edition. Minneapolis: University of Minnesota Press.
Balibar, Etienne. 2002. *Politics and the Other Scene.* Reprint edition. London: Verso.
Baumgartner, Frank R., and Bryan D. Jones. 1993. *Agendas and Instability in American Politics.* First edition. Chicago: University of Chicago Press.
BBC. 2016. "EU-Turkey migrant deal comes into force." *BBC News,* March 20, 2016, sec. Europe. https://www.bbc.co.uk/news/world-europe-35854413.
Bowker, Geoffrey C., and Susan Leigh Star. 1999. *Sorting Things Out: Classification and Its Consequences.* Cambridge, MA: MIT Press.
Broomfield, Matt. 2016. "Pictures of life for Turkey's 2.5 million Syrian refugees." *The Independent.* April 5, 2016. http://www.independent.co.uk/news/world/europe/pictures-of-life-for-turkeys-25-million-syrian-refugees-crisis-migrant-a6969551.html.
Butler, Judith, and Athena Athanasiou. 2013. *Dispossession: The Performative in the Political.* First edition. Malden, MA: Polity.
Calhoun, Craig. 2010. "The idea of emergency: Humanitarian action and global (dis)order." In *Contemporary States of Emergency: The Politics of Military and*

Humanitarian Interventions, edited by Didier Fassin and Mariella Pandolfi, 29–58. New York: Zone Books.

Council of the European Union, and European Parliament. 2013. "Directive 2013/32/ EU of the European Parliament and of the Council of 26 June 2013 on Common Procedures for Granting and Withdrawing International Protection (Recast)." *Official Journal of the European Union*.

Crawley, Heaven, and Dimitris Skleparis. 2017. "Refugees, migrants, neither, both: Categorical fetishism and the politics of bounding in Europe's 'migration crisis.'" *Journal of Ethnic and Migration Studies* 1–17.

De Genova, Nicholas. 2016. "The 'crisis' of the European border regime: Towards a Marxist theory of borders." *International Socialism* 150: 31–54.

Delcker, Janosch. 2017. "Architect of EU-Turkey refugee pact pushes for West Africa deal." POLITICO. July 28, 2017. https://www.politico.eu/article/migration-italy -libya-architect-of-eu-turkey-refugee-pact-pushes-for-west-africa-deal/.

Deutsche Welle. 2018. "The EU-Turkey refugee agreement: A review | DW | 18.03.2018." DW.COM. March 18, 2018. https://www.dw.com/en/the-eu-turkey -refugee-agreement-a-review/a-43028295.

Dijstelbloem, H., A. Meijer, and M. Besters. 2011. *The Migration Machine*. London: Palgrave Macmillan.

Dijstelbloem, H., A. Meijer, and F. Brom. 2011. "Reclaiming Control over Europe's Technological Borders." In *Migration and the New Technological Borders of Europe: Migration, Minorities and Citizenship*, edited by H. Dijstelbloem and A. Meijer, 170–185. London: Palgrave Macmillan.

The Economist. 2016. "Europe's murky deal with Turkey." *The Economist*, May 26. https://www.economist.com/europe/2016/05/26/europes-murky-deal-with-turkey.

European Center for Constitutional and Human Rights (ECCHR). 2018. "Case report. EASO's involvement in Greek hotspots exceeds the agency's competence and dis-regards fundamental rights." https://www.ecchr.eu/fileadmin/Fallbeschreibungen /ECCHR_Case_Report_Hotspots_Greece_EASO_March_2018.pdf.

European Council on Refugees and Exiles (ECRE). 2016. "Greece amends its asylum law after multiple appeals board decisions overturn the presumption of Turkey as a 'safe third country.'" 2016. https://www.ecre.org/greece-amends-its-asylum-law -after-multiple-appeals-board-decisions-overturn-the-presumption-of-turkey-as-a -safe-third-country/.

ekathimerini. 2015. "More than a third of migrants not fingerprinted, officials say | Kathimerini." August 20, 2015. http://www.ekathimerini.com/200728/article/ ekathimerini/news/more-than-a-third-of-migrants-not-fingerprinted-officials-say.

European Commission. 2016a. "Second report on the progress made in the implemen-tation of the EU-Turkey Statement." COM(2016) 349 Final.

European Commission. 2016b. "Implementing the EU-Turkey Statement—questions and answers." https://ec.europa.eu/commission/presscorner/detail/en/MEMO_16 _1664.

European Council and Council of the European Union. 2016. "EU-Turkey Statement, 18 March 2016 - Consilium." March 18, 2016. https://www.consilium.europa.eu/ en/press/press-releases/2016/03/18/eu-turkey-statement/.

European Parliament and Council of the European Union. 2010. "Regulation (EU) No 439/2010 of the European Parliament and of the Council of 19 May 2010 Establishing a European Asylum Support Office L132/11."

Gammeltoft-Hansen, Thomas. 2013. *Access to Asylum: International Refugee Law and the Globalisation of Migration Control.* Reprint edition. Cambridge: Cambridge University Press.

General Court of the European Union. 2017. "Press release No 19/17 Orders of the General Court in Cases T-192/16, T-193/16 and T-257/16 NF, NG and NM v European Council," February 2.

Gkliati, Marianna. 2017. "The EU-Turkey deal and the safe third country concept before the Greek asylum appeals committees." *movements* 3 (2): 213–24.

Gogou, Kondylia, and Amnesty International. 2017. "The EU-Turkey deal: Europe's year of shame." March 20, 2017. https://www.amnesty.org/en/latest/news/2017/03/the-eu-turkey-deal-europes-year-of-shame/.

Goulard, Hortense. 2016. "Angela Merkel: EU's Turkey deal a model for North African countries." POLITICO. August 23, 2016. https://www.politico.eu/article/angela-merkel-wants-refugee-migration-deals-with-northern-african-countries-migrants-migration-turkey/.

Greek Council for Refugees, European Council on Refugees and Exiles, Solidarity Now, and Αίτημα. 2016. "Letter to the European Commission." https://www.gcr.gr/en/news/press-releases-announcements/item/624-letter-to-the-president-of-the-european-commission-and-the-greek-minister-of-migration-policy.

Green, Sarah. 2010. "Performing border in the Aegean: On relocating political, economic and social relations." *Journal of Cultural Economy* 3 (2): 261–78.

Griffiths, Melanie. 2012. "'Vile liars and truth distorters'; Truth, trust and the asylum system (Respond to this article at http://www.therai.org.uk/at/debate)." *Anthropology Today* 28 (5): 8–12.

Griffiths, Melanie B. E. 2014. "Out of time: The temporal uncertainties of refused asylum seekers and immigration detainees." *Journal of Ethnic and Migration Studies* 40 (12): 1991–2009.

Guild, Elspeth. 2004. "Who is an illegal migrant?" In *Irregular Migration and Human Rights: Theoretical, European and International Perspectives*, edited by Barbara Bogusz, Ryszard Cholewinski, Adam Cygan, and Erika Szyszczak. Leiden and Boston, MA: Brill - Nijhoff.

Guild, Elspeth. 2006. "The Europeanisation of Europe's asylum policy." *International Journal of Refugee Law* 18 (3–4): 630–51.

Guiraudon, Virginie. 2018. "The 2015 refugee crisis was not a turning point: Explaining policy inertia in EU border control." *European Political Science* 17 (1): 151–60.

Heijer, Maarten den, Jorrit J. Rijpma, and Thomas Spijkerboer. 2016. "Coercion, prohibition, and great expectations: The continuing failure of the common European asylum system." SSRN Scholarly Paper ID 2756709.

Heyman, Josiah McC. 2001. "Class and classification at the U.S.-Mexico border." *Human Organization* 60 (2): 128–40.

Huffpost. 2017. "Επεισόδια Στη Μόρια." October 7, 2017. https://www.huffingtonpost
.gr/2017/07/10/eidiseis-koinwnia-moria-epeisodia_n_17450082.html.

Idriz, Narin. 2017. "The EU-Turkey Statement or the 'refugee deal': The extra-legal
deal of extraordinary times?" Asser Institute. Centre for International & European
Law, December 18.

in.gr. 2018. "Εκατοντάδες πρόσφυγες εγκατέλειψαν τη Μόρια μετά τα επεισόδια."
in.gr. May 26, 2018. http://www.in.gr/2018/05/26/greece/ekatontades-prosfyges
-egkateleipsan-ti-moria-meta-ta-epeisodia/.

International Organization for Migration. 2016. "Mediterranean migrant arrivals in
2016: 164,752; deaths: 531." March 29. https://www.iom.int/news/mediterranean
-migrant-arrivals-2016-164752-deaths-531.

Jeandesboz, Julien, and Polly Pallister-Wilkins. 2016. "Crisis, routine, consolidation:
The politics of the Mediterranean migration crisis." *Mediterranean Politics* 21 (2):
316–20.

Johnson, Corey, Reece Jones, Anssi Paasi, Louise Amoore, Alison Mountz, Mark
Salter, and Chris Rumford. 2011. "Interventions on rethinking 'the border' in border studies." *Political Geography* 30 (February): 61–69.

Agustín, Óscar García and Martin Bak Jørgensen. 2019. *Solidarity and the "Refugee
Crisis" in Europe*. Cham: Palgrave McMillan.

Kaiser, Robert J. 2012. "Performativity and the eventfulness of bordering practices."
In *Companion to Border Studies*, edited by Thomas M. Wilson and Hastings
Donnan, 522–37. Hoboken, NJ: Wiley.

Kingsley, Patrick, and Philip Oltermann. 2016. "'It took on a life of its own': How
one rogue Tweet led Syrians to Germany." *The Guardian*, August 25, 2016, sec.
World news. http://www.theguardian.com/world/2016/aug/25/it-took-on-a-life-of
-its-own-how-rogue-tweet-led-syrians-to-germany.

Koselleck, Reinhart. 2006. "Crisis." *Journal of the History of Ideas* 67 (2): 357–400.

Last, Tamara, Giorgia Mirto, Orçun Ulusoy, Ignacio Urquijo, Joke Harte, Nefeli
Bami, Marta Pérez Pérez, et al. 2017. "Deaths at the borders database: Evidence
of deceased migrants' bodies found along the southern external borders of the
European Union." *Journal of Ethnic and Migration Studies* 43 (5): 693–712.

Little, Adrian. 2015. "The complex temporality of borders: Contingency and norma-
tivity." *European Journal of Political Theory* 14 (4): 429–47.

Mau, Steffen, Fabian Gülzau, Lena Laube, and Natascha Zaun. 2015. "The global
mobility divide: How visa policies have evolved over time." *Journal of Ethnic and
Migration Studies* 41 (8): 1192–213.

Mbembe, A., and J. Roitman. 1995. "Figures of the subject in times of crisis." *Public
Culture* 7 (2): 323–52.

Mezzadra, Sandro, and Manuela Bojadžijev. 2015. "'Refugee crisis' or crisis of
European migration policies?" December 11, 2015. http://www.focaalblog.com
/2015/11/12/manuela-bojadzijev-and-sandro-mezzadra-refugee-crisis-or-crisis-of
-european-migration-policies/.

Mezzadra, Sandro, and Brett Neilson. 2012. "Between inclusion and exclusion: On
the topology of global space and borders." *Theory, Culture & Society* 29 (4–5):
58–75.

Mitsilegas, Valsamis. 2014. "Solidarity and trust in the common European asylum system." *Comparative Migration Studies* 2 (2): 181–202.

Nielsen, Nikolaj. 2016. "EU trying to bury report on Turkey migrant returns." EUobserver. June 15, 2016. https://euobserver.com/migration/133836.

Norwegian Association for Asylum Seekers. 2016. "A critical review of Turkey's asylum laws and practices-Seeking asylum in Turkey." https://www.noas.no/wp -content/uploads/2019/02/Tyrkia-2018-Update_Web.pdf.

Norwegian Refugee Council, International Rescue Commitee, and OXFAM. 2017. "The reality of the EU-Turkey Statement. How Greece has become a testing ground for policies that erode protection for refugees." https://reliefweb.int/ report/greece/reality-eu-turkey-statement-how-greece-has-become-testing-ground -policies-erode.

Oudshoorn, Nelly E. J., and Trevor Pinch. 2003. *How Users Matter: The Co-construction of Users and Technologies*. Cambridge: MIT Press.

Paasi, Anssi. 2009. "Bounded spaces in a 'borderless world': Border studies, power and the anatomy of territory." *Journal of Power* 2 (2): 213–34.

Payton, Matt. 2016. "Turkey is 'illegally forcing refugees back to Syria.'" *The Independent*, April 1. http://www.independent.co.uk/news/world/europe/turkey -is-illegally-forcing-refugees-back-to-syria-say-amnesty-international-a6963771 .html.

Redfield, Peter. 2005. "Doctors, borders, and life in crisis." *Cultural Anthropology* 20 (3): 328–61.

Reekum, Rogier van. 2016. "The Mediterranean: Migration corridor, border spectacle, ethical landscape." *Mediterranean Politics* 21 (2): 336–41.

Refucomm. 2016. "What happens to Syrians when they return to Turkey?" http:// refucomm.com/infopacks/greece-islands/assisted-voluntary-returns/what-happens -to-syrians-when-they-are-returned-to-turkey/en/greece-islands_assisted-voluntary -returns_what-happens-to-syrians-when-they-are-returned-to-turkey_EN.pdf.

Reinisch, Jessica. 2015. "'Forever temporary': Migrants in Calais, then and now." *The Political Quarterly* 86 (4): 515–22.

Roitman, Janet. 2011. "Crisis: Political concepts: Issue one." http://www .politicalconcepts.org/issue1/crisis/.

Roman, Emanuela, Theodore Baird, and Talia Radcliffe. 2016. "Analysis. Why Turkey is not a 'safe country.'" *Statewatch* 1–26.

Spanish Refugee Aid Commission. 2017. "Trapped in Greece. One year after the EU-Turkey Agreement." https://www.cear.es/wp-content/uploads/2017/06/ ATRAPADOS-EN-GRECIA_en_ok.pdf.

Strasser, Sabine. 2014. "Repressive autonomy discourses on and surveillance of marriage migration from Turkey to Austria." *Migration Letters* 11 (3): 316–28.

Strasser, Sabine. 2016. "The crises effect: Global moral obligations, national interventions and the figure of the pitiful/abusive migrant." *Ethnologia Balkanica* 18: 47–66.

themigrantfiles.com. n.d. "The migrants files." http://www.themigrantsfiles.com//

ThePressProject. 2016. "Επιστολή Μελών Επιτροπών Προσφυγών Για Την Τροπολογία Μουζάλα - ThePressProject." June 18. https://www.thepressproject.gr /article/96546/Epistoli-melon-Epitropis-Prosfugon.

Triandafyllidou, Anna. 2018. "A 'refugee crisis' unfolding: 'Real' events and their interpretation in media and political debates." *Journal of Immigrant & Refugee Studies* 16 (1–2): 198–216.

UN High Commissioner for Refugees (UNHCR). 2016. "Greece Data Snapshot - 29 Mar 2016." https://data2.unhcr.org/es/documents/details/47259.

van der Ploeg, Irma, and Isolde Sprenkels. 2011. "Migration and the machine-readable body: Identification and biometrics." In *Migration and the New Technological Borders of Europe*, edited by Huub Dijstelbloem and Albert Meijer, 68–104. London: Palgrave Macmillan UK.

Vigh, Henrik. 2008. "Crisis and chronicity: Anthropological perspectives on continuous conflict and decline." *Ethnos* 73 (1): 5–24.

Vlassis, Vasileios Spyridon. 2021. "Constructing Immobility: Border Work and Coercion at the Hotspots of the Aegean." In *Coercive Geographies*, edited by Johan Heinsen, Martin Bak Jørgensen, and Martin Ottovay Jørgensen, 42–62. London: Brill.

Wonders, Nancy A. 2006. "Global flows, semi-permeable borders and new channels of inequality." *Borders, Mobility and Technologies of Control* 63–86.

Woolgar, Steve. 1990. "Configuring the user: The case of usability trials." *The Sociological Review* 38 (S1): 58–99.

Worley, Will. 2016. "Turkish border guards 'shooting dead' Syrians fleeing war and terror." *The Independent*, March 31. http://www.independent.co.uk/news/world/ middle-east/turkey-shooting-dead-syrian-refugees-flee-civil-war-a6960971.html.

Zalan, Eszter. 2016. "EU pushes Greece to set up new asylum committees." June 15. https://euobserver.com/migration/133841.

Γιατροί Χωρίς Σύνορα. 2017. "ΕΝΑΣ ΧΡΟΝΟΣ ΜΕΤΑ ΤΗ ΣΥΜΦΩΝΙΑ ΕΕ-ΤΟΥΡΚΙΑΣ: ΑΜΦΙΣΒΗΤΩΝΤΑΣ ΤΑ «ΕΝΑΛΛΑΚΤΙΚΑ ΣΤΟΙΧΕΙΑ» ΤΗΣ ΕΕ." ΔΕΕ. 2015. "ΔΕΕ-Αποστολή."

Μπερση, Ευρυδίκη. 2017. "ΜΚΟ «αποδομούν» Τη Συμφωνία ΕΕ-Τουρκίας Για Το Προσφυγικό." March 17. http://www.kathimerini.gr/901067/article/epikairothta/ kosmos/mko-apodomoyn-th-symfwnia-ee-toyrkias-gia-to-prosfygiko.

Φωτιάδης, Απόστολος. 2019. "Πώς η Τουρκία . . . βαφτίστηκε από την Ε.Ε. «ασφαλής τρίτη χώρα» για τους πρόσφυγες." Η Εφημερίδα των Συντακτών. March 17. https: //www.efsyn.gr/kosmos/eyropi/187447_pos-i-toyrkia-baftistike-apo-tin-ee-asfalis -triti-hora-gia-toys-prosfyges.

PART III

Configuration of Migration Space

Chapter 6

Asylum Seekers Experiencing Forced Immobility as Offline and Online Actors

Claudia Lintner

INTRODUCTION

The chapter reflects asylum seekers' immobility experiences at the Brenner border (Italy) as offline and online actors. It is thus part of an emerging strand of research that focuses on studying migration not only as a physical experience (Schewel 2019; Khan 2016), but also as a virtual experience (Alencar 2020; Leurs 2019; Martin-Shields and Bodanac 2017). In doing so, the chapter places center stage the paradigmatic figure of the connected migrant (Diminescu 2020) that has gradually replaced and questioned the figure of the uprooted migrant. Diminescu (2020) describes in fact the connected migrant as "equipped with at least one digitalized device which enables him/ her to instantaneously switch between several lifestyles" (Diminescu 2020, 74). Thus, in contrast to the uprooted figure, the connected migrant is characterized by a constant presence that is becoming less physically linked to a particular territory and more affective (Witteborn 2012; Turkle 2011). New technologies allow asylum seekers both to stay in touch with family and friends left behind and to gather information about possible routes and ways to and through Europe in the shortest possible time (Dekker et al. 2018). As the chapter will show, the new possibilities also change how asylum seekers deal with and organize their everyday life in situations of forced immobility. In line with this, different scholars (Alencar 2017; Kaufmann 2018; Witteborn

2015; Lintner 2022) have outlined how connectivity widely compensates for the spaces of action, spaces of learning, spaces of interaction, and spaces for information that are missing offline, in the process of emplacing themselves in a new environment.

However, the figure of the connected migrant is at the same time exposed to new dangers and vulnerabilities given by an ever greater dependence on digital infrastructure like Wi-Fi hotspots, shops that sell SIM cards, or the physical offices of wire transfer services (Latonero 2016; Gillespie et al. 2018). As the results of the field study will clearly show, the digital infrastructure is not widely available or accessible to all, with vulnerable groups in society often being disadvantaged. In fact, the lack of digital accessibility, usability, and not least the affordability (Faith 2018) for refugees and asylum seekers leads to new forms of social and digital exclusion (Kaufmann 2020) as well as to information precarity (Wall et al. 2015) linked to access (missing or limited infrastructure) and to content (relying on untrustworthy sources, for example).

By taking the example of the Brenner border in northern Italy, the chapter analyzes how information and communications technology (ICT) changes the experiences of asylum seekers' mobility/immobility practices in a situation of forced immobility. In doing so, the chapter adopts the perspective of the so-called out-of-quota group, about two hundred to 250 applicants for international protection arrived in an autonomous way to the Brenner border zone (Italy) and not via the regular ministerial quota.[1] In order to regulate this group of asylum seekers, the northernmost Italian province adopted a restrictive regulation in 2016 (regulation Critelli) that does not give direct access to the reception system unless they are classified as vulnerable (families, pregnant women, and minors and unaccompanied minors) in accordance with the regulation. In particular, the regulation affects "the healthy man" who is not considered vulnerable—unless he has a serious illness or a vulnerability that is ascertained. Consequently, most of those potential asylum seekers considered non-vulnerable find themselves in precarious living situations. The study gives insight into how those "healthy men" make their living under extremely precarious conditions and use ICT to deal with and/or circumvent restrictive migration regimes. In doing so, the chapter is part of an upcoming strand of studies (Artero and Fontanari 2019; Wyss 2019) that shed light to the gaps in the current Dublin Regulation by providing ethnographic insights into precarious living conditions created by bureaucratic inefficiencies.

METHODOLOGY

The present study is part of the project "Digital border experiences of refugees: Understanding the use of ICT in the context of forced migration at the Brenner border–Italy (DIBO)," a cooperation between the Free University of Bolzano (Italy–Internal research fund CRC 2019), the University of Innsbruck (Austria), and the Technical University of Munich (Germany). The chapter reflects refugees' innovative use of ICT to deal with and/or circumvent restrictive migration regimes in the Brenner border area.

PARTICIPANTS

From December 2019 to May 2020, eleven semi-structured interviews and six narrative interviews with out-of-quota asylum seekers in the Italian northern border zone were carried out. Some informants spent a long time in Germany or a Scandinavian country, in some cases even years, before being forced to leave the country by the Dublin Regulation. Others arrived directly from the Balkans or Austria (Afghans, Pakistanis, and Bangladeshis) without ever having applied for asylum. They are now in the northern border zone, waiting for full entry into the reception system, to which they are entitled but where there are few possibilities. The seventeen out-of-quota asylum seekers interviewed for this study came from Nigeria (four), Gambia (five), Afghanistan (three), Pakistan (three), and Bangladesh (two). They all came in an autonomous way to South Tyrol: nine out-of-quota asylum seekers from southern Italy and eight out-of-quota asylum seekers from Germany/Austria.

DATA COLLECTION

The study is based on a qualitative research approach. In the first research phase, six narrative interviews were conducted. This approach helped to encourage the interviewees to reflect upon their experiences and their strategies to organize their everyday lives. While the influence of the interviewer was minimal, importance was given to the idea of reconstructing individual life experiences from the point of view of informants. The narrative interviews served as the basis for the structure of the eleven semi-structured interviews. The most important issues pertaining to the research focus of the study were examined in more depth during the semi-structured interviews. The narratives and the semi-structured interviews lasted from sixty to 120 minutes each. The interviews were conducted in English and German. Due to the first outbreak of the COVID-19 pandemic in northern Italy and the related containment measures, seven semi-structured interviews out of eleven interviews were carried out via phone.

DATA ANALYSIS

The analysis of the data was based on the coding processes described by Strauss and Corbin (2008), which involves three levels of analysis: open coding, axial coding, and selective coding. During the open coding phase, the researchers constantly compared interview transcriptions and the questions asked. In this first phase, different categories were developed, the properties and dimensions of which were recorded in document memos. During axial coding, parts of interviews of note were pieced together in new ways, which allowed bringing new issues and perspectives into the process of analysis. Finally, during selective coding, core categories were defined and connected to other categories by looking for similarities and relationships between the categories. The findings of this paper focus on the following core categories: "border management" (policies/performances), crossing borders (role of smartphone/trying,_attempting), "being stuck" (living situations/everyday life/role of smartphone), and "accessibility" (opportunities/hindering and enabling structures).

ETHICS

All interviewees participated voluntarily. They were informed about the purpose of the study, the data collection process, and how the data would be treated. Before the data collection started, all interviewees gave their written informed consent to participate. Furthermore, it was made clear from the beginning that all participants could withdraw from the study at any time. Finally, all participants agreed that the interviews would be recorded, transcribed, and used in academic publications. In the presentation of the findings, the names of the participants have been removed and replaced by pseudonyms.

CROSS-BORDER MOTILITIES IN MATERIAL SPACE

Border Management

Since 2015, and in particular after the closing of the west Balkan route in March 2016, the Brenner border between Italy and Austria has become one of the main passages for refugees arriving in southern Italy and continuing their path toward northern Europe. Consequently, due to the increasing number of refugees present in the border zone, the Austrian government introduced a restrictive border management in 2015/2016, which provided for a 370-meter-long fence (that could be raised at any time if necessary), a so-called registration center, increased control activities, and personnel deployment in the area close to the border. In August 2017, despite the decreasing number of refugees, Austria kept up the border management and sent seventy soldiers to the Brenner border to control border crossings. In line with this, in October 2017, Austria and Germany confirmed that border controls in the Schengen area would be extended for another six months until May 2018. Hence, although the number of refugees who tried to cross the border decreased, the state authorities continued with their "border spectacle" (De Genova 2002, 493) or "exemplary theater" (De Genova 2002, 436), two terms with which De Genova describes how the state demonstrates its sovereignty through practices of enforcement on the border. Linked to this, border performance in this period was highly symbolic as it reproduced social, political, and economic relations and stressed the privileges as well as the limitations of citizenship (Anderson 2013). This is particularly reflected in the practices of "racial profiling" experienced by several interview partners and confirmed as a common practice of control by the group of activists that monitored the situation on the Brenner pass from 2015 to 2018. Antenne migranti more than once during their final report mentioned this practice as "Infringement of the legislation on the prohibition of discrimination, including Article 14 of the ECHR, would constitute a form of systematic control at internal borders prohibited by Article 22 of the Schengen Borders Codex" (2017, 76). Racial profiling as a frequent control practice has been observed especially on the trains going from Verona to Munich. Personal controls are part of a trilateral agreement (installed in 2015) between the railway police of Rosenheim (Germany), Innsbruck (Austria), and Bolzano (Italy) on the express trains, in order to prevent refugees from crossing the Italian border into Austria and then further to the German border. Even today, five years after the so-called crisis, this practice of personal control is still carried out by police officers on the trains and the railway stations along the Brenner route. In doing so, an emergency status and security status is upheld and reproduced in 2020 when the number of refugees crossing the border by train has been extremely reduced. In 2019, local media proudly report on the so-called success of these initiatives. The online portal stol.it, for example, headlines in April 2019: "Refugees avoid train over the Brenner Pass. Due to the intensive controls, there are now hardly any illegal immigrants trying to reach Germany by express train from Italy via the Brenner route." However, the monitoring of the border management by activists as well as the interview narratives show a different reality, namely that of alternative (and often more dangerous) ways of crossing as well as an increase of immobility experiences characterized by precariousness and an ulterior extension of the civic stratification system among the refugee groups present in the border zone.

From Immobility to New Mobilities

In line with this, Farim, a twenty-three-year-old man from Gambia, reports on his experiences of being unable to cross the border in a legal way. In 2016, Farim came to Italy by boat. He spent five months in Sicily. There he applied for asylum. His destination was not Italy, but Germany, where a friend and part of his family already live. So he left the accommodation center in south Italy and made his way north on his own. His destination was the Brenner border and then on to Germany. Without being in possession of documents that allow him to cross the border he has been forced to interrupt his mobility trajectory being now stuck in the border area: "Now, it's very difficult to go to Austria, Germany. They control on the trains. For me it's almost impossible. So now, I'm here, two years already. You have to wait here, think, look, talk to people until it's possible again." Two years that seem lost. Focused on what will be and less connected to the now. As Fontanari (2018) writes, asylum seekers like Farim are "deprived of their lifetime: they experience a present time without linearity, which is characterized by wait, judicial uncertainty, and impossibility to settle." Thus, by waiting, asylum seekers experience a sense of dislocation and disempowerment which leads to a "suspended identity," caught between the former life and the life they want to begin in the host country. However, in contrast to Lennartsson (2007), who defines this process of waiting as a vulnerable and powerless position characterized merely by passivity, Farim in his interview shows how he is eager to keep himself mobile and active even during his physical stuckedness, for example by building networks and planning further steps. Consequently, he describes the act of crossing borders as having to be considered as a series of experiences, skills, and networks that involve the individual as a both mobile and immobile actor (De Genova 2016). Thus, in this redrawing/rethinking process, they do not only rely on their own experiences but also on the experiences of others by weighing them up, imitating or rejecting them: "A friend of mine crossed the border by foot then. Now most people take the Flixbus or pay a taxi. They take bus from here to the border. They go Brennero. Then you walk and walk and you enter in Austria or Swiss. And then you take bus." To the question if this is a possible strategy also for him he says: "No, it's too dangerous, there are high mountains I don't know the right way." In this way, moving forward and crossing borders can be understood as part of new learning processes that are based on experiences. This follows the phenomenological view that learning is not understood as the initiative of a goal-oriented act. Rather, it proves to be a kind of awakening triggered by a foreign demand (Meyer-Drawe 2003), as it is outlined in the next quote: "I have to move on, I don't know how, that's why I talk to people who know the way to Germany and they tell you, so you can change plans."

By extension, interview partners often use the terms "to try" and/or "attempt" in order to describe the experiences of crossing borders as part of their new normalities. In the narrative of Salim, a twenty-six-year-old man from Nigeria, for example, the act of crossing borders is described as lived experience during his flight. Salim's journey took him from Nigera via Niger to Libya. "I have crossed so many borders," he says. In Libya, the police took him to prison as he did not have any documents with him: "In Libya it was terrible, I was in prison. If you didn't do what they said, they shoot you. So I said nothing. I survived." In late 2016, on the coast of Libya, he boarded a boat that would take him to Europe. A friend organized this crossing for him. Territorial borders in Europe no longer trigger any fears in him. Borders are simply obstacles he tries to overcome without fear. They have become part of his life: "I'm not afraid about crossing borders in Europe. If you want to go through Europe you have to cross borders. Here, I'm not afraid, I try." In fact, Salim in his narrative often makes use of the verb "to try" in describing uncertain structural environments that constantly surround them and impact their physical mobility experiences: "You never know how it ends. If I think on how I crossed the sea. It was so dangerous. But at that time I didn't see the danger, it was my only possibility, so I just did it, it was my second attempt to cross the sea." At the same time, the verb "to try" as well as the noun "attempt" expresses agentic action and thus personal strategies in order to circumvent/escape from power regimes and limiting structural circumstances. Similar to this, Kleist and Jansen (2016), for example, outline that the several attempts to cross a border (attempted cross-border mobility) can be seen as "one—contested—response to existential immobility and 'stuckedness.'" Similar to Salim, Hadim, a young man from Gambia, came to Italy by boat. From southern Italy he continued his journey north toward Sweden, where his brother lives with his family. Also Hadim associates the act of crossing borders as a lived normality in the refugee context, which is not characterized by fear but by negotiations:

So I go Austria three times. I'm not afraid to try again and again. After the third time they tell me this is the last time. I'm going but with the next train I'm coming back. So they tell me: you have to go to jail. I say just do it now. They say: why do you behave like this? I say: Because I don't want to live in Italy. There is no good for me, I'm sick. So, I don't have treatment. So I have to go. I can't live. So they asked me, you want to stay here or you want to go Germany? I say I don't want to stay here, I want to go Germany. So they let me pass through.

The quote shows how border practices have a strong performative dimension, which is reflected in concepts such as doing borders or doing frontiers (Heinze et al. 2015). This doing process is an embodied experience, and it is reflected in multiple encoded boundaries of access.

Forced Immobility and Living Situation

Leaning on different experiences made by interview partners, the restrictive border management at the Brenner pass has shifted the geographical border to the city of Bolzano that has become a hub for (unauthorized) asylum seekers and thus to all effects a border town where border practices are performed: "When the police catch you at the border, they put you on the train and send you back to Bolzano." That this is a common development is underlined by Wonders (2006, 66) who argues that "border performances occur in locations that may be far from the actual geographic border" and that the day-to-day decisions by government agents, police officers, and others "play a critical role in determining where, how, and on whose body a border will be performed." Due to the Critelli regulation, which denies direct access to the reception system to asylum seekers who arrive independently in South Tyrol, most of the so-called out-of-quota asylum seekers have no choice but to look for a place to sleep on their own. Halim, from Afghanistan, first fled to Italy, where his fingerprints were registered, then he continued his journey to Austria and then to Germany. Here he worked and lived for two years until he was checked by the police and sent back to Italy:

When I came to Bolzano I slept out about five months, you have to wait six months to get a place. If you come with family right away, if you're alone you have to wait six months, eight months, always outside, if it's cold, it doesn't matter, very difficult. During the day it was better because I went to the library and at night it was difficult because it was cold and I didn't have a place and I didn't even have many blankets, very difficult.

When Halim has to leave one place, he either keeps traveling or starts moving through the streets, parks, or the spaces below bridges:

I slept under the Roma bridge or even slept here many times (Talvera bridge), but the police came here and did not allow me to sleep here. Even on the Rome bridge two or three times, the police brought my luggage, my blanket and they didn't want to give it back to me. They said that it's not allowed to sleep there and I said "but where do I sleep," they said we don't know.

This "roaming around" the city, streets, and streambeds is turned into the quintessential "other" by local authorities. "I asked them: but excuse me, where can I go? Where do you think I can go? And they said we don't know, we just know that you can't stay here, you have to go. And there are so many guys who have the same situation." The interview quote suggests that during their experience of forced immobility, they are contemporarily forced to mobility by policies and practices of exclusion and marginalization: "you can't stay here, you have to go." So, what from the outside is seen as a vagabond attitude of people who have nothing to do, just roaming around, from the inside is filled with concrete and active steps. Being mobile while being in a situation of immobility can thus be interpreted as a daily survival strategy while being stuck in a limbo.

KEEPING MOBILE WHILE BEING IMMOBILE—
THE RELEVANCE OF THE VIRTUAL SPACE

The restrictive measures are pushing irregular asylum seekers more and more to the margins of society, restricting their freedom of mobility not only within the material but also within the virtual space that is equally important and vital for their survival. Accordingly, in 2016, due to the growing number of asylum seekers "roaming around" in public spaces, the local authorities in the border city of Bolzano have become more restrictive and adopted several policies of exclusion. One of the biggest consequences for the irregular refugees was certainly the restrictions on free internet access. Different public and private institutions like the university and the museum of modern art in fact used to offer their visitors free internet access and the possibilities to charge digital devices. This policy was changed in 2016 when several institutions in the territory decided to eliminate their free Wi-Fi hotspot in order to prevent the accumulation of refugees before or within the institution. In line with this, Rashid refers to his own experiences of discrimination in public space: "When they see two or three black men together they become afraid, so they switched off the power in this area." Most of the interview partners report that this decision has hit them hard, as most of them are not able to afford to buy internet access on a regular basis. Rashid goes on to say that when he first came to Bolzano, he had no work. His money was exhausted. To get in touch with his parents and to orientate himself in this new environment, he had to use his mobile phone. For him, free Wi-Fi hotspots in the city were of utmost importance: "Before I always was at the university. I used the Wi-Fi. Now this is not possible. Now they ask you ten euros to buy internet free Wi-Fi. I don't always have money so sometimes I charge it for one or two euros." Thus, more than others, asylum seekers without the possibility to directly access the reception centers have heavily depended on public institutions and their offer to use free internet as well as charge their smartphones with electricity. With the preposition "before," the interview partner refers to the period before the restrictions in 2016, when many institutions became self-active in exclusionary practices. In his narrative, Rashid shows the influence such external decisions have on his everyday life. The smartphone is the only way to get in touch with his friends and relatives in his country of origin:

> There is no possibility. I cannot call my family, my friends. This is not nice. Also I used to listen to music, but if I don't have the possibility to charge it with power. I can't do it in order to save battery. It's difficult for me, sometimes I go to my friend's house and charge it there. Or, I give it to my friend who is living in an accommodation center they charge it for me. But there is always the risk that they steal it. . . . Now for example my phone does not work. I don't have power. I have to wait until my friend is coming back from Trento. He has an apartment.

Also Faith (2018) underlines how keeping mobile phones charged with power is one of the most important elements that contributes not only to social inequality but also to digital inequalities. In line with this, exclusive policies that restrict the virtual space can be interpreted as an ulterior institutional act of discrimination by denying them a fundamental human right (UN, Article 12, 2016) to accessing, using, creating, and publishing on digital media. Following this, the narratives confirm the high importance of ICT in their everyday lives that has changed their experiences of forced immobility. As such, smartphones are a constant companion in everyday life, as Rashid explains. He describes their smartphones in this period of physical forced immobility as one of the most important things they own and which they have to protect from those who want to steal it: "I always have my phone in my jacket. I always take it with me. In this situation here, my phone is so important to me. Here are many thieves, so you have to be careful. I always take care of it." Rashid, similar to others, comparatively invest a lot of money in phones and smartphones: "They have stolen my phone twice. Now I have a new one. I spent a lot of money about 180 Euro. For me this is very much. But I need it and now it's always here in my pocket. It's one of the most important objects I own."

The main argument here is that ICT endangers national borders via facilitating information transfer across borders. Different researchers link the importance of smartphones to their usability as main digital devices to stay in contact with family and friends in a transnational context. In addition to this, the narratives give insight into how smartphones are also the main digital devices used to deal with the refugees' everyday struggles. Following this, Farim, the young man from Gambia, outlines that smartphones are one of the main communication and organization channels to support each other in their daily battle for legitimacy: "When the police has vacated our sleeping place under the bridge, my friend called me and told me not to return there. We communicate usually via phone. When there was the police it is better not to return so you're safe. Otherwise you never know what happens." As the results show, the communication within their community is not only limited to the local reality of immobility, but extends itself to the transnational context across borders. As such, refugees report that phones and smartphones are the main communication channels to remain in contact with community members across European borders. The communication on how border regimes work, for example, or on how the possibilities are to cross the borders is usually negotiated via phone, as Hadim explains: "I also communicate with my friends who are already in Germany. They always tell me about the situation at the border, than I see. . . . I use Facebook and WhatsApp, yes. We are always in contact." As the interview quote shows, even if they are physically stuck in a border area, virtual platforms like WhatsApp and Facebook turn into extremely important virtual spaces to keep active, to organize, and redraw their trajectories. In addition, and despite their knowledge of possible police surveillance of their phone content, the interview partners consider the virtual space as a more "secure" space of acting during their forced immobility experience. In line with this, in order to organize border crossings, for example, they prefer online services to physical contact with service collaborators and the possible direct contact with police and thus authorities that "control and look at every step we are making." Thus, in the interviews, the virtual space is generally described as a sort of protected space that escapes control from the outside. In the virtual space, they feel free to communicate and to act without being restricted, as Salim outlines in the next quote: "Next time I'll make the reservation online, as my friend told me, very quick then you pay and you go to the border with the Flixbus. You don't meet the police."

CONCLUSION

The chapter gave insights into how asylum seekers, coming in an autonomous way to the Brenner border zone, make their living under extremely precarious living conditions by using ICT to deal with and/or circumvent restrictive migration regimes. In doing so, the chapter adopted a multi-dimensional understanding of mobility, both as a physical and virtual experience. However, in order to understand mobility/immobility as an online and offline experience, the individual level has to be related to the structural context that shapes it as a personal experience. Following this line of argument, the chapter adopted a relational perspective on agency and vulnerability. Accordingly, vulnerability is not something that someone has or possesses, but a status that has been attributed from the outside. Consequently, the "agency-vulnerability nexus" has the potential to break through stereotypical views of people who have experienced migration and flight and focuses on the processes of social inequality in conjunction with the resources of actors. In particular, focusing on social inequality lays bare a system of stratification "based on the relationship between different categories of individuals and the state, and the rights thereby granted or denied" (Morris 2003, 76). Following Zetter (2007), this fractioning/stratification of the refugee label is part of globalized processes and mixed migration flows that increase the development of stratified migration management patterns as well as bureaucratic practices with the aim to control mixed migration flows.

As the results show, the denied right of having access to the reception system and the interventions adopted by different institutions and actors have reduced and limited systematically the refugees' physical mobility and thus spaces where they are legitimated to be and to go. Thus, social needs have been turned into security threats via security measures such as evictions (policies of "disturbing") and urban re-development policies with the goal to eliminate the "unwanted" refugees. Following this, they have no other choice than "roaming around"—be mobile in order to survive. However, policies and practices of exclusion have long stopped to be discriminating and marginalizing only on a physical level, but have been effective also in reducing the virtual dimension that characterizes mobility. In order to exercise this form of mobility, however, having access to connectivity as well as electricity and thus to rely on digital infrastructures that are accessible for all (e.g., free internet provided via Wi-Fi hotspots throughout the city) is crucial. Instead, as the mapping and analyses of the data show, public connectivity provided by public Wi-Fi hotspots changed from a human right into an instrument of power that installed new inequalities and new exclusion forms, allowing free access to Wi-Fi only to those who can afford it and leaving those at the bottom of the civic stratification system behind. This contradicts the 2030 sustainability goals that promote the idea of ending extreme poverty in all its forms, and reducing inequalities among both individuals (vertical) and groups (horizontal). Key to "leaving no one behind" is the prioritization and fast-tracking of actions for the poorest and most marginalized people and not vice versa, which the border area testifies.

REFERENCES

Alencar, A. 2018. "Refugee integration and social media: A local and experiential perspective." *Communication and Society* (online) 21 (11): 1588–603.

Alencar, A. 2020. "Mobile communication and refugees: An analytical review of academic literature." *Sociology Compass* 14 (8): e12802.

Anderson, B. 2013. *Us and Them? The Dangerous Politics of Immigration Control.* Oxford: Oxford University Press.

Antenne Migranti. 2017. *Lungo la rotta del Brennero. Rapporto di monitoraggio della situazione dei migranti a Bolzano e al Brennero.* https://www.asgi.it/wp-content/uploads/2017/09/2017_Report_Monitoraggio_Bolzano_Brennero_25_09.pdf.

Artero, M., and E. Fontanari. 2019. "Obstructing lives: Local borders and their structural violence in the asylum field of post-2015 Europe." *Journal of Ethnic and Migration Studies* 47 (3): 631–48.

Corbin, J. M., and A. L. Strauss. 2008. *Basics of Qualitative Research: Techniques and Procedures for Developing Grounded Theory.* Thousand Oaks, CA: Sage Publications, Inc.

De Genova, N. 2002. "Migrant 'illegality' and deportability in everyday life." *Annual Review Anthropology* 31: 419–47.

De Genova, N. 2016. *Detention, Deportation, and Waiting: Toward a Theory of Migrant Detainability.* https://www.globaldetentionproject.org/wp-content/uploads/2016/12/De-Genova-GDP-Paper-2016.pdf.

Dekker, R., G. Engbersen, J. Klaver, and H. Vonk. 2018. "Smart refugees: How Syrian asylum migrants use social media information in migration decision-making." *Social Media and Society* 4 (1): 2056305118764439.

Diminescu, D. 2020. "Researching the connected migrant." In *The SAGE Handbook of Media and Migration*, edited by K. Smets, K. Leurs, M. Georgiou, S. Witteborn, and R. Gajjala. London: Sage Publications Ltd.

Faith, B. 2018. "Maintenance affordances and structural inequalities: Mobile phone use by low-income women in the United Kingdom." *Information Technologies & International Development* (Special Section) 14: 66–80.

Fontanari, E. 2018. *Lives in Transit. An Ethnographic Study of Refugees' Subjectivity across European Borders.* London: Routledge.

Gillespie, M., S. Osseiran, and M. Cheesman. 2018. "Syrian refugees and the digital passage to Europe: Smartphone infrastructures and affordances." *Social Media and Society* 4 (1): 1–12.

Heinze, T., S. Illigens, and M. Pollok. 2016. "Doing frontiers: On the performativity of the European border and migration regime." DNGPS Working Paper, Hanover, Germany.

Kaufmann, K. 2018. "Navigating a new life: Syrian refugees and their smartphones in Vienna." *Communication & Society* 21 (6): 882–98.

Kaufmann, V. 2002. *Re-thinking Mobility*. Burlington, VT: Ashgate.

Khan, N. 2016. "Immobility." In *Keywords of Mobility: Critical Anthropological Engagements*, edited by N. Salazar and K. Jayaram, 93–112. New York: Berghahn.

Kleist, N., and S. Jansen. 2016. "Introduction: Hope over time—crisis, immobility and future-making." *History and Anthropology* 27 (4): 373–92.

Latonero, M. 2016b, February 1. "Refugees' new infrastructure for movement: A digital passage." *Data & Society*. https://points.datasociety.net/refugees-new -infrastructure-for-movement-d31c3ab53b20#.wxiltwxst.

Lennartsson, R. 2007. "You are nobody while you are waiting: Asylum seekers' experiences of nothingness." *Ethnologia Scandinavica* 37: 21–34.

Leurs, K., and K. Smets. 2018. "Five questions for digital migration studies: Learning from digital connectivity and forced migration in(to) Europe." *Social Media and Society* 3: 1–16.

Lintner, C. 2022. "Being (co-)present: Reflecting the personal and public spheres of asylum seeking in relation to connectivity." *Ethnography* 23 (1): 60–82.

Martin-Shields, C. P., and N. Bodanac. 2017. "Peacekeeping's digital economy: The role of communication technologies in post-conflict economic growth." *International Peacekeeping* 34 (3): 420–45.

Meyer-Drawe, K. 2003. "Lernen als Erfahrung." *Zeitschrift für Erziehungswissenschaft* 6 (4): 505–14.

Morris, L. 2002. *Managing Migration: Civic Stratification and Migrants Rights*. London: Routledge.

Schewel, K. 2019. "Understanding immobility: Moving beyond the mobility bias in migration studies." *International Migration Review* 54 (2): 328–55.

Turkle, S. 2011. *Alone Together: Why We Expect More from Technology and Less from Each Other*. New York: Basic Books.

Wall, M., M. Otis Campell, and D. Janbek. 2015. "Syrian refugees and information precarity." *New Media and Society* 19 (2): 240–54.

Witteborn, S. 2015. "Becoming (im)perceptible: Forced migrants and virtual practice." *Journal of Refugee Studies* 28: 350–67.

Witteborn, S. 2012. *Forced Migrants, New Media Practices and the Creation of Locality. The Handbook of Global Media Research, Supra-and Sub-National Spheres: Researching Transnational Spaces*. Oxford, UK: Wiley-Blackwell.

Wonders, N. A. 2006. "Global flows, semi-permeable borders and new channels of inequality: Border crossers and border performativity." In *Borders, Mobility and Technologies of Control*, edited by S. Pickering and L. Weber, 63–86. Dordrecht, The Netherlands: Springer.

Wyss, A. 2019. "Stuck in mobility? Interrupted journeys of migrants with precarious legal status in Europe." *Journal of Immigrant & Refugee Studies* 17 (1): 77–93.

Zetter, R. 2007. "More labels, fewer refugees: Remaking the refugee label in an era of globalisation." *Journal of Refugee Studies* 20 (2): 172–92.

NOTE

1. The so-defined out-of-quota group is heterogeneous and comprises several groups with different legislative backgrounds. There are, for example, those who voluntarily left an Italian reception center/hotspot and decided to come to Bolzano. Another group of refugees and asylum seekers constitutes those who re-entered Italy because of pending deportations out of other EU states (such as from Germany or Austria) that issue negative asylum decisions. Finally, there are those who return to Italy from other EU member states, according to the Dublin procedure. As their fingerprints were first registered in Italy via the Eurodac system, Italy was identified as the state responsible for following the asylum procedure.

Chapter 7

Navigating the Resources of the Migrant Digital Space

Luca Rossi

INTRODUCTION

This chapter investigates the resources that different types of actors shared on social networking sites (Facebook) during the period surrounding the 2015 surge in migration toward Europe.

The role that digital technologies and digital media play in contemporary migration is at the center of the growing field of digital migration studies (Siapera 2014; Leurs and Smets 2018a). Migrants use digital technologies for a wide range of scopes: from accessing relevant information before and after the journey (Dekker et al. 2018) to establishing or maintaining social capital (Almenara-Niebla 2020). By doing so, migrants create what Kok and Rogers defined as a transglocal network (Kok and Rogers 2017), a network of individuals as well as resources that exists alongside the national and transnational dimension.

While these transglocal networks are not technologically determined, social networking platforms by facilitating the creation of connections by an unprecedented number of people and by facilitating the connection with weak(er) ties have certainly played a major role in shaping the contemporary migratory experience. These technologically supported networks have long been studied in the context of digital diasporas (Siapera 2014; Laguerre 2010; Kok and Rogers 2017) while having received less attention in the context of digital migration studies.

Nevertheless, the explosive worldwide adoption of social media and social networking sites (e.g., Facebook, Twitter, Instagram, Telegram, etc.) has produced long-lasting changes in the migratory process that cannot be overlooked. On the one side, social media and social networking sites provide an easier independent access to information for those people who are planning on or considering migrating. The number of resources available to future or potential migrants has exploded as well as their practical availability.

On the other side, social media and social networking sites resulted in a much larger number of actors that are now able and willing to provide information to those who are considering migrating (e.g., through dedicated websites, YouTube channels or Facebook groups created by solidarity groups, small local nongovernmental organizations [NGOs], etc.). Within this perspective, the production and sharing *at scale* of information about the journey (e.g., about how to cross a border or apply for asylum) are no longer exclusively possible for governments or structured groups of activists but also for voluntary associations.

It is worth considering what the consequences are when the ability to become producer or gatekeeper of content aimed at facilitating or supporting the migratory process is granted to a wide range of widely different actors. Della Porta (2009) suggests the distinction between social movements—conceptualized as conflictual actors—and consensus movements—characterized by a dialogue-oriented vision of politics. In the contemporary context of actors supporting migratory processes, conflict and consensus movements are both possible: large international NGOs might operate within a consensus framework when they try to mediate and operate within the legal boundaries of existing immigration policies, while other alternative actors might position themselves within a conflictual framework when they share information or resources or actively facilitate illegal migrations. Following Dessewffy and Nagy (2016), this chapter argues that the political nature of some of these actors is often shaped in relation to the surrounding institutional context and the political attitude surrounding them. If we observe, as done in this chapter, a period sufficiently long, it is easy to see how actors' political positioning on the conflict-consensus axis might change.

By having allowed a larger number of diverse actors to become providers of information resources for migrants, social networking sites produced what Gillespie, Osseiran, and Cheesman defined as a paradox (2018). While available information for migrants has grown at an unprecedented rate due to the growing number of subjects that are now able to provide and make public this information, its reliability has declined. Gillespie and colleagues observe how information provided online is often outdated, lacks references to primary sources, or does not adhere to any fact-checking standard. Overabundant information does not necessarily translate, for the people willing to migrate, into more reliable information, as the challenge of finding relevant information is replaced by the challenge of deciding which piece of information one should trust.

As Dekker points out (Dekker et al. 2018), access to social media while looking for information takes place together with many other information-seeking activities both online and offline. The result is often an abundance of information that needs to be evaluated. Separating facts (and reliable information) from rumors is the key challenge for many migrants, especially when dealing with what is often perceived as an increasingly hostile environment.

Given these premises it should appear clear that mapping the types of actors that provide online information for migrants as well as understanding their strategies, activities, and motivations is crucial to understanding contemporary migration. Makrygianni and colleagues (Makrygianni et al. 2021) have initiated this effort by developing a methodological approach to map what they define as Migrant Digital Space (MDS). The MDS is the assemblage of actors, resources, and platforms available, at a specific moment in time, for a specific migrant population. In their attempt to map the MDS, Makrygianni et al. (2021) categorize the actors that act in the MDS according to their organizational level: institutional (institutional organizations, governmental or intergovernmental agencies active in the field of migration and refugees, e.g., UN High Commissioner for Refugees), semi-institutional (medium and large organizations, often NGOs, that have an organized and permanent structure, e.g., Médecins Sans Frontières, Sea-Watch, etc.), and informal (loosely organized actors run on voluntary work with an unclear temporal stability).

This categorization grasps some of the complexity that we have described so far. If, on the one side, large institutional organizations might appear more reliable, researchers have shown how informal actors—often managed by solidarians with close personal connections to the experience of migration (Alencar 2018; Alencar 2019)—can easily be perceived as more trustworthy due to an often-common background between the migrants and the solidarians. In addition, informal and familiar actors can be less frequently associated with the fear of online surveillance compared to large organizations of state actors (Dekker et al. 2018). Different perceptions of informal actors by the migrant population could allow the informal actors to play a complementary or alternative role to larger and most institutional actors.

On these premises, we hypothesize that informal actors will share different sets of resources compared to institutional or semi-institutional actors.

This will be explored through two research questions:

- How similar, in terms of online domains, are the online resources shared by institutional, semi-institutional, and informal actors operating within the MDS in Europe?

- What additional characteristics of the pages can explain the similarity between the online resources that are shared?

To answer these questions, the chapter builds on the data collected during the DIGINAUTS project (Makrygianni et al. 2021). The project aimed, among other things, at mapping the digital resources publicly available to migrants on Facebook in four European countries (Greece, Germany, Denmark, and Sweden). This assemblage of resources was defined as MDS (Makrygianni et al. 2021), and Facebook pages were manually coded according to several different characteristics. A detailed description of the data is provided in the section "Methods and Data."

RELATED WORKS

Despite the growing popularity of digital migration studies (Leurs and Prabhakar 2018a; Leurs and Smets 2018b), quantitative approaches are still relatively rare. This is probably due to the epistemological closeness that the newborn field shares with many methodological approaches within the humanities and the qualitative part of social sciences (ethnography, participatory observation, interviewing) (Leurs and Prabhakar 2018b). Despite being less popular, quantitative approaches to digital migration studies are present and have often been used to map the migratory phenomenon, frequently through the data produced by migrants (Kok and Rogers 2017). Within this perspective, the goal has often been to map the migrant or diasporic community (Rodica et al. 2020) as it evolves and develops meaningful social connections that are increasingly mediated by digital technologies (Rosenau 2003). These social connections between migrants or migrant organizations form networks that have frequently been framed in terms of social capital and access to resources. Despite these connected actors commonly being referred to as networks, the adoption of methods taken from network analysis and of related concepts has been extremely limited, as noted by a special issue published of the journal *Social Networks* that aimed at exploring this "missing link" and reinforcing the connection between migration research and network methods (Bilecen, Gamper, and Lubbers 2018).

It is worth observing how the core of the special issue focuses on the network dynamics underlying the social processes of integration in a new country (e.g., Vacca et al. 2018) or on the structural properties of transnational networks (e.g., Cachia and Maya Jariego 2018) while there is no research that builds on online or digital data that were the key element of the concurrent explosion of digital migration studies. Within this perspective, it seems fair to say that while network analysis has been used in migration studies to understand the social structure of connections that are able to shape and support various phases of the migration process, the use of network analysis in the context of digital migration studies is still in its early stages.

This chapter, building on digital social media data and adopting methods from network analysis, starts filling this gap and will hopefully be followed by more research in the future.

METHODS AND DATA

The DIGINAUTS research project defined the MDS as an unstable set of social relations, practices, and resources that migrants navigate before, during, and after their journey (Makrygianni et al. 2021). Within this perspective, the MDS is formed by (a) digital subjects (accounts, pages, hashtags, channels) and (b) migrant-related topics (such as discussions on migration routes, language lessons, football conversations, university enrollment, job seeking) through conversations across (c) various digital platforms. This theoretical definition can be easily mapped into a precise set of digital data to be collected, which in the case of DIGINAUTS resulted in (a) a series of public pages (b) retrieved looking for a set of manually selected relevant keywords (c) on Facebook.

To preserve privacy and minimize potential harm to the subjects, only public pages were included in the selection, and usernames were anonymized. The pages were identified using a user-centric perspective (Makrygianni et al. 2021). This means that the research team simulated migrants' information-seeking practices by using keywords and research terms "as if they were migrants looking for information" (Makrygianni et al. 2021). These terms and keywords have been used both in the languages of the destination countries investigated by the project (German, Greek, Danish, Swedish) as well as in Arabic and English. Once online resources were identified through this process, the list was integrated by additional resources identified through pilot interviews conducted in Greece, in the Öresund region, and in Germany. This approach produced a final dataset composed of two hundred Facebook pages that were then manually coded with additional information such as the type of actor behind each Facebook page, the physical location of the actor, the date when the page was created, as well as the language used on the page (Arabic, domestic, English, multilingual). At the same time, all the content (posts, comments, and reactions) publicly available on the pages was downloaded using Facebook's API. This produced a final dataset totaling two hundred pages, 84,359 posts, and 2,254,923 comments, produced between December 20, 2010, and September 24, 2018.

For the analysis presented in this chapter, the dataset was filtered to iso-late only pages that published content from January 1, 2014, to December 31, 2017 (N = 154). Because this chapter only focuses on the informational resources shared by actors managing the Facebook pages, we first removed all the comments (that could have also contained links to online resources) and selected only the posts that contained a link to an external website (N = 7,851). These posts contained links toward 7,079 distinct URLs and 1,384 domains. Due to the absolute number of links, we will focus our attention on the internet domains that were shared by the Facebook pages rather than considering the specific URL. This means that, in the context of this chapter, the online resource is identified by the domain rather than by the specific html page/PDF document/YouTube video. While this was done due to practical reasons given the sheer number of links, it clearly limits the level of detail that the description can provide.

In order to address RQ1, we represent the data into what is known as a bipartite network. A bipartite network is a type of network characterized by the presence of two types of nodes (pages and domains in our case), and where connections are only possible between nodes of different type

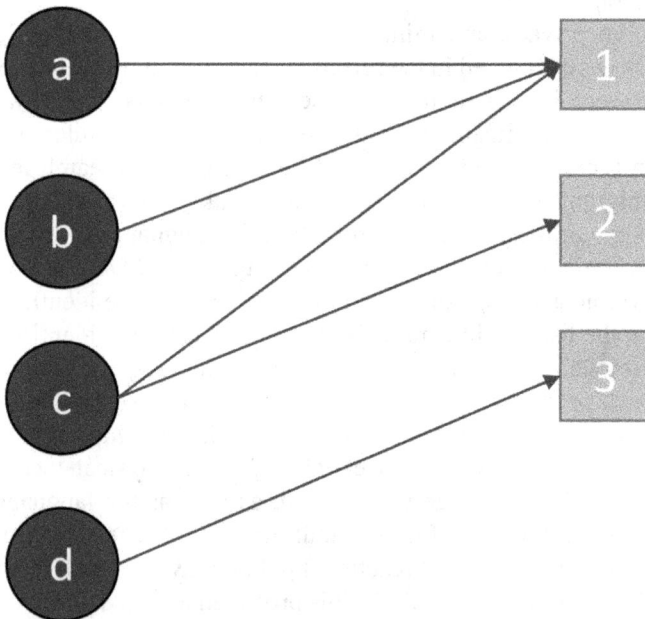

Figure 7.1. A bipartite network. Facebook pages (circles) are connected to the online domain they have shared (squares). Only connections between circles and squares are possible. *Source:* Authors.

(e.g., pages can link domains, but domains cannot link domains). This means that we will represent the data as in Figure 7.1.

Bipartite networks are widely used in the analysis of social activity since "common action," "common participation," or, as it is in our case, "the use of common resources" is often a sign of proximity or similarity between the social actors (Tucker et al. 2018).

Following this assumption made by Tucker and colleagues (2018), this chapter will use the similarity of the online domains shared by the Facebook pages to infer about the similarity between the pages. In other words, we will ask (RQ2) what other characteristics of the pages lead them to share similar resources. To study this, it was necessary to perform an additional transformation of the network called projection. A projected network is a bipartite network where two nodes (two pages in our case) are connected if they have a common connection (in our case, if they have shared a link to the same domain). From a bipartite graph containing 154 pages and 1,384 domains, we obtained a projection. Subsequently, given the known tendency of projected networks to have an extremely high number of connections that bear very little information (Coscia and Rossi 2019), we extracted its signed backbone.[1] Extracting the backbone of a network means to preserve only those connections that are statistically significant. In our case, the backboning of the network retains a connection between two pages only if the connection (two pages having shared the same domain) occurred significantly more (alpha = 0.01) than what was expected from a null model (Neal 2013). The resulting projected network has 154 pages connected through 1,591 connections (see Figure 7.2).

This procedure has been performed on the whole dataset (from 2014 to 2017) as well as on the yearly data.

Table 7.1 reports the dimension of the bipartite network (pages and domains) in total and for every year of the analysis as well as the number of connections between nodes of the projected network (the number of nodes in the projected network is equal to the number of pages of the corresponding year).

Table 7.1. Nodes and Connections in the Bipartite and in the Projected Networks

	Nodes	Connections	Unique Pages	Websites	Proj_connections
Total	1,538	7,851	154	1,384	1,591
2014	336	1,103	47	289	106
2015	541	1,812	78	463	142
2016	662	2,324	106	556	188
2017	664	2,612	118	546	317

Figure 7.2. Visualization of the bipartite network. Several pages link to the same online resource. *Source*: Authors.

CO-SHARING ANALYSIS

Before we move further, it is important to highlight that while the analysis is based on a large quantity of longitudinal data, it is nevertheless hard to claim generalizability for the results. The way in which the MDS is defined makes it a convenience sample, thus the results should always be interpreted as limited to the dataset. Moreover, the construction of the dataset made only a minimal effort to balance the actors within the various countries of the study. This results in significant differences between different countries and between different types of actors (Figure 7.3). Overall, all the countries have more informal actors and fewer semi-institutional and institutional actors. Germany is the country with most actors, followed by Sweden, Greece, and Denmark.

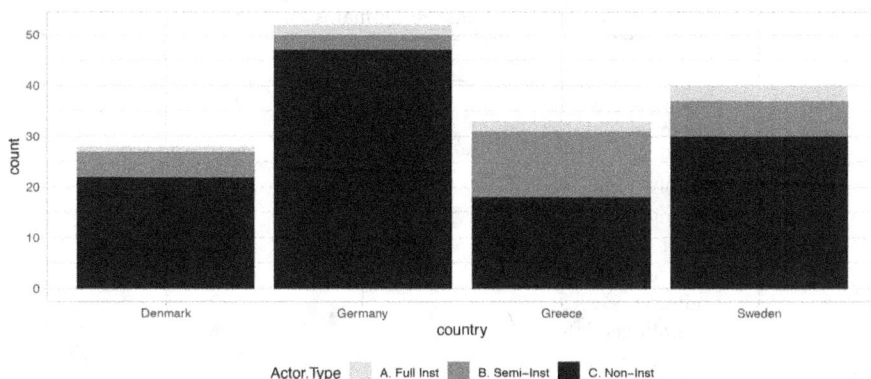

Figure 7.3. Number of Facebook pages per country (N = 154). *Source*: Authors.

These differences can be due to many concurrent factors: larger migrant population, larger internet adoption, or Facebook penetration in the country, as well as unknown biases during the data collection. While the statistical analysis we describe later in the chapter is not affected by these differences in size, it is still worth knowing that they exist.

A first element of interest is to study which websites are the most linked to. Table 7.2 and Table 7.3 show the top ten most linked to domains both overall and for each country. It is interesting to observe how Swedish domains, shared by Swedish pages, occupy the first three positions despite the fact that Sweden is not the most represented country in the data, suggesting that the countries within our sample had an overall different level of Facebook activity or were reliant on Facebook communication to different degrees.

When we look at the different countries, it is interesting to observe how the overall picture is remarkably similar when it comes to what kinds of websites are shared. In every country, the top ten of the most shared domains is characterized by a mix of sites dedicated to migrants (most of them no longer active or available) (e.g., arabeurobe.com, for-syrians.de, refugeesupport.eu, lifeeu. info), news media (dr.dk, ndr.de), a few large NGOs (msf.gr, sosmediterranee. org), and links to other social media resources (YouTube).

As expected, due to the 2015 explosion in migrant activity, the volume of shared links increases over the years (Figure 7.4), it peaks in 2016, and it declines for some countries (Sweden and Germany) in 2017. It is interesting to observe how overall the links shared by informal actors keep growing throughout the period (Figure 7.5), peaking in 2017, while institutional or semi-institutional actors peak in 2016: the year after the peak of the crisis that coincides with the agreement between the European Union and Turkey. While these differences could be properly explained only through a qualitative analysis of the links—that is outside of the scope of this chapter—it is

Table 7.2. Top Ten Most Shared Domains

Name	No. of Links
sverigesrost.se	1,063
alkompis.se	611
malmo.se	327
youtube.com	203
lifeeu.info	203
msf.gr	200
for-syrians.de	151
youtu.be	150
blog.refugee.info	136
lojo2.com	122

possible to shed some light on these differences by looking at the five most shared domains per each type of page over time (Figure 7.6).

There are a few things that are worth noticing. On the one side, institutional actors share links to large NGOs or local and national authorities (e.g., msf.gr, malmo.se). Both semi-institutional and informal actors share links to social media platforms (mainly YouTube). Both informal and semi-institutional pages share links to ad hoc pages and resources (e.g., refugeesupport.eu, for-syrians.de, refugee.info), while only semi-institutional pages share links to news media domains (e.g., politiken.dk, information.dk). These differences suggest a different type of focus between these actors: institutional actors were more engaged sharing resources that were relevant during the peak of the migration crisis (e.g., links to NGOs and rescue operators), while semi-institutional and informal actors shared resources aimed at supporting migrants when they were settling down in Europe (e.g., relevant news, legal advice, etc.). Moreover, some kind of temporal stability of the type of domain

Table 7.3. Top Ten Most Shared Domains within Each Country

Germany	Greece	Sweden	Denmark
for-syrians.de	msf.gr	sverigesrost.se	lifeeu.info
lojo2.com	blog.refugee.info	alkompis.se	danmarkliv.com
sosmediterranee.org	mydonate.bt.com	malmo.se	information.dk
arabeurobe.com	refugeesupport.eu	centersweden.com	trampolinehouse.dk
youtube.com	youtu.be	m.facebook.com	youtube.com
thevoiceforum.org	drive.google.com	oresundspuls.com	dr.dk
ndr.de	support.msf.gr	youtube.com	politiken.dk
alloeurope.com	refugee.info	on.fb.me	youtu.be
taz.de	refugeerescue.co.uk	migrationsverket.se	drc.dk
youtu.be	bit.ly	youtu.be	danskherognu.dk

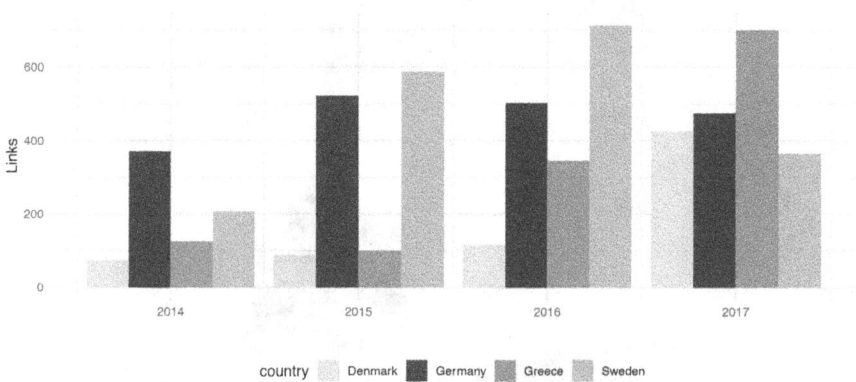

Figure 7.4. Temporal evolution of links to external domains in the four countries. *Source*: Authors.

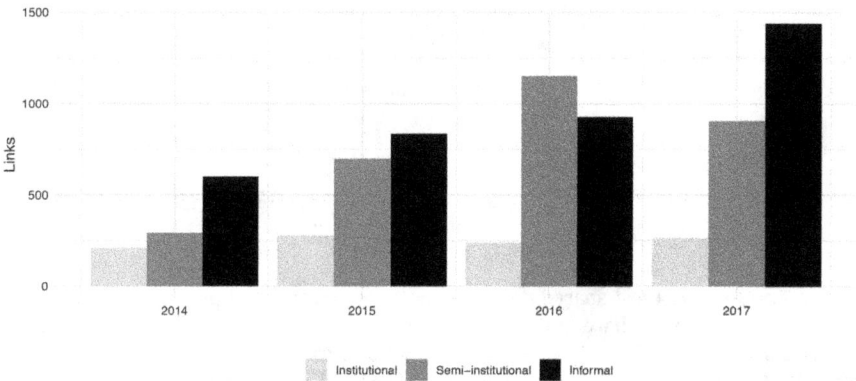

Figure 7.5. Temporal evolution of links to external domains shared by various types of actors. *Source*: Authors.

(e.g., news organization, ad hoc pages, official pages) shared by the different types of actors can be observed.

While this initial intuition comes from a visual exploration of the data, it can be further investigated by quantitatively addressing RQ1.

If, as we suggested earlier, the focus of the various types of actors is different with institutional pages more focused on the actual moment of migration and semi-institutional and informal pages more focused on the post-migration phase of settling down in Europe, we will expect to observe a quantifiable difference between the domains shared by these different types of actors. Given the diversity in size of the sets of links shared by the various types of actors, we decided to measure the difference (or the similarity) between the links to domains shared by the various types of actors using the overlap coefficient (Vijaymeena and Kavitha 2016). Overlap coefficient is not affected

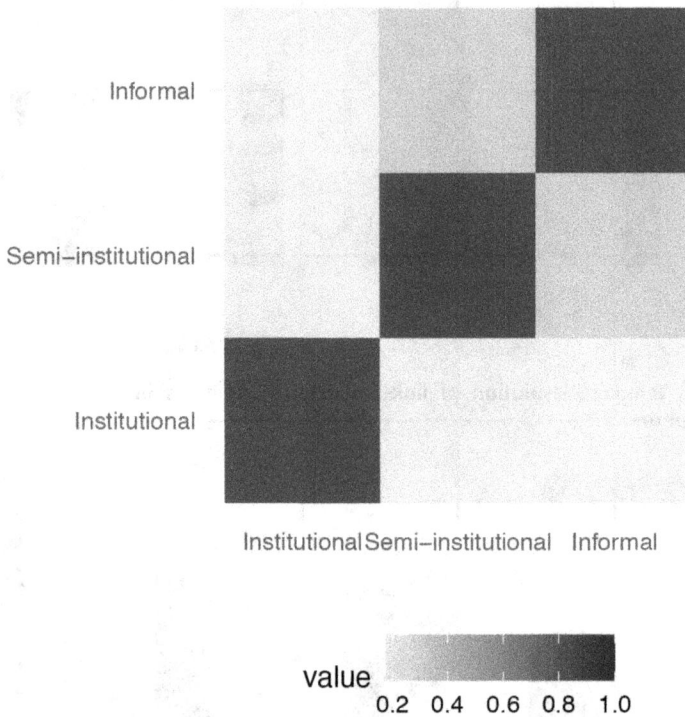

Figure 7.6. **Top five most shared domains per each country and per type of page, over time. If a domain was shared by more than one type of page, it would appear twice in the visualization. Notice how semi-institutional and informal pages are mostly shared after 2016, and how the type of domain that is shared does not change.** *Source*: Authors.

by differences in size between the two groups we are comparing (opposite to other similarity metrics that are often used, e.g., Jaccard coefficient), and it is expressed as

$$overlap(X, Y) = \frac{X \cap Y}{min|A||B|}.$$

Overlap coefficient measures the overlap between two sets of elements (domains in our case), meaning that if two groups of actors (e.g., institutional and semi-institutional pages) had shared only links to exactly the same set of domains, the overlapping coefficient between them would be 1. Figure 7.7 shows the overlap of domains shared between the three groups of actors we are observing. The overlap is quite small between domains shared by institutional pages and those shared by semi-institutional (0.18) and even smaller with informal pages (0.17). The overlap is higher (0.32) between

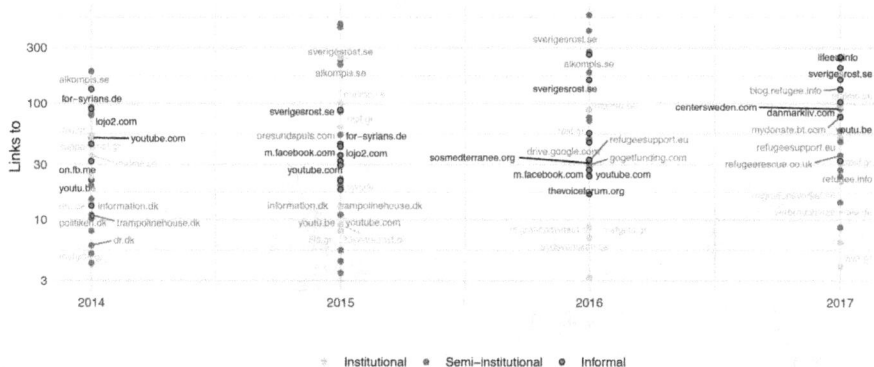

Figure 7.7. Overlapping coefficient between the domains shared by the various types of pages. *Source*: Authors.

semi-institutional and informal pages. This allows us to confirm and quantify our initial intuition. The three types of actors share links to different types of online resources with minimal level of overlap between institutional pages and the other two categories. The overlap, thus the similarity between the domains shared, between the two other groups of pages (semi-institutional and informal) is higher.

NETWORK ANALYSIS

As described in the previous sections, we perform network analysis on the projection of the bipartite network Pages-> Domains. Because the projected network connects two pages when they have shared the same domain, our RQ2 (What additional characteristics of the pages can explain the similarity between the online resources that are shared?) is equivalent to asking what characteristics of two pages can explain their being connected in the projected network (Figure 7.8). In network analysis, the problem of understanding which individual characteristics of the nodes of a network are driving the formation of connections (in our case, which characteristics of the pages drive the sharing of similar links) is framed as an attempt to understand the homophily of the network. Homophily is a well-known social principle that states that similar social actors are more likely to be connected to each other than dissimilar ones (McPherson, Smith-Lovin, and Cook 2001). While homophily has been observed in a wide range of social networks both offline and online (Halil, Agarwal, and Xu 2010), the actors' characteristics that explain the homophily we observe might change from case to case.

In the context of this chapter, studying what drives the homophily in the network means to ask on which of the characteristics of the pages (Country,

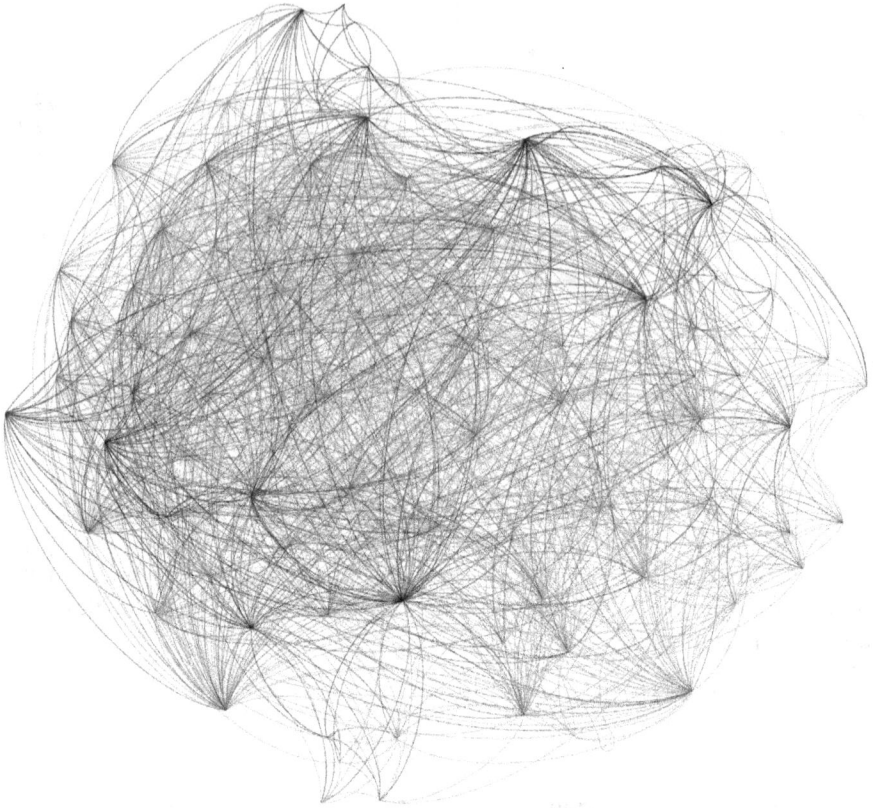

Figure 7.8. Projected network. When projected, the nodes that in Figure 7.2 were linking to the same online resources are now connected. *Source*: **Authors.**

Language of the page, Type of organization) we can observe the tendency of connecting to similar pages in a higher degree than what would be expected by random connections (Coscia 2021). This property can be measured using the nominal assortativity defined by Newman (2002). Nominal assortativity returns a value from –1 to 1 where –1 corresponds to a perfectly disassortative network where actors only connect with actors that do not share the tested characteristic, and 1 corresponds to a perfectly assortative network where actors only connect with actors that share the tested characteristic.

Figure 7.9 shows the existing value of nominal assortativity within the network for Country, Type of actor, and Language for the years from 2014 to 2017.

There are several interesting aspects to notice. Almost every year—with the exception of 2016—the characteristic with the highest level of nominal

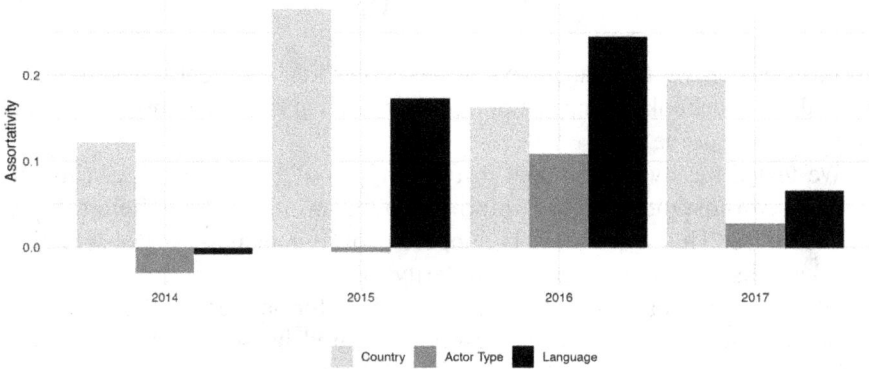

Figure 7.9. Nominal assortativity over type for country, type of actor, and language. *Source*: Authors.

assortativity is for the page to be located in the same country. This means that pages managed by actors located in the same countries were more likely to share similar resources. This is expected and hardly surprising because most of the resources that target migrants apply, from a legal and bureaucratic point of view, to a specific country. Nominal assortativity for Actor type (institutional, semi-institutional, informal) is negative in 2014, almost zero in 2016, and positive in 2016 and 2017. This means that in the first year of our data, the pages were sharing resources shared also by pages of a different type more frequently than resources shared by pages of their own type. This stops in 2016 when assortativity for Actor type becomes clearly positive, meaning that pages of a specific type share more frequently resources shared also by similar pages. The evolution of the nominal assortativity value for the language used on the page is probably the most interesting aspect of this analysis. Starting from a value very close to zero in 2014, it rises to almost 2 in 2015 and becomes the highest type of nominal assortativity in 2016. It is worth remembering that the attribute language represents the main language used by the page in its activities, and it can be Arabic, domestic (when a page uses the language of where it is located), English, or multilingual (when multiple languages are constantly used in the posts). The growth of the nominal assortativity value for language suggests that language-specific resources emerged as a relevant destination to link between 2015 and 2016, and that the linguistic dimension was even more relevant than the country where the page was located to explain the co-sharing of resources. This hints toward the emergence, between 2015 and 2016, of language-specific resources (may be in Arabic or in English) that were providing useful information outside of the national border of relevance.

DISCUSSION

In this chapter, we have analyzed the resources that different types of actors shared on Facebook during the period surrounding the 2015 surge in migration toward Europe.

We tested the hypothesis that different types of Facebook pages (institutional, semi-institutional, and informal pages) would share different types of resources. This hypothesis is supported by our quantitative observation that has observed only a small similarity between the resources shared by institutional pages and semi-institutional and informal pages. The similarity is higher when we observe the resources shared by semi-institutional and informal pages.

While this different level of similarity between the resources shared by the three types of pages is clearly observable in the data, we showed how there were additional dynamics at play. We observed how pages tended to share similar resources also on a geographical principle (pages located in the same country were sharing the same resources) as well as on a linguistic principle (pages communicating in a specific language were sharing the same resources).

Taken as a whole and combined with the temporal perspective, these results show quantitative evidence to understand what drives the sharing of information resources on social networking sites and, ultimately, shapes a considerable part of the digital migrant experience. We have observed how different types of actors provide access to different types of resources and how these differences exist along various dimensions: Country, Type of organization, and Language. This confirms the paradoxical situation where easy access to information production resulted in a large diversity in available information that must then be navigated by the migrants. The main challenge that migrants face is to evaluate the trustfulness of the sources they rely on, and this applies both to online sources (Dekker et al. 2018) as well as to offline situations (as Mollerup and Sandberg show in this present volume). Within this perspective, we observe how the emergence of specific sets of resources shared uniquely by pages communicating in a specific language seems to play into that perception of common background that both according to Dekker (2018) and Alencar (2018) is necessary to trust unknown online actors. Hence, we can imagine that pages that write in the home language (e.g., Arabic) and explicitly mention a common background with the migrant population (e.g., Araberne i Danmark, The Iraqis in Malmo, the Syrian Community in Denmark) aim at facilitating the establishment of this relation of trust by providing the perception of a bounding capital technologically mediated (Lee 2013) even if in a foreign country.

Nevertheless, it should be noted that the perceived trustfulness of these sources does not necessarily mean that they are trustworthy or updated. The difference in shared resources between institutional actors and semi-institutional/informal actors suggests that these actors do not rely on the same information if not for a very small part. Whether both sets of information are reliable or if one is, willingly or not, unreliable is impossible to say with the analysis that we have performed, but it remains a key question for research and a key challenge for the migrant population.

REFERENCES

Alencar, Amanda. 2018. "Refugee integration and social media: A local and experiential perspective." *Information, Communication & Society* 21 (11): 1588–603.

Alencar, Amanda. 2019. "Digital place-making practices and daily struggles of Venezuelan (forced) migrants in Brazil." In *The Sage Handbook of Media and Migration*, edited by Kevin Smets, Koen Leurs, Myria Georgiou, Saskia Witteborn, and Radhika Gajjala, first edition, 503–13. Thousand Oaks, CA: Sage Inc.

Almenara-Niebla, Silvia. 2020. "Making digital 'home-camps': Mediating emotions among the Sahrawi refugee diaspora." *International Journal of Cultural Studies* 23 (5): 728–44.

Bilecen, Başak, Markus Gamper, and Miranda J. Lubbers. 2018. "The missing link: Social network analysis in migration and transnationalism." *Social Networks* 53 (May): 1–3.

Bisgin, Halil, Nitin Agarwal, and Xiaowei Xu. 2010. "Investigating homophily in online social networks." In 2010 IEEE/WIC/ACM International Conference on Web Intelligence and Intelligent Agent Technology, volume 1, 533–36.

Cachia, Romina, and Isidro Maya Jariego. 2018. "Mobility types, transnational ties and personal networks in four highly skilled immigrant communities in Seville (Spain)." *Social Networks* 53 (May): 111–24.

Coscia, Michele. 2021. *The Atlas for the Aspiring Network Scientist.* Self-published.

Coscia, Michele, and Luca Rossi. 2019. "The impact of projection and backboning on network topologies." In 2019 IEEE/ACM International Conference on Advances in Social Networks Analysis and Mining (ASONAM), 286–93.

Dekker, Rianne, Godfried Engbersen, Jeanine Klaver, and Hanna Vonk. 2018. "Smart refugees: How Syrian asylum migrants use social media information in migration decision-making." *Social Media + Society* 4 (1): 205630511876443.

della Porta, Donatella. 2009. "Consensus in movements." In *Democracy in Social Movements*, edited by Donatella della Porta, 73–99. London: Palgrave Macmillan UK.

Dessewffy, Tibor, and Zsófia Nagy. 2016. "Born in Facebook: The refugee crisis and grassroots connective action in Hungary." *International Journal of Communication* 10: 2872–94.

Domagalski, Rachel, Zachary Neal, and Bruce Sagan. 2021. "Backbone: An R package for extracting the backbone of bipartite projections." *PLOS ONE* 16 (1): e0244363.

Gillespie, Marie, Souad Osseiran, and Margie Cheesman. 2018. "Syrian refugees and the digital passage to Europe: Smartphone infrastructures and affordances." *Social Media + Society* 4 (1): 2056305118764440.

Kok, Saskia, and Richard Rogers. 2017. "Rethinking migration in the digital age: Transglocalization and the Somali diaspora." *Global Networks* 17 (1): 23–46.

Laguerre, Michel S. 2010. "Digital diaspora: Definition and models." In *Diasporas in the New Media Age: Identity, Politics, and Community*, edited by Andoni Alonso and Pedro J. Oiarzabal, 49–64. Reno: University of Nevada Press.

Lee, Hun-Yul. 2013. "Bonding and bridging migrant workers to Korean society: A study of migrant workers' television as a counterpublic sphere." *International Journal of Communication* 7: 2609–29.

Leurs, Koen, and Madhuri Prabhakar. 2018a. "Doing digital migration studies: Methodological considerations for an emerging research focus." In *Qualitative Research in European Migration Studies*, edited by Ricard Zapata-Barrero and Evren Yalaz, 247–66. Cham: Springer International Publishing.

Leurs, Koen, and Kevin Smets. 2018a. "Five questions for digital migration studies: Learning from digital connectivity and forced migration in(to) Europe." *Social Media + Society* 4 (1): 205630511876442.

Makrygianni, Vasiliki, Ahmad Kamal, Luca Rossi and Vasilis Galis. 2021. "Migrant digital space, building an incomplete map to navigate the public online migration in research methodologies and ethical challenges." In *Digital Migration Studies: Caring For (Big) Data?*, edited by Marie Sandberg, Luca Rossi, Vasilis Galis, and Martin Bak Jørgensen, 25–57. Lanham, MD: Rowman & Littlefield.

McPherson, Miller, Lynn Smith-Lovin, and James M. Cook. 2001. "Birds of a feather: Homophily in social networks." *Annual Review of Sociology* 27 (1): 415–44.

Mollerup, Nina, G. and Marie Sandberg. 2022. "'Fast trusting': Practices of trust during irregularized journeys to and through Europe." In *The Migration Mobile: Border Dissidence, Sociotechnical Resistance and the Construction of Irregularised Migrants*, edited by Vasilis Galis, Martin Bak Jørgensen, and Marie Sandberg, 143–162. Lanham, MD: Rowman & Littlefield.

Neal, Zachary. 2013. "Identifying statistically significant edges in one-mode projections." *Social Network Analysis and Mining* 3 (4): 915–24.

Neumayer, Christina, Luca Rossi, and Björn Karlsson. 2016. "Contested hashtags: Blockupy Frankfurt in social media." *International Journal of Communication* 10: 5558–79.

Newman, Mark E. J. 2002. "Assortative mixing in networks." *Physical Review Letters* 89 (20): 208701.

R Core Team. 2021. *R: A Language and Environment for Statistical Computing.* Vienna, Austria: R Foundation for Statistical Computing.

Rodica, Ciobanu, Rosca Mariana et al. 2020. "Moldovan diaspora's social networks: Political mobilization and participation." *Central and Eastern European eDem and eGov Days* 338: 323334.

Rosenau, James N. 2003. *Distant Proximities: Dynamics Beyond Globalization.* Princeton, NJ: Princeton University Press.

Siapera, Eugenia. 2014. "Diasporas and new media: Connections, identities, politics and affect." *Crossings: Journal of Migration & Culture* 5 (1): 173–78.

Tucker, Joshua, Andrew Guess, Pablo Barbera, Cristian Vaccari, Alexandra Siegel, Sergey Sanovich, Denis Stukal, and Brendan Nyhan. 2018. "Social media, political polarization, and political disinformation: A review of the scientific literature." *SSRN Electronic Journal.*

Vacca, Raffaele, Giacomo Solano, Miranda Jessica Lubbers, José Luis Molina, and Christopher McCarty. 2018. "A personal network approach to the study of immigrant structural assimilation and transnationalism." *Social Networks* 53 (May): 72–89.

Vijaymeena, M. K., and K. Kavitha. 2016. "A survey on similarity measures in text mining." *Machine Learning and Applications: An International Journal* 3 (1): 19–28.

NOTE

1. Backbone extraction was performed using the *backbone* package (Domagalski, Neal, and Sagan 2021) for the R programming language (R Core Team 2021).

Chapter 8

"Fast Trusting"

Practices of Trust during Irregularized Journeys to and through Europe

Nina Grønlykke Mollerup and Marie Sandberg

INTRODUCTION

The smugglers had lied. As Noor describes their deceit, his calm and pleasant demeanor was once again taken over by a palpable anger as when he spoke about Bashar Al Asad. They had promised there would be life vests for the trip. Yet when Noor stood on the beach of the Mediterranean Sea, the armed smugglers had given a bag with twenty life vests to a random man and told him to distribute them. The man had taken one for himself and given life vests to children and the sick, though "not to the Africans," Noor said, scorning the intrinsic racism he saw unfold so many times during his journey. As the hundreds of people settled into the much too small boat, a smuggler hit a man, who asked to sit next to his elderly father. Few others dared to dissent.

Irregularized migrants who travel to Europe do so unable to rely on safe, established infrastructures and modes of travel. Whereas regularized travelers can lean on their passports, flight tickets, and travel itineraries, these kinds of established infrastructures for international travel are suspended for those who are forced to travel irregularly. Instead, irregular travelers depend on illegalized modes of travel and cannot seek help if assaulted or threatened or similar. Therefore, as in the vignette with Noor, a Syrian refugee we interviewed, irregularized migrants need to manage issues of trust, navigating between slender promises and potential lies. The establishment of trust is

143

essential for human, societal, institutional, and transactional interaction, and it needs to be continuously established—repeatedly and over time—for societies to function (Jimenéz 2011; Hynes 2003, 1). However, in the context of irregularized migration, regular ideas of trust break down. In an environment characterized by danger, uncertainty, and continuously changing realities, the decisions irregularized migrants make along the way regarding which route to take, which smugglers to travel with, and more can be a matter of life and death, yet it is rare that they have a reliable foundation on which to base their decisions (Khosravi 2010). In other words, trust in these situations is crucial for people to act, yet it is exceptionally difficult to establish continuously. Furthermore, with the suspension of conventional dependence on structures of mobility, trust often needs to be established in extremely short encounters with strangers. Irregularized migration, then, is dependent on what one of our research participants referred to as "fast trusting." The question is therefore how is trust established in a context of its improbability, when lives are at stake, encounters are brief and superficial, and the situation is highly volatile?

In this chapter, we investigate the notion of *fast trusting* by focusing on the trust practices of irregularized migrants and solidarity workers who help them during these journeys. Following Jiménez, we do not pursue the task of defining what trust is, but rather examine what kind of work the notion does (Jiménez 2011, 178f). Taking the lead from Jiménez, we contend trust to be not only a cognitive category but an inter-subjective as well as an interobjective relational phenomenon established through practice (Jiménez 2011, 178f). This means that practices of trust establish themselves not only in the interfaces between humans but also in the entangled relations between humans, materialities, and technology. Based on ethnographic fieldwork with previous irregularized migrants and solidarity workers carried out in the Öresund region encompassing the Danish-Swedish borderlands, in 2018 and 2019, we show that there are different yet related trust practices enacted in the various ways irregularized migrants move through the European border regime. By way of our analysis of the complex stories about navigating irregularized, border-crossing journeys depicted in retrospective accounts by our research participants, we find that at least four different ways of practicing fast trust are significant in the ethnographic material. We term these *relay trust, positional trust, institutional trust*, and *desperate trust*. While we acknowledge the particularly challenged situations in which the irregularized travelers are positioned, we understand these different practices of fast trusting to cut across practices of migrants and solidarity workers. In scrutinizing what the notion of trust does in a context of its breakdown, the meticulous and often taken-for-granted work of practicing trust is rendered visible.

We argue that trust is practiced not merely through interpersonal relations, but also through socio-material connections established between social media platforms, digital devices, smartphones, solidarity networks, narratives, and information flyers—what we term *hybrid alliance building*. As we unfold these different heterogeneous trust practices, we engage theoretically with a socio-material understanding of materiality and performativity as suggested within the field of science and technology studies (Latour 2005) as well as recent studies within anthropology, migration studies, and related fields, which we here dub *anthropology of uncertainty* because they share a concern with the implications of crisis, borders, and precarity (Kleist and Jansen 2016; Janeja and Bandak 2018).

In the following section, we elaborate on our methodological approach and how we have encountered trust practices not only in our research participants' stories but also in our own relations with them. Next, we give an overview of anthropology of uncertainty in order to place ourselves in relation to current research. In the following section, we develop our understanding of trusting as hybrid alliance building and introduce the four modes of fast trusting. Subsequently, we analyze a handful of concrete stories told by our research participants about their perilous journeys (cf. Mollerup 2020b) through the analytical lens of different trust practices. In conclusion, we suggest that the four different yet related modes of practicing trust can be used as a hopeful tool for understanding irregularized migrants' navigation of the European border regime as well as provide more succinct explorations of the kind of work the notion of trust does.

METHODOLOGICAL REFLECTIONS ON RESEARCHING IRREGULARIZED MIGRATION AND TRUST PRACTICES

Our analysis is based on ethnographic fieldwork carried out with Syrian refugees and solidarity workers of different nationalities in and around the Danish-Swedish borderlands, the Öresund region, mainly in 2018 and 2019. The refugees we spoke with arrived in Denmark and Sweden as irregularized migrants between 2014 and 2016 and had since obtained refugee status. We present the term *migrant* here in a general, not juridical, sense, and likewise we use the term "irregularized" to stress that these arriving migrants are unable to travel through normal, safe, established means, but rather they are forced to find illegalized and often highly dangerous routes to safety. During fieldwork, we were particularly interested in how migrants navigated during irregularized journeys to Europe, the role of solidarity workers in this navigation, and the significance of digital practices among our research participants. Therefore, we mainly used in-depth, retrospective interviews in which we, in the case of the refugees, looked back on their journeys and, in the case of the solidarity workers, revisited their work to help irregularized migrants (cf. Sandberg 2020). While we introduced our interest in digital practices to our research participants and while we at times asked specifically about direct engagements with phones and other digital knowledge-seeking in interviews, we also made a point of emphasizing that our interest was broader than the digital. Therefore, the digital was absent or peripheral in large parts of our interviews. This oscillation between a direct focus on the digital and a broader focus on the journey and the reasons for fleeing has allowed us to place the digital *alongside* people (Mollerup 2020a) in boats, on highways, in smugglers' houses, and more. In some of the interviews, we included what we term *device tours* (Mollerup 2020b, 98) in which research participants showed us old conversation threads, pictures, apps, and more on their phones and computers, allowing these to become focus points in the interviews. We established initial contact in a variety of ways, including through personal and professional networks and through contacting people on Facebook, based on their engagements in public discussions. Some interviews lasted half an hour; others lasted several hours and were woven together with meetings and socializing with family members and others. We interviewed some people only once, whereas we interviewed others several times. We stayed in contact with most interviewees through different text-based communication channels and at times asked follow-up questions and received feedback on our analyses. We carried out the interviews in Danish, English, and Arabic.[1] In total, we did sixteen interviews with refugees and sixteen interviews with solidarity workers.

The topic of our research necessitated that we spoke with our research participants about illegalized activities and deeply disturbing experiences. Thus, while trust was a theme in our interviews, it was also crucial for us to establish trust with our research participants, many of whom were traumatized by their experiences, both in the cases of refugees and solidarity workers (Hynes 2003, 13). However, while the trust irregularized migrants and solidarity workers needed to establish in the context of irregularized journeys was characterized by severe precarity, transient encounters, and extremely high stakes, we were able to engender trust on very different terms. Spending time with people, returning to interview the same people several times, ensuring anonymity, and engaging in discussions about issues important to them were some of the ways we sought to create trust. We also asked our initial research participants to suggest and establish contact with other potential research participants. In this way, the trust we were able to establish with our initial research participants was passed on to new research participants, drawing on a mode of trusting that can also be relevant in the context of irregularized migration, namely what we describe later as relay trust. Interviewing different members of family networks, we were given different accounts of shared journeys, and this enabled us detailed insights into the significance of family members having gone before.

The retrospective nature of our research approach meant that we were bound to engage with re-collections of trust after it had been tested. That is, the uncertainty which our research participants experienced on their journeys was differently configured when they described their journeys to us, knowing when trust had been honored and when it had been broken. Our device tours, though complicated by people having acquired new devices, at times played a role in bringing up memories and emotions, which gave us glimpses of the uncertainty and fear experienced on the journeys beyond narrative accounts.

ANTHROPOLOGY OF UNCERTAINTY

As we aim to unfold the different practices of trust enacted by irregularized migrants and solidarity workers, we engage with various strands of research, which we here designate *anthropology of uncertainty*. This heading covers a broad range of studies mainly from within anthropology and the social sciences including refugee studies and critical border and migration studies, which take uncertainty as a point of departure rather than as an exceptional circumstance added to people's livelihood. Whereas previous research on uncertainty in anthropology derives mainly from within forensic anthropology and medical humanities focusing on insecurities and risk connected to health and medicine (cf. Samimian-Darash 2013) or magic and religion (Dein 2016), the studies included here all share a concern with living on the edges (of society, of welfare or prosperity), within crisis (economic, political, planetary), or at the Othered side (of the border, of normality). Muehlebach has called this research concern as engaging with the precarity of life itself, as "a shorthand for those of us documenting the multiple forms of nightmarish dispossession and injury that our age entails" (Muehlebach 2013, 298). As Kleist and Jansen (2016) observe, research strands concerned with precarious issues of uncertainty also contain dimensions of hope and working for bettering the future, for instance when migrants are leaving homes and family in order to make for a better living. Kleist and Jansen even identify a profound "hope-boom" within anthropology concerned with uncertainty and suggest that grounded knowledge on future-making is a necessary other side of the coin when researching despair and crisis (see also Khosravi 2017; Hage 2016). On a similar note, Bandak and Janeja (2018) confer that "where despair, ruin and pain all are prevalent figures in the contemporary world, an anthropological engagement ought to explore such situations as diverse forms of interacting with the world" (p. 9). By suggesting four different modes of fast trusting in this contribution, we aim to foreground not only the diversity of trust in the practices of irregularized migrants and solidarity workers try-ing to navigate the landscape of European bordering. We also aim to present a more hopeful account of the ways trusting is made possible in a context of its improbability.

In refugee studies, attention toward trust in relation to migratory jour-neys has so far been limited. Lyytinen reviews the field of "trust research" in social sciences, emphasizing how social trust and institutional trust have been highlighted, yet with a main focus, on the one hand, on the question of the extent to which the "migrant experience" entails dimensions of mistrust due to high degrees of violence and conflict in the country of origin and, on the other hand, the degree of trust establishing in the country of exile (2017, 491). Drawing on insights into the flight of Congolese refugees from the Democratic Republic of Congo to Mapala, Lyytinen has suggested a new analytical framework for examining refugees' journeys from the perspective of trust (Lyytinen 2017, 491). Building on Brugger et al. (2013), Lyytinen proposes trust as an "emotion concept" defined as "a positive feeling about or evaluation of the intentions or behaviour of another" and "a discursively created emotion and practice which is based on the relations between the 'trustor' and the 'trustee'" (Lyytinen 2017, 489f). Yet in the context of irregu-larized migration, trust practices are seldom divided neatly into roles of being either trusted or trustful. Furthermore, the assigning of roles is entangled with digital and material actors like smartphones, dinghys, life vests, lorries, and more. In the following, we will therefore show how trusting is not only either an interpersonal or institutional matter (social trust), but also a matter of building hybrid alliances between socio-material actors, including humans.

REGIMES OF MIS/TRUST—TRUSTING AS HYBRID ALLIANCE BUILDING

Trust is essential to democratic societies and a keyword for political and social sciences working in particular with social cohesion in civil society and national economy (Häkli 2008, 15). According to Häkli, interpersonal as well as social trust is center-stage in democratic deliberation processes in order to prevent social conflict (Häkli 2008). Trust is also considered intrinsic to efficiency of economic transactions, and often mistrust in market relations is associated with developing countries in contrast to so-called high-trust societ-ies: "with higher trust, economic transactions become more efficient, as there is less need to invest time, effort, and money in establishing written contracts or other kinds of guarantees for business transactions" (Häkli 2008, 16).

Jiménez (2011) instead directs our attention toward the notion of *mis*trust as a foundational premise for neoliberal market societies. As he argues, the markets' obsession with radical openness and transparency builds on a political epistemology of trust which presupposes that if you (or your corporation) are not willing to "show it all" then you are in principle suspicious. Assessing the trustworthiness of a person is thus intrinsically linked to global standards for accountability and transparency established in order to create trustworthiness for corporations: "Transparency, accountability and trust (diaphaneity) have been mobilized against the dark forces of secrecy, uncertainty and risk (opacity)" (192). In Jiménez's words, "[t]here is, in a sense, no trust in society except in an 'after-trusting' mode" (193). The contestation of trust is further sustained by what Peter Dahlgren (2018, 20) identifies as "an 'epistemic' crisis in public spheres that threatens to undermine political agency" related to the magnitude and speed of information spread in the digital age (see also Farkas and Schou 2019). With a similar sentiment, Matthew Carey (2017, 8f) develops an ethnographic theory of *mis*trust. On the basis of fieldwork conducted in the Morroccan High Atlas, he explores reasons for assuming general attitudes of mistrust and the social implications thereof.

In the case of irregularized journeys, the idea of "high-trust societies" collapses twofold when it comes to migrants arriving at the European border regime. Placed at the margins, they are suspended from trust, considered not trustworthy per se by European governments; a threat to the market and the welfare of European states. They participate in informal economies of smugglers and traffickers. The solidarity workers on their side are obviously not (necessarily) marginalized citizens, but they too need to navigate flows of information which can be seen as false, "weird," imprecise, true, etc., and they need to maneuver between friends and infiltrators when using digital platforms for helping migrants on their journeys. In that sense, solidarity workers and migrants are both involved in practicing trust in related ways.

Promoting Danish philosopher Løgstrup, Pedersen and Liisberg highlight trust as "the original moral sentiment" which would form the basis for all human encounters (2015, 4). Yet, during irregularized journeys, we suggest that trust as a basic moral sentiment is challenged. Irregularized migrants during flight simply cannot rely on the ethical demand which would suggest that any vulnerable life placed in another person's hands will be taken care of (Løgstrup, Pedersen, and Liisberg 2015, 3). As we will illustrate, trust is neither a character disposition nor something installed in social relations. Rather, as we contend, in the context of irregularized migration, trust is a practice which means that trust needs to be continuously established. Speaking of trust in the context of asylum seekers in England, Hynes (2009, 97) argues that "trust is an ambiguous term; it is complex and multifaceted and, once lost, it takes time to restore." While we agree that time is crucial for trust practices, in the context of irregularized migration, there is seldom time to build relations of trust. That is, trust is rarely there to be lost. Instead, trust mainly has to be continuously established within very short timespans, often with people with whom the irregularized migrants have had no prior interactions. Face-to-face encounters may be extremely brief and even when they last longer, they are often marked by danger and fatigue framing the human encounters. Concurrently, trust is fundamental to the very ability to act and make decisions. Pedersen and Liisberg argue that trust implies "a move toward the future that depends on the imaginary anticipation of the imminent" (2015, 1). We contend that this anticipation of the imminent is vital for the ability to act. Yet, in the context of these irregularized journeys, anticipating the imminent is extremely difficult and points toward potential death. Trust in the context of irregularized migration, then, is vulnerable, fleeting, precautious, and essential.

We approach the study of irregularized migrants' digital practices from a non-media-centric and non-representational point of departure (Moores 2018). Thus, we wish to give primacy to practice and movement over the symbolic and the cognitive (Moores 2018, x). Accordingly, we use the term "digital-related practices," drawing on Mark Hobart's (2010) term "media-related practices." Hobart uses the term to draw attention to the way the significance of practices related to media extends well beyond actual engagements with media, arguing that in order to capture the significance of media we must look beyond people's direct engagements with media. This insight is particularly relevant when dealing with the digital, as conceptualizations of the digital have tended to disregard its emplacement. We do not understand digital practices as limited to direct engagements with digital media devices (cf. Dekker et al. 2018). Whereas Dekker et al. (2018, 9) call for a more extensive focus on which digital social ties are considered to be trusted, we are interested in how the digital folds into practices well beyond such engagements. Taking the lead from Meinert's point that trust is "a tricky social achievement" (2015, 119), we further suggest that the repertoire of relevant actors in trust practices is broadened from interpersonal relations to also include engagements with environments, materialities, and technologies (Ingold 2000). Within anthropology, ethnology, and related fields, the material turn has encouraged an analytical approach to studying meaning-making practices, which includes not only discursive levels but also the inclusion of objects and technologies in conceptualizing practices (Miller 2010; Hodder 2012). Material objects are considered as not only inscription devices but are rather acknowledged for their transformative effect for meaning-making practices (Latour 2005). When we conceptualize trusting as *hybrid alliance building*, we are thus inspired by the performative point significant for science and technology studies, in which discursive utterances along with the handling of material and technological objects co-perform the world. Science and technology studies has a long-standing research discussion on trust in technologies (Jasanoff 2015), yet here we are more concerned with the socio-material connections that enable decisions in/of fast trusting. We thus suggest an attentive look toward *hybrid alliances* between irregularized migrants, solidarity workers/activists, and digital platforms alike—each contributing to establishing the trust that enables the migratory decision of how to cross the border.

FOUR MODES OF FAST TRUSTING

We approach the complex relations of trust as hybrid alliance building in order to highlight that the trust irregularized migrants depend on to navigate through unknown, shifty, and often hostile environments needs to be established over short timespans. Such modes of trusting cannot rely solely on relations and experiences established over a long period of time. Rather, it depends on a broader repertoire of actors and often involves digital-related practices. Based on our ethnographic research with irregularized migrants and solidarity workers who have helped them, we suggest four modes of trusting that are particularly significant in the precarious and uncertain situations on the journeys during which irregularized migrants continuously need to establish trust in order to navigate. Significantly, neither of these modes of trusting relies on reciprocity. Rather, they depend on very imbalanced asymmetrical trustiness in which one part has very limited opportunities for action if agreements are broken while simultaneously placing their very lives in the hands of the trusted person. We refer to the four modes of trusting as *relay trust, positional trust, institutional trust,* and *desperate trust.* We do not contend that the modes of trusting presented here form an exhaustive list of all kinds of trust practices, but we suggest that these four modes of trusting can help us understand better precarious border navigation. As irregularized migrants navigate to and through the European border regime, their various trust practices play into their navigational decisions. It is important to stress that while the four modes of trusting are established empirically, they are not ontological categories "out there." Together, the four modes present a register of fast trusting so it is not possible to attach one mode of trusting to one single individual person or case. Rather, as we shall see, specific situations can be analyzed through several or a combination of the different modes of trusting suggested here. The four modes of trusting can therefore work ideal-typically as analytical strategies for creating more nuanced knowledge on what complex decisions irregularized migrants face when navigating the European border regime.

Relay trust is a mode of trusting that can be "passed on" from one person to another, so a person can assume another person's trust in a third person. It thus ties into other modes of trusting and cannot stand on its own as it depends on previously established, reenacted trust. That is, *relay trust* depends on existing networks of trust in which some layers of trust have been established previously, often under very different circumstances, which can enable more durable relations of trust. As *relay trust* depends on previously established relations of trust, it is a mode of trusting that can be passed on quickly through different links in a chain. *Relay trust* can be granted to people, migrants, and solidarians alike, who through word of mouth have been established as reliable. *Positional trust* is a mode of trusting that relies on the trusted person's reputation based on experience or background. *Positional trust*, then, can be granted to people regardless of personal relations though it does necessitate a recognition of (or trust in) the position enabling the trust. *Positional trust* can be established, for example, in people who have experience with the journey from having made it, people who have a certain reputation for instance as leaders of a solidarity network or similar, people who by virtue of their personal background are expected to be sympathetic, and people who perform certain practices, such as solidarity work. *Positional trust*, then, is a mode of trusting particularly focused on social roles that can be attributed by organizational skills. *Institutional trust* is grounded in perceptions of established entities such as the United Nations, the police, or companies, which can enable trust in people and situations beyond these entities. Institutional trust is thus not about trust in institutions as such, but can also be directed toward digital platforms. This mode of trusting particularly takes into account principles imposed by such institutions, such as established means of payment (e.g., in an app) and legal significance of signatures. Such measures "exist to guard against interpersonal mistrust" (Voutira and Harell-Bond 1995, 220), enabling relative trust between people grounded in trust in an institution. At times, *institutional trust* interestingly can make digital platforms work for new purposes. Lastly, *desperate trust* is a sporadic mode of trusting which is not based on relations with people or entities, but rather on a need for urgent solutions to basic needs and a lack of alternatives. It is thus a mode of trusting that is less related to past experiences and in contrast to the other modes of trusting, this one proves foremost relevant for migrants and not solidarian practices. *Desperate trust*, then, is a mode of trusting that enables action in situations where it is hard to know or trust anyone or anything. And it might be fair to say that most decisions made by irregularized migrants during their journeys feature some element of desperate trust.

As illustrated in Table 8.1, the modes of trusting each enact a different kind of relationality and mobilize different effects. Together, the four modes of trusting suggested here emphasize that trust cannot solely be seen from a first-person perspective or merely be understood as an intersubjective

Table 8.1. Main Features of Each Mode of Fast Trusting

Fast Trusting Mode: Feature:	*Relay trust*	*Positional trust*	*Institutional trust*	*Desperate trust*
Relationality Mobilization effect	Network Mobilizes a track record beyond the actual moment	Social Mobilizes organizational role, relying on reputation, experience, and/or skill	Structural Mobilizes established juridical, political, technological measures	Individual Mobilizes impulse

Note: Modes are organized into type of relationality and which kind of effect the trust practice mobilizes.

relationship, but should rather be conceived as hybrid alliance building mobilizing a broad range of actors.

PRACTICING FAST TRUST

In the following, we aim to illustrate how fast trust is practiced in different ways and through different alliances between a hybrid set of actors in the context of irregularized journeys to and in the European border regime. As the analysis will show, in order to unfold particular situations of trust-making, we need to draw on all four modes of fast trusting. Further, we show how this repertoire of trust also plays into solidarity workers' trust practices in situations when trust needs to be established quickly.

Wael

Wael,[2] a young man traveling on his own, had made it safely across the Aegean Sea in a small dinghy and was hoping to make it to Denmark where his brother lived. Trust was not an easy currency to come by for Wael. As we were sitting down together in a café in the middle-range town in Denmark where Wael lived at the time, he explained to us again and again how frightened he had been. In order to understand how he nevertheless made it across Europe's borders, several modes of trusting need to be activated including a varied range of actors. Wael was traveling on his own but in the sense of building alliances along the way, he was never alone. Some of the people who had crossed the sea with him had relatives who had previously made the journey. During the journey they communicated digitally, and they had established contact with a smuggler who offered to take Wael's group to northern Europe in the back of a truck. The relatives, who had previously made the journey, said that this man would not cheat them. Many irregularized migrants had indeed experienced being cheated in similar arrangements. And the high stakes in such arrangements are illustrated by the tragic incident in 2015, when a large group of irregularized migrants suffocated in the back of a truck in Austria. We conceptualize the trust Wael established in the people he had traveled with as positional trust. That is, through acknowledging that they as irregularized migrants were in the same position as himself, literally in the same boat, he was able to trust them. Moreover, their trust in their relatives was passed on to Wael, which we designate as relay trust in them. This, in turn, enabled relay trust in the smuggler. The relay trust in the relatives was strengthened by a positional trust in them, as they also had shared Wael's position as irregularized migrants. Thus, by assuming a trust that had been established by other people previously, he was able to quickly establish a level of trust that enabled him to make difficult choices. So, though he was petrified to do so, Wael decided to pay the money for the smuggler and get in the truck. While the organization of irregularized traveling in the European border regime did not invite for much trust as an institution, there were certain measures that could at times be imposed to guard against interpersonal mistrust, allowing Wael a level of institutional trust. For instance, Wael and his fellow travelers agreed with the smuggler that they paid the money in installments along the way as they crossed various borders, reducing the risk of them getting left behind after having paid the full amount. In this way, the trust Wael was able to establish through his journey did not only tap into his relations with other people, but also depended on socio-material connections. For instance, the boat and the truck were part of the establishment of similar positions and thus of positional trust just as the payments in installments tapped into a larger system that ensured the value of money. Wael did eventually make it to Denmark though it was a scary and difficult journey. His fear, which he so carefully described to us, is important to consider as it points both to the limitations of trust and the trust that was nevertheless established on these journeys. The trust Wael was able to establish fast and on the spot enabled him to act, yet it did not enable him a security that allowed him to relax. Nor did it enable him to rely on Løgstrup's original moral sentiment, discussed earlier, which would suggest that any vulnerable life placed in our hands will be taken care of. Rather, the trust Wael was able to build along the way was a fleeting and reserved trust that needed to be continuously established, enacting different, intersecting modes of trust, and a variety of socio-material actors.

Jens and Mahmoud

A while before the summer of 2015, that is, when the border between Denmark and Germany was still open, Jens was going home to Denmark from Germany.

He offered a ride through a German rideshare app, *Mitfahrgelegenheit*, and a young man named Mahmood booked a ride. Mahmood was from Syria and had asylum in Germany, so he said. He further explained to Jens that he was on his way to Sweden to propose to his girlfriend. When they had boarded the ferry, Mahmood confided that he did not actually have asylum but was traveling as an irregularized migrant and had needed help getting on the ferry without proper ID. This story was told to us by Jens, as we met him for a chat on his dedicated engagement in the European "refugee crisis" later to be dubbed the "long summer of welcome" (Karakayali and Kleist 2015), stressing the many acts of solidarity with arriving refugees that also took place during 2015 (Sandberg and Andersen 2020). For irregularized migrants, often traveling with large sums of money and having little opportunity to seek help from police if robbed or assaulted, getting in a car with someone completely unknown poses a risk. However, in the case of Mahmoud and Jens getting in a car together, this risk was managed through institutional trust. That is, we understand the trust needed for two strangers to get in a car together as institutional, as it is initially established through the confidence in the app. This trust allowed for exchange of practical information while also setting a frame for the encounter between Jens and Mahmood, in a sense taking the irregularity out of the initial establishment of trust between the two. As such, institutional trust assisted in Mahmood becoming able to cross the border in a regular fashion. In this situation, Mahmoud's smartphone, which enabled him access to the app, was crucially entangled in his trust practices. What is further interesting, then, is that institutional trust in this case involves an appropriation of digital platforms for new purposes. Mahmood was enabled to get in the car, trusting that he would not be robbed or taken to the police because of the relation established through the app; an app which was not designed for the purpose of irregularized migration. Concurrently, Mahmoud's narrative about pursuing courtship could also be read as a tactic for establishing positional trust by emphasizing their human commonality through the known trope of romantic love.

Jens recalled how, as they shared a cigarette—and a human encounter—on the ferry, Mahmoud thanked Jens for his help. Mahmoud said that he would make it on his own from here, saying he was worried that Jens could be imprisoned for helping him cross the border knowingly. However, Jens refused to let Mahmoud continue on his own, saying if there was one thing he would go to prison for, it was helping another human being to safety. When the ferry docked, they both entered Jens's car again. Unlike the trust that enabled their initial shared ride, the trust that enabled their continued ride was differently temporally configured. That is, at this time, they had had the time to build up a relationship of trust beyond fast trusting.

Ghada and Ziad, and Daham Alasaad

As we argue in this contribution, trust is a particularly important currency for irregularized migrants because they cannot rely on access to conventional infrastructures and modes of traveling. For this reason, institutional trust is at times challenged by the risk that institutions might work against irregularized migrants, even when this undermines the customary purpose of these institutions, leading to institutional mistrust. Ghada and Ziad, a married couple, traveled together in 2015 aiming to reach Denmark or Sweden. They told us of their travels as we met them separately at their workplaces, Ziad entertaining their two-year-old daughter while we spoke. When they had arrived in Germany, they were told that all irregularized migrants should get on a specifically designated train. Under different circumstances, institutional trust in a railroad company would allow travelers to rely on a train to travel to its designated destination. However, having heard from other irregularized migrants who were apprehended on such trains, Ghada and Ziad did not trust that this train would take them to their desired destination. Instead, they made a point out of appearing like regular travelers, changing their clothes, which had become dirty and worn from the trip, and boarded a regular train. That is, their ability to enact institutional trust—and get on a train trusting it would take them to the train's purported destination—was dependent on their ability to disassociate themselves from the category of irregularized migrants. Their trust practices were thus bound up with, among other things, their physical appearance, including their clothes.

Institutions are particularly known to work against their customary purpose in the context of irregularized migrants' sea crossings. Syrian journalist Daham Alasaad told us how he had worked on a story in Izmir for a European media outlet. As he sat with his European colleague at a café in Basmany Square, their camera placed on the table, a man with a badly burned leg noticed the camera and called Daham over. The man had been trying to cross to Greece by boat, he told Daham, but the engine had caught fire and the boat was forced to return. Though he had been burned, he could not go to the hospital, he explained, because the following day, he would try to cross again. He asked to exchange numbers and said he would write, if he made it. At five o'clock in the morning, Daham's phone rang. On the other end of the phone he heard screams. Still half asleep, he thought he had a nightmare. Yet slowly awakening, he realized the severity of the situation. It was the man from the café who was calling; he was at sea again and the boat was taking in water. The people on the boat were fearing they would drown. Daham asked the man to send their location. As they were close to Lesvos, he looked up the number for the Greek coast guard and called them to alert them to the emergency. Their response was blatant indifference. He then called Refugee

Rescue, whose number he had saved on his phone. They asked for the location and assured him they would send help. Later that day, Daham told us, he saw that the man had logged on to Viber, convincing him that the boat had indeed been saved. We see several intertwined modes of trusting at play here, implicating cameras, apps, and more. In the initial encounter, the camera supports the irregularized migrant's establishment of positional trust in Daham in that he is someone who potentially has an ability to get stories out. Meanwhile, his Syrian background positions him as someone who would understand and care. However, while in the urgent and dramatic situation in water, it is just as much situational trust that makes the man call Daham. That is, it is a desperate situation with a lack of alternatives and does not allow for a careful assessment of phone contacts. Daham initially calls the Greek coast guard, at a time before stories of the Greek coast guard attacking and deterring irregularized migrants' boats abounded, with an institutional trust that they will respond to people in distress at sea. However, this trust is sorely betrayed. While Daham is not a solidarity worker in a strict sense, this story also speaks to the similarities in terms of trust repertoires between irregularized migrants and solidarity workers. Though there were significant differences in the reciprocity of trusting of irregularized migrants in smugglers or solidarity workers and *between* solidarity workers, we see a repertoire of trust practices enacted across the irregularized migrants and solidarity workers in situations when trust needed to be established quickly. And as the journalist experienced, institutional trust is complicated by the context of irregularized migration in which institutions often come to work against their declared purpose. This was particularly visible through the shifting national approaches and the ambiguity of policies, which the next and final story aims to illustrate.

Kareem

Kareem, a solidarity worker from Sweden, explained to us how he had helped with reception of the unprecedented amount of people seeking asylum in Sweden. While he was not officially requested to do so by authorities, he did get an unofficial request for help from a friend who worked at the municipality. The Swedish response to the wave of irregularized migrants arriving in Europe in 2015 was, unlike Denmark, initially an open-door policy, and Kareem and other volunteers had no perception of doing something potentially illegal. As Kareem explained about the time, "I never thought about being wrong. Not morally and not legally." However, as the situation shifted and Sweden changed its policy and started prosecuting people who had helped irregularized migrants crossing borders, the institutional trust of solidarity workers came to be challenged in the same way as that of irregularized migrants. That is, national policies are not merely a context for trust practices, but ties into their very core.

In the uncertain and shifting context with occasional infiltrations by neo-Nazis and other right-wing groups, trust was crucial for solidarity workers to establish. They were at times able to establish relations of trust through sustained engagements with the same people, for instance when working for longer periods at train stations or in Facebook groups. Kareem explained,

> And we—the people that joined—were like strangers from the internet, and it was kind of hard to recognize who is a friend and who is not or who is someone not helping, or someone making the job more difficult. And in [the initial] phase, there was a lot of misinformation; it was a lot of information that if we say something that was wrong, it goes down through the network and to other groups to a lot of people, so it made the work really, really hard. And after a few days, you know which persons are serious, and you get closer and closer. I knew for my group.

That is, solidarity workers were able to establish trust over time through their sustained engagement, which allowed them to see who was actually doing the work to help. But they also found themselves in need of establishing trust quickly, for instance when urgently collaborating across borders with people they had never met. Kareem explained to us how such trust could be established in such situations, describing it as "fast trusting": "If I know someone in Sweden that knows this person in Bosnia, for example, I can call my friend in Sweden: 'Do you know him?' 'Yeah, I met him, da da da da da.' And because of that, we can fast trust each other fast also." He elaborated how this would at times involve capricious connections: "I remember a woman in northern Germany, she needed help. And a friend, a guy I met at a party in Holland like a couple years ago, he called me. So the trust became like—it's weird, it's weird. I don't believe in destiny or fate, or like that. But it was really weird." In this way, solidarity workers were also able to enact relay trust, building on trust entangled in events that were seemingly disconnected from the moment of solidarity, such as a party taking place years ago. In this regard, relay trust could be embedded in digital practices which both facilitated direct connections with people, solidarity workers as well as irregularized migrants, in other locations "on the route," but also because they allowed a tracking of people with whom relay trust could be built, including old acquaintances.

CONCLUSION

In this contribution, we have argued that in the context of irregularized migration trust is something vulnerable that needs to be established not only continuously but also over extremely short timespans. During these precarious journeys, to put it simply, there is seldom time to build up human sentiment through interpersonal relationships as the "high-trust societies" hypothesis would have it. Face-to-face encounters may be extremely brief and social media provides only temporary connections. Spurred by the emic notion of "fast trusting" presented to us during fieldwork, we have explored the kind of work this notion does in a context where common infrastructures and the trust they enable are suspended. It is exactly the suspension of trust that renders visible the meticulous work of establishing trust and gives us the cue to further explore the kind of work trust does. By ethnographically qualifying and theoretically refining the work of fast trusting, we have suggested at least four different modes of trusting: relay trust, positional trust, institutional trust, and desperate trust. These modes of trusting are not in any way exhaustive, but when used together as analytical tools, they can offer a more subtle understanding of people's precarious crossing of borders during flight as well as of the work the notion of trust does.

We have conceptualized trusting as hybrid alliance building that is not merely an interpersonal relation, but a socio-material engagement, which includes smartphones, digital platforms, institutions, networks of people, and more. We have done so by establishing four different modes of trusting as enacted by irregularized migrants and solidarity workers alike. Focusing on these different trust practices and the ways they intertwine helps us unfold how borders are navigated through migrants' movements well beyond the physical realms of borders.

Further, as the analysis has revealed, "the digital" cannot be maintained as one singular or separate domain. Rather, digital relations extend beyond and weave into relations established between socio-material actors (apps, platforms, infrastructures). Approaching the meticulous work of trusting in this way as a hybrid alliance building shows that the more heterogeneous the repertoire of actors involved in trust work is, the better the opportunities are for fast trusting on the spot. For refugees during flight, it is not a matter of avoiding the breakdown of trust, because trust was not "there" from the outset. Rather, the work fast trusting does is to create momentary connections that make the next fragile move possible. This possible next move contains a hopeful step toward safer ground, sounder protection, a better future. As a contribution to *anthropology of uncertainty* we have thus provided grounded knowledge on future-making practices during extremely precarious circumstances. Rather than merely documenting precarity of life itself, we contend that our ethnographically informed insights into fast trusting as hybrid alliance building will enhance the possibilities for keeping up the hope that despite states of dispossession, injury, and despair, trust is on the horizon.

REFERENCES

Bandak, Andreas, and Manpreet Kaur Janeja. 2018. "Introduction: Worth the wait." In *Ethnographies of Waiting: Doubt, Hope and Uncertainty*, edited by Manpreet Kaur Janeja and Andreas Bandak, 1–39. London: Bloomsbury Academic.

Brugger, J., K. W. Dunbar, C. Jurt, and B. Orlove. 2013. "Climates of anxiety: Comparing experience of glacier retreat across three mountain regions." *Emotion, Space and Society* 6: 4–13.

Carey, Matthew. 2017: *Mistrust. An Ethnographic Theory.* Chicago: Hau Books.

Dahlgren, Peter. 2018. "Media, knowledge and trust: The deepening epistemic crisis of democracy." *Javnost* 25 (1–2): 20–27.

Dein, Simon. 2016. "The anthropology of uncertainty: Magic, witchcraft and risk and forensic implications." *Journal of Forensic Anthropology* 1:1.

Dekker, Rianne, Godfried Engbersen, Jeanine Klaver, and Hanna Vonk. 2018. *Smart Refugees: How Syrian Asylum Migrants Use Social Media Information in Migration Decision-Making.* sagepub.com.

Farkas, Johan, and Jannick Schou. 2019. *Post-Truth, Fake News and Democracy: Mapping the Politics of Falsehood.* New York: Routledge.

Hage, Ghassan. 2016. "Afterword. Questions concerning a future-politics." *History and Anthropology* 27 (4): 465–67.

Häkli, Jouni. 2008. "Geographies of trust." In *Social Capital and Urban Networks of Trust*, edited by Jouni Häkli and Claudio Minca, 13–36. Surrey: Ashgate Publishers.

Hobart, Mark. 2010. "What do we mean by 'media practices'?" In *Theorising Media and Practice*, edited by Birgit Bräuchler and John Postill, 55–75. Oxford: Berghahn.

Hodder, Ian. 2012. *Entangled: An Archaeology of the Relationships between Humans and Things.* Malden, MA: Wiley-Blackwell.

Hynes, Patricia. 2003. "The issue of 'trust' or 'mistrust' in research with refugees: Choices, caveats and considerations for researchers." New Issues in Refugee Research Working Paper 98, UN High Commissioner for Refugees, Evaluation and Policy Analysis Unit. Middlesex University, London.

Hynes, Patricia. 2009. "Contemporary compulsory dispersal and the absence of space for the restoration of trust." *Journal of Refugee Studies* 22 (1): 97–121.

Ingold, Tim. 2000. *The Perception of the Environment: Essays on Livelihood, Dwelling and Skill.* Oxon: Routledge.

Janeja, Manpreet Kaur, and Andreas Bandak, eds. 2018. *Ethnographies of waiting: Doubt, hope and uncertainty.* London: Bloomsbury Academic.

Jasanoff, Sheila. 2015. "Future imperfect: Science, technology, and the imaginations of modernity." In *Dreamscapes of Modernity. Sociotechnical Imaginaries and the Fabrication of Power*, edited by Sheila Jasanoff and Kim Sang-Hyun, 1–33. Chicago: University of Chicago Press.

Jiménez, Alberto Corsín. 2011. "Trust in anthropology." *Anthropological Theory* 11 (2): 177–96.

Karakayali, Serhat, and Olaf Kleist. 2015. "Strukturen und Motive der ehrenamtlichen Flüchtlingsarbeit (EFA) in Deutschland." *Berliner Institut für empirische Integrations-und Migrationsforschung.* http://www.fluechtlingshilfe-htk.de/uploads/infos/49.pdf

Khosravi, Shahram. 2010. *Illegal Traveller: An Auto-Ethnography of Borders.* Basingstoke: Palgrave Macmillan.

Khosravi, Shahram. 2017. *Precarious Lives. Waiting and Hope in Iran.* Philadelphia: University of Pennsylvania Press.

Kleist, Nauja, and Stef Jansen. 2016. "Introduction: Hope over time—crisis, immobility and future-making." *History and Anthropology* 27 (4): 373–92.

Latour, Bruno. 2005. *Reassembling the Social.* Oxford: Oxford University Press.

Lyytinen, Eveliina. 2017. "Refugees' 'journeys of trust': Creating an analytical framework to examine refugees' exilic journeys with a focus on trust." *Journal of Refugee Studies* 30 (4): 489–510.

Meinert, Lotte. 2015. "Distrust as a starting point and trust as a social achievement in Uganda." In *Anthropology and Philosophy: Dialogues on Trust*, edited by Sune Liisberg, Esther Oluffa Pedersen, and Anne Line Dalsgård, 118–36. New York: Berghahn.

Miller, Daniel. 2010. *Stuff.* Cambridge: Polity Press.

Mollerup, Nina Grønlykke. 2020a. "What violent conflict tells us about media and place-making (and vice versa) - Ethnographic observations from a revolutionary uprising." In *Theorising Media and Conflict*, 181–95. Oxford: Berghahn.

Mollerup, Nina Grønlykke. 2020b. "Perilous navigation. Knowledge making with and without digital practices during irregularized migration to Öresund." *Social Analysis* 64 (3): 95–112.

Moores, Shaun. 2018. *Digital Orientations: Non-Media-Centric Media Studies and Non-Representational Theories of Practice.* New York: Peter Lang.

Muehlebach, Andrea. 2012. "On precariousness and the ethical imagination: The year 2012 in sociocultural anthropology." *American Anthropologist* 115 (2): 297–311.

Pedersen, Esther Oluffa, and Sune Liisberg. 2019. "Trust and hope: An introduction." In *Anthropology and Philosophy: Dialogues on Trust*, edited by Sune Liisberg, Esther Oluffa Pedersen, and Anne Line Dalsgård, 1–20. New York: Berghahn.

Samimian-Darash, Limor. 2013. "Governing future potential biothreats: Toward an anthropology of uncertainty." *Current Anthropology* 54 (1).

Sandberg, Marie. 2020. "Retrospective ethnographies. Twisting moments of researching commemorative practices among volunteers after the refugee arrivals to Europe 2015." In *Challenges and Solutions in Ethnographic Research. Ethnography with a Twist*, edited by Tuuli Lähdesmäki et al., 117–30. London: Routledge.

Sandberg, Marie, and Dorte J. Andersen. 2020. "Europe trouble: Welcome culture and the disruption of the European border regime." *Nordic Journal of Migration Research* 10 (4): 1–9.

Voutira, Eftihia, and Barbara Harrell-Bond. 1995. "In search of the locus of trust: The social world of the refugee camp." In *Mistrusting Refugees*, edited by E. V. Daniel and J. C. Knudsen, 207–24. Berkeley: University of California Press.

NOTES

1. The interviews in Arabic were conducted by Nina Grønlykke Mollerup in non-native, Egyptian Arabic, which is largely mutually intelligible with Syrian Arabic. The interviews were recorded, and we are indebted to Alaa Almeiza for translating and transcribing these interviews.

2. All names of irregularized migrants and solidarity workers are made up for their protection.

PART IV

Reconfiguring the Border Regime(s) and Emancipation of Space

Chapter 9

Counter-Narrating the Mediterranean Border Regime and Reclaiming Rights

Refugee Voices in Libya and Across the Sea

Sara Creta and Chiara Denaro

INTRODUCTION

In August 2018, dozens of Ethiopian and Eritrean asylum seekers and migrants commenced a rare protest in a detention center, twenty kilometers away from Tripoli, Libya.[1] Trapped in a country devastated by civil war and at daily risk of human trafficking, they asked for help to get out of Libya, as their requests to the UN High Commissioner for Refugees (UNHCR) were unheeded. Among them there was a twenty-one-year-old man who was kidnapped, sold, and exploited before ending up in detention after escaping from traffickers. On Sunday, August 12, the group posted photos and videos of the protest on Facebook in the hope that they would be shared widely. They articulated their message using the same vocabulary as that of international organizations: "human rights," "refugees," "assistance," "protection," "justice." In a few hours, their post reached a hundred thousand people around the world, including journalists and activists who have been mobilizing to ask for their evacuation. This protest was not an isolated event. Seeking for better conditions and for evacuation to safe countries, refugees in Libya have been performing embodied practices, and putting their bodies on the line to exert political pressure on UN agencies and expose the violence of contemporary EU border practices of externalization. These struggles—regularly organized in detention centers in Libya—are an example of the many political struggles for rights undertaken by refugees, migrants, and activists across the world.

The autonomy of migration approach provides us with the theoretical background to understand how the struggles for movement—through a multiplicity of practices and tactics—"escape and subsequently delegitimize and derail sovereign control" (Papadopoulos and Tsianos 2007; 2013, 12). Furthermore, it stresses how these struggles can create "other forms of life" which are defined as "mobile commons," namely the ability to cultivate, generate, and regenerate the contents, practices, and affects that facilitate the movements of mobile people (Papadopoulos and Tsianos 2013, 21). According to Papadopoulos and Tsianos, part of these mobile commons are "transnational communities of justice," which take shape through forms of "thick everyday performative and practical justice" that make mobility possible (2013, 22). From this perspective, in addition to being definable as acts of citizenship (Isin and Nielsen 2008) and "acts of resistance" (Hess 2017), border crossings became "acts of immediate justice" for sustaining migrants' everyday life (Papadopoulos and Tsianos 2013, 17).

In Libya, like elsewhere, protests have become a new form of "contentious politics" (Ataç, Rygiel, and Stierl 2016) and justice claims-making questioning bordering policies and politics of visibility. Bordering and re-bordering policies are made of different components, such as externalization, search and rescue (SAR), asylum, reception, and detention policies (Kriesi et al. 2021).

Politics of visibility are at the core of bordering policies, in the Central Mediterranean region and worldwide. While on the one hand, some components of the border regimes are intentionally ostentatious—through what De Genova (2014) has defined as "the border spectacle"—others are explicitly obscured and invisibilized, such as border violence. Beyond detention, torture, systematic rapes, and other human rights violations that take place every day in Libyan detention centers (United Nations 2018; Al-Dayel and Anfinson 2021), lethal sea crossings that migrants choose to go through are a meaningful expression of this border violence (Brambilla and Jones 2020). Part of this violence continuum, from detention to choosing to risk one's own life, are the interceptions at sea and related pushback operations toward unsafe countries. So are those cases in which EU authorities are informed but choose not to intervene—known as "left to die boats" cases (Heller and Pezzani 2012).

As for Libyan detention centers, these sea crossings become battlefields (Denaro 2015; Mezzadra and Stierl 2019) in which visibility and fundamental human rights, such as among others the right to life, the right to leave, and the right to asylum, are at stake.

In this chapter, after providing an overview of the invisibilization continuum that people on the move go through from Libyan detention centers and urban settings until sea crossings, interceptions, and pushback to Libya, we examine those practices of voice and resistance through which they refuse their forcibly imposed condition of "speechless emissaries" (Malkki 1996). We examine how people speak up by documenting, photographing, videoing, and sharing their own experiences of the border regime, as well as by reaching out to possible "listeners" (Couldry 2009), organizing protests and demonstrations, and claiming for rights and justice.

For this purpose, on the one hand, we explore the ways in which refugees in Libya strategically mobilize resources, claims, and networks and develop political strategies through digitally supported processes of (counter-)narrative and justice seeking; on the other hand, we analyze "voice through exit" processes of people on the move in the frame of Central Mediterranean Sea crossings by examining the different tools, messages, and strategies that they decide to use to challenge their invisibility, asking for help, denouncing possible violations, and claiming for rights (Denaro 2020; 2021). Pictures and videos produced and shared by people on the move are mainly taken with smartphones, so they are of low quality.

In particular, we highlight how digital media, in combination with supportive social relationships with activists, journalists, and researchers, provide powerful tools for giving voice to agentive selves, mediated by digital interaction and connectivity. The conceptual framework brings together literature on critical border and migration studies with citizenship studies, and recent scholarship on narrative, identity, and digital media, with an eye toward agency. When it comes to the digital future and its consequences for refugees in Libya, multiple points demand our attention: The challenges to human rights and visibility that refugees encounter in the digital era cannot be circumscribed or analyzed without considering algorithms and platforms and the consequences that these technological assemblies can have on people's lives. Exploring the use of digital technologies as tools for self-expression becomes a strategic tool by which to get to the other side of the Mediterranean, and to claim new forms of collective action in which resistance and daily struggle are required. In this battlefield for visibility, voice, and recognition, the relationship between political self-construction, digital storytelling, and identity needs to be explored further. There is a need to shape and advance the current debate on the relationship between the claim for rights, freedom, and dignity in countries of origin—especially in revolutionary contexts—and the attitude to documenting, counter-narrating, and denouncing experienced violence and violations during migration pathways as a part of "voice through exit" processes (Denaro 2020).

In precarious spaces such as detention centers in Libya, where violence and abuse are widespread, how can access to communication or social media expand the practices of contesting power structures? And furthermore, during sea crossings where human lives are at risk, often de-humanized, and confronted with violent bordering politics of (in)visibility, which tools can be used to claim for visibility, rescue to a place of safety, and access to human rights? And finally, how do the whole of these efforts for challenging the forced invisibility to which migrants are exposed, by showing the violence and violations which feature the central Mediterranean border regime, facilitate access to justice?

BORDERING PRACTICES AND THE VIOLENCE CONTINUUM: POLITICS OF (IN)VISIBILITY AND FORCED IMMOBILITY IN LIBYA AND BEYOND

The Mediterranean space has been characterized by structural migration by sea for more than two decades. Main routes are articulated around three main corridors, namely the Western Mediterranean, the Eastern Mediterranean, and the Central Mediterranean one. Jointly with Tunisia, Libya remains the main country of departure for migrants who attempt to reach Europe by sea, especially after the partial closure of the so-called Egyptian route to Italy (Ciabarri 2014; Denaro 2016a; Squire et al. 2017). Migrants' situation in the country has been worsening over time, especially post-2011. Most of them are detained in formal and informal prisons, in which access to international organizations, journalists, and researchers is prevented. Tortures, rapes, and other forms of intentional violence are carried out on a daily basis, against women, children, and men. These kinds of mistreatment and abuse are finalized to extort money to detained people, who can be released only after a ransom has been paid by relatives and friends. Migrants report how they are often required to call relatives during the torture in order to make them listen to their screams and sufferings and to push them to find money to release them. In Libyan detention centers, which have been defined as places characterized by a "state of impunity" (Beşer and Elfeitori 2018), migrants are daily imprisoned after interceptions at sea and are still exposed to the risk of deportation to countries of origin, in full violation of the non-refoulement principle, as part of what has been defined as a "deadly refoulement industry" (Andrijasevic 2010; Godwin-Gill 2011; Stierl 2019).

While scarcely addressed by recent literature, refugees' living conditions outside detention, so in urban settings in Libya, are also worthy of attention. For years, migrant communities living in urban contexts have been facing multiple kinds of discriminations, abuse, and threats (Hamood 2006; Creta

2021). Full access to international protection for those who are in search of asylum is prevented as Libya is not a signatory of the 1951 refugee convention; even those who are registered with UNHCR as refugees have access to neither services, nor resettlement procedures. International organizations who manage resettlement procedures do apply very strict selection criteria which contribute to making legal migratory pathways a residual and unreachable opportunity. According to the International Organization for Migration (IOM) and UNHCR, as of November 2020, at least thirty-two hundred people were being held in eleven detention centers—although many more were likely also detained in "unofficial" facilities in western Libya.

UNHCR statistics refer to 43,113 refugees and asylum seekers who are part of their "population of concern" and who live in urban settings. However, these numbers are scarcely representative of the whole refugee population in Libya, as some nationalities are not registered with the organization. Main recorded nationalities shift from the Horn of Africa (Eritrea, Ethiopia, Somalia, Sudan, and South Sudan) to West Africa and sub-Saharan countries (Senegal, Gambia, Ivory Coast, Mali, Guinea, Cameroon, and many others), up to the Middle East and North Africa region (Syria, Egypt, Tunisia, and Morocco).[2]

The perception of Libya as an unlivable place is widespread among refugees, and most of them dream of reaching safety in Europe. Unfortunately, due to the almost complete unavailability of legal pathways, lethal sea crossings remain their only chance to do it (Scheel and Squire 2014).

Looking at Table 9.1, it is possible to grasp the relevance of Libya as a departure and transit country for those who want to reach Europe. In addition, the increase of interception at sea and pushbacks indicates the growing cooperation efforts carried out by the European Union and its member states to contain arrivals. EU-Libya cooperation dates back to the 2000s, but it has been progressively strengthened starting in 2009 and 2010, in the frame of the close relationship between the then Italian prime minister Berlusconi and the Libyan dictator Gaddafi, with the main aim of "outsourcing and off-shoring the borders of Europe" (Hamood 2008; Human Rights Watch 2009; Bialasiewicz 2012).

Table 9.1. Central Mediterranean Sea Crossing

	2018	2019	2020	2021–August
Arrivals Italy	23,371	11,471	34,134	37,260
Arrivals Malta	1,445	3,406	2,281	244
Pushbacks to Libya	14,949	9,000	11,891	20,799

Data Source: UN High Commissioner for Refugees, International Organization for Migration, and Italian Ministry of Interior.

The "Treaty of Friendship" agreement had the containment of migration flows as a main goal, which was pursued through the reinforcement of Libyan shores surveillance, and the cooperation between Italian and Libyan authorities in intercepting people at sea and pushing them back to Libya. Human rights violations entailed by the systematic pushback policy were acknowledged by the European Court of Human Rights in 2012, with the renowned Hirsi case.[3] Notwithstanding that and the relevant impact of EU-Libya cooperation on the respect of the non-refoulement principle and other human rights violations (Gammeltoft-Hansen and Hathaway 2014; Giuffré 2017), in 2017 a three-year agreement was signed by Italy and Libya, and renewed in 2020. This Memorandum of Understanding[4]—being grounded on the recognition of a "Libyan Search and Rescue Zone"—implicated the training, funding, and equipment of the so-called Libyan Coast Guard.[5] This externalization project should have included the creation of a Libyan Maritime Rescue Coordination Center, which has never been realized.[6] At the European level, more efforts were made in the direction of preventing departures from Libya, as well as with the aim of strengthening southern Libyan borders, to reduce the possibility of entering Libya for those willing to reach Europe. Against a total budget of around seven hundred million euros, which the European Union dedicated to "supporting" Libya over the last few years through various funding instruments—including the EU Trust Fund for Africa (EUTF), the European Neighbourhood Instrument, the humanitarian assistance, and the Instrument contributing to Stability and Peace—the EUTF has mobilized so far €455 million, €57.2 million of which have been dedicated to "Integrated border management" activities.[7]

In this context, the European Union states exercise a "contactless control" (Moreno Lax-Giuffrè 2017) on Libyan authorities through externalized but EU-funded and-led border infrastructures. This kind of control may lead to a "contactless responsibility" of the European Union for violations carried out by Libyan authorities, according to what has been defined as extraterritorial jurisdiction. In this regard, the main critical point of the picture is the very nature of Libya which—as claimed by innumerable nongovernmental organizations and international intergovernmental organizations over the years, and recently remarked by UNHCR (2020)—does not meet criteria to be considered a safe third country or a place of safety. Therefore, a rescue operation being considered concluded only after the disembarkation of people in a place of safety, which Libya is not, does not apply to Libyan Coast Guard intervention at sea. Here, words such as *interceptions*, *captures*, and *pushbacks*, in full violation of the non-refoulement principle, look more appropriate. This wording allows to partially unveil border violence experienced during sea crossings, as well as during sea interceptions in which people are forcibly returned to the place they fled from, meanwhile risking their lives.

Deaths at the border—and deaths at sea—are clear expressions of borders as violent entities, as well as more explicit recourse to violence by border surveillance authorities (Jones 2016; Pécoud 2020). However, while "regional solutions of migration management rest on a reified notion of the Mediterranean as a coherent regional borderland," the solutions "obscure both the instability of this place as well as the violence that occurs there" (Mountz and Loyd 2014). This is particularly true in the Libyan context, as well as during lethal sea crossings, interceptions, and pushbacks: bodies and identities are invisibilized, violence is obscured and kept out from official narratives on migration and border management policies, as well as from reporting activities on how EU funds are effectively spent.

In particular, taking Libya as case study, and looking into it from our multiple perspectives of research, activism, and journalism, it is possible to highlight a (border) violence continuum, from detention to sea crossings, which can develop through circular and never-ending pathways if people are intercepted at sea, forcibly returned back to Libya and again detained.

However, people on the move do challenge their forced invisibilization—and immobilization—every day through a multiplicity of tools, interactions, and messages, as well as collective and individual acts which make border violence finally visible and explicit. As suggested by Rygiel (2014), even the choice to risk life at sea can be seen as an act of "transgressive citizenship" that challenges the border regime. People on the move continuously find ways to challenge those borders that try to reduce them to speechless emissaries, and to speak up, showing themselves as political subjects and claiming for rights and justice. New technologies, social media, and instant messages play a key role in these processes, and smartphones, as well as other digital communication devices, have been recognized as primary needs good for people on the move (Leurs and Smets 2018).

In this chapter, we first outline the state of the art on social media and migration studies, with a focus on scholars' contributions on refugees and new technologies as well as inspiration from postcolonial critique and citizenship studies. Second, we provide an in-depth analysis of some responses by people on the move to what we define as a border violence continuum, from detention in Libya to lethal sea crossings, and possibly onward through interceptions and pushbacks.

REFUGEES' DIGITAL RESISTANCE AND "VOICE THROUGH EXIT": FROM "SPEECHLESS EMISSARIES" TO "POLITICAL SUBJECTS"

Refugees are definitely part of those "subaltern" populations whose right to speak was deeply questioned by Chakravorty Spivak in her essay "Can the subaltern speak?" The mainstream narratives on human mobilities often depict them as "speechless emissaries" (Malkki 1996), by obscuring their agency and political subjectivity and focusing more on them as "needy and vulnerable populations" than on their struggles, resistance, and voice.

In this chapter, while contesting the misrepresentation of refugees as voiceless, we try to shed light on the processes, the contexts, the tools, and the ways in which refugees' voices emerge, as part of interlocutions between them as "speakers" and a wide plethora of "listeners" (Couldry 2009). Moreover, we stress the relevance of new digital technologies and communication devices as key tools in these interlocution processes, both in conditions of "immobility" and while refugees are "on the move." In particular, while the relevance of mobile communication for refugees, as well as the key role of smartphones and social media for those on the move, has already been underlined by the academic literature (Alencar 2020; Gillespie et al. 2018; Denaro 2016), less is known about refugees' aptitude for documenting border violence and denouncing human rights violations (Denaro 2021). Likewise, less is known about how these practices—which take place in the frame of wider visible and invisible struggles for safe passages and claims for justice—can challenge the infrastructure of the existing border regimes, contributing to debordering processes (Kriesi et al. 2021; Denaro 2021b).

Early studies suggest that the reduction of participation costs enabled by information and communication technologies can promote participation and challenge conventional collective action theories, but given that smartphones became ever more mobile and pervasive even in developing countries (Bennett and Segerberg 2012; Earl and Kimport 2011), little is known about how internet access can affect the ability of marginalized groups to be part of mobilization processes. In the last decades, the question of who has the "right to have rights" has become ever more important. The integration of digital connectivity into people's lives, often celebrated as liberating and empowering for marginalized groups, raises questions on how online engagement could bring about political change (Papacharissi 2015). New technologies and new forms of connectivity are enhancing the creation of digital publics where the paradoxically precarious, speechless emissaries and humanitarian subjects (Malkki 1996) assume new forms of resistance practice using digital tools. This effort to understand active agency, access, and power begins with the recognition that the existence and visibility of refugees in Libya in the "new media, cultural and socio-economic order" (Appadurai 2006) allows the interpretation of new "forms of existence" that are shaping political subjectivities from the margins. According to Papadopoulos and Tsianos (2013), these new "forms of life," which they define as mobile commons, comprise four main aspects: the invisible knowledge of mobility that circulates between people on the move, an infrastructure of connectivity which helps share and distribute this knowledge, a multiplicity of informal economies, and transnational communities of justice. Beyond having a key role in the transmission of mobile commons (Trimikliniotis et al. 2015), Creta (2021) highlights how migrant digitalities can become what Arendt defined as a "space of appearance" (1958, 195) that allows people on the move to reclaim their narrative and to convey their struggles to exist in the European's communicative order (Georgiou 2018). At the same time, social media platforms like Twitter, Facebook, and YouTube have provided a space for civic engagement where the collective production creates a self-organized social system that can mobilize people (Lindgren and Johnson-Glenberg 2013) and offer opportunities to construct a "new distribution of power" (Borkert et al. 2009). Similar scholarship also found that exiled communities and activists play an important role in mediating political practices and mobilization (Andén-Papadopoulos 2013). In this global network of information flows, rethinking the public sphere concept is fundamental, as digital technologies have brought distant "others" into the space of deliberation. These developments have transformed many aspects of economic, social, and political life (Castells 2001; Silver et al. 2006), facilitating socioculturally marginalized voices to be expressed, heard, and shared in public space. Transnational media flows have mediated people's participation in the public sphere, allowing a deliberation of sociopolitical issues, developing transnational connections that create a sort of cross-border dialogue.

In discussing transnationalism, and the way exiled communities can use social media for "transnational justice" (Hodzic and Tolbert 2017), it is important to analyze how this can enable a process championing victims' rights to truth and justice. Or ensure that systematic violence does not recur. Previous research has found that media and communication technologies are important both to the perpetration of mass rights violations and to the promotion of transitional justice responses to them—as Price and Stremlau put it, they "often serve as both a weapon and a mirror of violence" (2012, 1078).

Questions of access, digital capabilities, infrastructures, platforms, and agency need to be discussed when developing new theories on how digital media and the ongoing struggles of people on the move intersect with new forms of freedom and agency in our global era, in particular in precarious settings like in refugee camps or situations of forced exile. This is particularly interesting for refugees in Libya as well as other groups living in exile outside of Europe. What does the new digital media ecosystem offer? How does it create collective identities and actions that can enable mobilization? In particular, it is interesting to understand how user-generated content has emerged as a key mode of mediation, allowing an eyewitness view of events taking place in worldwide locations (Andén-Papadopoulos 2013; Bruns 2018; Meikle 2018). Critically, however, sustaining practices of bearing witness is fundamental to understanding how suffering and violence become an aesthetic presentation of the self-narrative. Zelizer (2002, 698) suggests that one of the key functions of bearing witness is that it helps return a community to a state of unity that existed prior to whatever trauma might have befallen it. Similarly, Chouliaraki (2006) has suggested that media coverage of suffering must be brought into a narrative—or else audiences will not be morally activated. In what follows, how do political self-construction, digital storytelling, and identity play a role in the formation of publics? And how can the political act of reclaiming voice expand the idea of "the political" through Arendt's understanding of political action as narrative? Finally, how can refugee voices—aimed at documenting and denouncing human rights violations and border violence, in the frame of a wider claim for justice—work as de-bordering practices?

REFUGEE VOICES AS ACTS OF CITIZENSHIP: FROM LIBYAN DETENTION FACILITIES TO LETHAL SEA CROSSINGS AND PUSHBACKS

In this section, we analyze three examples of how refugees dealt with the southern European border regime, by challenging politics of (in)visibility, narrating violence, and claiming rights from Libyan detention facilities and urban settings, until sea crossings and pushbacks. In particular, we argue that their voices and practices of resistance to border violence emerged as transgressive "acts of citizenship" (Isin and Nielsen 2008; Rygiel 2012). According to Isin and Nielsen's conceptualization, these acts consist of dynamic and relational processes of subjectivation, unrelated to national belonging to a determined country, in which people constitute themselves as citizens. Acts of citizenship can be made of overlapping and interdependent components, in which people claim for justice, rights and responsibility (Isin and Nielsen 2008, 10). They are moments of creative rupture that allow the social transformation and which "cannot be reduced to practices [of citizenship] because to enact oneself as a citizen involves transforming oneself from a subject into a claimant, which inevitably involves a break from habitus" (Farnell 2000). Being grounded on the Arendtian definition of citizenship as "right to have rights," these acts of citizenship take shape through claims for rights, which in the analyzed cases are the right to life, the right to leave, the right to seek asylum, and the right to find adequate protection in a safe country. Lethal sea crossings from Libya to Europe, which are the main factor forcing refugees to go through detention and dangerous living conditions in Libya, are the only option to exercise them.

Finally, being inspired by more recent revisions of the autonomy of migration approach (Papadopoulos and Tsianos 2013)—which overcome the attempt to re-align migrants with the working classes (Mezzadra 2001; Papadopoulos and Tsianos 2007) and focus on the claim for freedom of movement by people on the move—we engage with the concept of "acts of immediate justice," which seems useful to provide a deeper understanding of refugees' attempts to make their voices heard, with the aim of documenting border violence, counter-narrating the border regime, and claiming for rights.

Detention Centers

While access to Libyan detention facilities remains limited for journalists or human rights organizations, social media platforms and phones become important tools (when available) for detained asylum seekers to connect with journalists, advocates, activists, legal representatives, and families. Access to social media networks has enabled detained asylum seekers and refugees to expose violations in an attempt to protest their situation and record human rights abuses. Considering the way "self-represented witnessing" (Rae et al. 2018) is performed, circumventing the usual mediation of their stories, refugees in Libya have documented their own suffering and communicate this directly to online audiences. This practice, similar to the strategy developed by asylum seekers in other places like Manus and Nauru (Australian-managed offshore detention centers), has enabled collaborative filtering that allows an effective engagement for the public. Their pictures and videos from detention centers and their attempts to protest their situation have been posted on social media platforms, such as Facebook, or their personal walls, to capture their experiences over time and create a community of support. This collective experience of shared feelings and traumas has also developed the path for a strong appeal to human rights claims and social justice.

"I am giving my words by putting my life in danger. I posted my pictures on facebook so the world can see our situation," wrote an Eritrean refugee, held in Khoms detention center. This appeal on his Facebook personal wall was accompanied by a self-shot and edited video in which refugees' bodies were seen on the beach nearby the detention center. Using a hidden phone, the Eritrean refugee who has been detained in Khoms for several months managed to go out to the beach and record a video of him digging up sand in an attempt to cover the body of a dead migrant. With the main desire to expose and challenge the EU deadly border practices, as they are directly affecting their personal lives, detained Eritrean refugees in Libya have used social media as a platform to communicate their struggle and their experience in detention. A similar message has been posted by another Eritrean asylum seeker being held in Qasr Ben Ghashir detention center, south of Tripoli.

> Merry Christmas and Happy New Year, from the Libyan detention center. WE REALLY MISS TO SEE OUTSIDE OF LIBYA. Would they resettle us from this hell this year? What will they tell us? Wait in dark, get torture, experience terrible sexual violence, rape or not? What are the European countries doing so far? What's UNHCR's aim? Dear new year, we have been going through an awful life. What will you say to us? We don't know. We can try to survive because we have our family waiting for us.

An important element must be considered regarding how digital tools are affecting and fostering new networks to facilitate the diffusion of the Eritrean refugees' claims, but also supporting their demands of visibility: the main request of tangible solutions, provided by States and by the UNHCR. Both examples hold the promise of storytelling but also a pressing matter dominating the public sphere while addressing refugees' storytelling. While for years, agencies such as the UNHCR have mediated refugees' narratives, these self-represented refugees' narratives offer a significant counter-narrative to the attempts to erase or flatten individual stories. At stake there are issues of ethics, power, and agency, which are all entwined in the refugee's struggle to make their voices heard. "I have been looking for help after I was released from prison. But unfortunately, I didn't get any help from the UNHCR. They did nothing more to me. Can you please help?" wrote another Eritrean refugee on his personal wall.

By using the EU logo or UN representative Filippo Grandi's picture to create a meme, as well as by writing "EU don't give attention to the deaths of migrants in Libya, in legal detention centers, due to brutal daily biting by militias," they define a space for claims-making; re-defining who is allowed to speak as a political subject. While at the national—and international—level the political and social rights of refugees are put into question, here they articulate their demands for recognition from the margins. The space in detention, therefore, witnesses the emergence of a practice of articulation, claiming and renewing group rights in and through the appropriation of a narrative as the act of posting and denouncing violations allows detained Eritrean refugees to capture their experiences over time to create a community of support (see Photo 9.1).

Photo 9.1. Facebook post. *Source*: Facebook.

This was the case in August 2018, when an Eritrean refugee, after an escape attempt from captivity conditions by human traffickers west of Bani Walid, Libya, posted the pictures of the people getting shot on his Facebook wall. He, together with dozens of asylum seekers and migrants, was wounded after trying to escape captivity and was referred to the General Hospital of Bani Walid. After a few weeks, while still in need of help and support, he publicly shared his story. "We are in Tripoli. Please share our problem and pray for us," wrote one of the survivors while publishing the pictures on his Facebook wall. The Eritrean refugee explained the vital role the internet played in reaching out for help. "This was our true life. We decided to post it as we couldn't get any help from UNHCR and we wanted to move from that hell," he said. Other protests followed in Zintan, Tajoura, Zawya, Sabha, and Tariq el Sikka Sika detention centers in Tripoli. "In Zintan we organized a lot of protests. We urged UNHCR, Human right organizations, IOM and others to see our sufferings. It was heard and even some representatives from different organizations like UNHCR and IOM visited us. They made a promise to see our case in priority. But no positive result on the ground," said Yonas in an interview in Zintan in December 2020.

Across the Mediterranean

In continuity with struggles and resistance practices that take place in Libya, refugees' attempt to break their forced immobility and invisibility materialize during sea crossings. Requests for help and rescue when in distress are voices which are then amplified by their listeners. Starting in 2014, Watch the Med Alarm Phone network[8] has progressively come to represent a key interlocutor for people on the move. After the end of Mare Nostrum operation, the space of intervention of EU SAR assets was shrunk up to thirty NM from the Italian coasts. This event was followed by the withdrawal of EU SAR assets, the increased delegation of SAR responsibility to Libya, and the increase of pushbacks to this unsafe country. For these reasons, even if refugees kept calling the EU coast guards, their trust in EU SAR authorities was deeply undermined, and the presence of an "independent" interlocutor to which address their SOS request—especially in case of protracted non-assistance by the institutional actors—was very relevant for them. Nowadays, the Mediterranean Sea represents a transnational and political space, which is daily crossed both by persons and by individual and collective struggles to reach a safe place, to exercise their rights—to life, to fleeing, to asylum, to protection from violence—as well as to choose where to live. The interlocution between refugees and Alarm Phone during sea crossings is the infrastructure for refugee voices to emerge, both in order to "become visible" to EU authorities and those subjects who could perform a rescue, as well as to denounce possible lack of assistance and other forms of violence during sea crossings. Even if during Mediterranean Sea crossings from Libya, this kind of communication mainly takes place through satellite phones, which only allow refugees to claim for visibility through their own voice and by facilitating geo-localization processes, people on the move do often travel with smartphones, which help them document violence and violation through

Photo 9.2. Malta's dangerous maneuvers at sea. *Source*: **Alarm Phone (one of the authors).**

audiovisual material and share it after disembarkation in order to plea for justice. An example of these processes are events that occurred between April 10 and 12, 2020, to a group of 101 people[9] on a boat in the Maltese SAR zone, which provided testimonies and footage of the dangerous maneuvers performed by the Maltese Coast Guard after a failed attempt to force the people to go back to Libya. As reported by Alarm Phone,[10] "instead of proceeding to immediately rescue those overboard, and as is visible in the video footage, the survivors state that the AFM drove dangerous manoeuvres close to people in the water, further endangering their lives and those still on the rubber boat" (see Photo 9.2).

After the resistance performed by those onboard and their refusal to invert the route and go back to Libya, reportedly Maltese authorities provided them a new engine and fuel, and indicated to them the route to Italy; they autonomously arrived in Pozzallo.

Pushed Back

According to the available data, the Mediterranean Sea crossing attempts from Libya which end up in pushbacks to the country refugees were fleeing from exceed the number of arrivals to Italy and Malta of boats that left from there. According to the mainstream narrative, operational activities carried out by the Libyan Coast Guard are defined as SAR operations; however, this definition does not properly correspond to reality. According to international maritime law, a rescue should be concluded with the disembarkation in a place of safety, which—as underlined by UNHCR itself and other relevant international bodies and organizations—Libya is not (UNHCR 2020). Therefore, it is more correct to talk about interceptions and pushbacks in violation of the non-refoulement principle because, as it is known, Libya does not meet criteria to be considered a safe country—neither of origin, nor of transit (UNHCR 2020). The frequently reported protests and suicide attempts performed by migrants at sea after they realize that Libyan authorities are intervening to intercept them back to Libya are often related to testimonies in which they say to prefer to die instead of being returned to the country from which they were fleeing. Reports by people who are back in Libya after a sea crossing attempt show concern about the pushback operations themselves, the possible use of violence by Libyan authorities, the loss of lives before or during the "rescue" operations, as well as the structural violence and deprivation they suffer in detention facilities.

Through these testimonies, they counter-narrate the "rescues" toward Libya, challenging the EU definition of Libya as a "third safe country" and documenting how the Libyan Coast Guard is quick to carry out interceptions of moving boats at sea. Coast guards systematically delay interventions when people are in drifting, their engine has stopped working, and their boat risks capsizing at every moment. Survivors speak up—supporting their narrative through audiovisual materials and allowing their "listeners" to spread their voices—which opens breaches in the politics of invisibilization of border violence by making it visible (see Photo 9.3).

A shipwreck occurred between August 14 and 16, 2020, when a boat carrying eighty-two people,[11] after being shot at by a group of five men, caught fire.[12] According to testimonies collected by Alarm Phone, forty-five people were killed, while the remaining thirty-seven people were found by a local fisherman and brought back to Libya. After the disembarkation, the survivors—including several injured and burned people—were brought to a detention facility without being granted prompt access to medical care. "There are some who are in the room, they can't walk, some can't see anymore, all their hands are burned," a survivor says in the video. Despite the alert to all EU SAR authorities by Alarm Phone, and despite the lethal

Photo 9.3. Shipwreck survivors speak up. *Source*: Alarm Phone (one of the authors).

situation they experienced a long time of non-assistance was reported. "I can't believe it. I can't believe what happened to us. We drowned and there was fire everywhere! Nobody came! Some ships could have saved us! But no one came. Thanks to the fisherman who saved us, we are still alive." These voices, which include denouncing of suffered violence and parallel claims for justice, often expose them to possible repercussions and punishments. In this case, the aforementioned Eritrean refugee's words, "I give you my voice by putting my life in danger," was particularly true, because the survivors who spoke up about the August 16 fire and shipwreck were arrested after the publication of the video.

CHALLENGING INVISIBILITY, NARRATING BORDER VIOLENCE, CLAIMING RIGHTS IN THE DIGITAL POLITICAL SPACE: VOICES AS DE-BORDERING PRACTICES

Despite the presence in Libya of agencies such as the UNHCR, who should have the role of "providing the means for [refugee] voices to be heard" at the core of its mandate, many refugees consider themselves voiceless individuals (UNHCR 2014). However, their "digital traces," speaking up about processes and acts of citizenship, are able to deeply challenge the UNHCR narrative. A criticism could be that by focusing on their plight, UN agencies and humanitarian organizations may have been oversimplifying in their claims, while erasing vital geopolitical stakes, idealizing and representing refugees only by focusing on their vulnerability, and complicating the mediation of their lives. A few questions arise while observing the digital practices performed in Libya. Can this self-represented witnessing foster some common ground that allows for a better understanding of the other? Can these self-represented narratives manage to bring readers/audiences closer to the person whose life is often being retold by others? If these life narratives—broadly understood as memoirs or digital traces on social media to record atrocities—are geared toward denouncing injustice while calling for change, it is interesting to explore if they can also reveal an attempt to resist power, thus constituting borders in different forms and different spaces, in a logic of control, questioning restrictive migration regimes. The lived experience shared via social media provides a window into their personal being in detention that runs counter to dominant discourses and representation and can be considered "reclaimant narratives" to contest for rights under conditions of oppression (i.e., forms of activism from the margins).

To investigate the ways in which the visual is mediated by refugees in Libya, it is necessary to recognize why people want to "capture" or share their lived experience. Although the practice of storytelling can become a "healing" aspect of narration, it can also be a collective identity frame being used to shape online political identity construction. At any level of analysis, from the individual to the collective effort to mobilize, narratives and visual elements play a central role in the formation of the ties that constitute networks. They become matters of vital necessity, offering visibility to ensure survival or to expand the visual and discursive modes of expressing politics. From these mediated performances of collective action in detention centers, refugees have built their new forms of political interactions from the margins. The idea that human rights are shaped through collective action fits with Arendt's (1958) view of human rights and political resistance. For Arendt, the most fundamental right, and a precondition for other rights, was the right to have rights or the right to membership of a political community. This membership meant having "a place in the world which makes opinions significant and actions effective" (Arendt 1958, 296).

Other tools to read the complex interconnection between struggles for mobility and claims for justice are provided by the autonomy of migration approach, as revised by Papadopoulos and Tsianos (2013). The conceptualization of border crossings as "acts of immediate justice," grounded on an immediate feeling and judgment about what is just and unjust in relation to everyday life conditions, is of great inspiration to read refugee voices in Libya and across the sea. Detention conditions, violence and torture, limited access to food and water, as well as sea-crossings conditions, where people are exposed to death and pushbacks, are all perceived as unjust. Therefore, the decision to document, denounce, and speak up can be considered "acts of immediate justice," through which people on the move seek to change their situation by struggling against forced immobility, by trying to be released from detention, to be rescued at sea, and to access fundamental rights.

Looking at the previously analyzed cases of refugees speaking up from Libyan detention centers, as well as during lethal sea crossings and after pushback operations to the country from which they attempted to flee, it is possible to identify some common features. The first one is a smart and innovative use of digital technologies with the aim to challenge the politics of (in) visibility entailed by the border regime. Pictures, videos, audio recordings, as well as the phone calls to ask for help and rescue at sea (e.g., to Alarm Phone) are powerful tools of visibility, through which refugees' voices emerge by showing their presence in places where their lives are at risk. These voices are able to counter-narrate Libya as a (not) safe country, the border regime as violent infrastructure instead of a tool for protecting people's lives from human trafficking and smuggling, and the asylum policies, which far from facilitating access to safe countries keep people in detention, prevent them from safely reaching countries of asylum and expose them to violence and forced immobility.

Moreover, testimonies by people on the move—especially when supported by audiovisual materials—provide the ground for possible formal claims for justice through strategic litigation processes[13] and for a multiplicity of advocacy actions, and political pressure activities aimed at facilitating their access to rights, such as to be released from detention, to be promptly rescued and disembarked in a place of safety, or to receive urgent medical assistance.

To conclude, what we argue is that all these de-bordering practices—which take shape through refugee voices, practices of resistance, and acts of citizenship—could never take place without the essential intermediation of digital technologies.

CONCLUSION

Being inspired by the autonomy of migration approach and its assumption of human mobility as a political and social movement, the chapter has focused on how digital technologies are essential tools in refugee struggles for movement and claims for justice. In particular, we argue that active citizenry and online participation among refugees in Libya and during sea crossings to Europe, mediated by smartphones and tempered by platforms, are valuable sites of production of counter-narratives on border violence and the border regime, which are essential components of a wider claim for rights and justice. As for a "physical" border crossing, speaking up for requesting help, for denouncing rights violations, and for narrating violence can maybe be considered what Papadopoulos and Tsianos (2013) define as "acts of immediate justice," due to their intrinsic potential to challenge existing power structures by claiming rights.

These insights provoke questions about how new technologies enhance new forms of connectivity for people on the move and may contribute to challenge some of the border regimes' infrastructures, such as mainstream narratives and politics of visibility, but also denied access to rights and justice. In particular, as provision of technology and/or media outlets does not by itself necessarily enable security, freedom, or emancipation, it is interesting to explore how refugees' voices—often mediated by humanitarian organizations or media—and hence channeled in ways that perpetuate their image of dependency and powerlessness (Kisiara 2015, 163), become an opportunity to "potentially enable both new ways of being political and new visions for the type of politics we wish to imagine in the world" (Nyers and Rygiel 2012, 9). More specifically, the chapter contributes to research on voice and citizenship by introducing collective digital performance as a way to speak beyond expected voicelessness, and it suggests that any attempt to theorize and study connectivity, especially when refugees are trapped in abusive and violent experiences, should encapsulate a social justice lens, echoing Leurs and Smets' (2018, 10) view on the "particular urgency to assert more firmly our social justice orientation" as researchers dealing with questions of migration. To a large extent, the social expectations associated with mobile connectivity have only partly questioned whether and how refugees' experiences go beyond precarity. If oppression, exclusion, and injustice are not researched, scholars can fall into what Georgiou (2018, 46) calls, "symbolic bordering," and which she describes as "the hierarchical ordering of Europeans' and migrants' humanity that subjects migrants to danger, controlled mobility, and conditional recognition." When focusing on struggles for mobility, debordering practices, and how refugee voices are able to challenge politics of invisibilization of their bodies and identities, documenting border violence, counter-narrating the cornerstones of contemporary border regimes, and claiming rights and justice can be a necessary step in the opposite direction.

ACKNOWLEDGMENTS

One of the authors gratefully acknowledged funding from the European Union's Horizon 2020 research and innovation program under the Marie Skłodowska-Curie grant agreement No 765140.

The work of the other author has been realized as part of the PRIN 2017 project "De-bordering activities and citizenship from below of asylum seekers in Italy. Policies, practices, people," in the frame of which she works as a postdoctoral researcher at Trento University.

REFERENCES

l-Dayel, N., A. Anfinson, and G. Anfinson. 2021. "Captivity, migration, and power in Libya." *Journal of Human Trafficking* 1–19.

Alencar, A. 2020. "Mobile communication and refugees: An analytical review of academic literature." *Sociology Compass* 14 (8): e12802.

Andén-Papadopoulos, K. 2013. "Media witnessing and the 'crowd-sourced video revolution.'" *Visual Communication* 12 (3): 341–57.

Andrijasevic, R. 2010. "Deported: The right to asylum at EU's external border of Italy and Libya." *International Migration* 48 (1): 148–74.

Appadurai, A. 2006. *Fear of Small Numbers: An Essay on the Geography of Anger.* Durham, NC: Duke University Press.

Appadurai, A. 2010. "How histories make geographies." *The Journal of Transcultural Studies* 1 (1): 4–13.

Arendt, H. 1958. *The Human Condition*. Chicago: University of Chicago Press.

Ataç, I., K. Rygiel, and M. Stierl. 2016. "The contentious politics of refugee and migrant protest and solidarity movements: Remaking citizenship from the margins." *Citizenship Studies* 20 (5): 1–18.

Bennett, W. L., and A. Segerberg. 2012. "The logic of connective action: Digital media and the personalization of contentious politics." *Information, Communication & Society* 15 (5): 739–68.

Beşer, M. E., and F. Elfeitori. 2018. "Libya detention centres: A state of impunity." https://www.academia.edu/38458295/Libya_Detention_Centres_A_State_of_Impunity.

Bialasiewicz, L. 2012. "Off-shoring and out-sourcing the borders of Europe: Libya and EU border work in the Mediterranean." *Geopolitics* 17 (4): 843–66.

Borkert, M., P. Cingolani, and V. Premazzi. 2009. *The State of the Art of Research in the EU on the Uptake and Use of ICT by Immigrants and Ethnic Minorities (IEM)*. Siviglia: European Commission, Joint Research Centre, Institute for Prospective Technological Studies.

Brambilla, C., and R. Jones. 2020. "Rethinking borders, violence, and conflict: From sovereign power to borderscapes as sites of struggles." *Environment and Planning D: Society and Space* 38 (2): 287–305.

Castells, M. 2001. *The Power of Identity*. Oxford: Blackwell.

Ciabarri, L. 2014. "Dynamics and representations of migration corridors: The rise and fall of the LibyaLampedusa route and forms of,obility from the Horn of Africa (2000–2009)." *ACME: An International Journal for Critical Geographies* 13 (2): 246–62.

Chouliaraki, L. 2006. *Media, Globalization and Ethics*. London: Sage.

Couldry, N. 2009. "Rethinking the politics of voice: Commentary." *Continuum* 23 (4): 579–82.

Creta, S. 2021. "I hope, one day, I will have the right to speak." *Media, War & Conflict*, 1750635221989566.

Creta, S. 2021. "Libya fails to stop migrant detention abuses, as EU-backed returns soar." *The New Humanitarian*. https://www.thenewhumanitarian.org/news-feature/2021/6/24/libya-fails-to-stop-migrant-detention-abuses-as-eu-backed-returns-soar.

De Genova, N. 2014. "Extremities and regularities: Regulatory regimes and the spectacle of immigration enforcement." In *The Irregularization of Migration in Contemporary Europe. Detention, Deportation, Drowning*, edited by Y. Jansen, R. Celikates, and J. de Bloois, 3–14. London: Rowman & Littlefield.

Denaro, C. 2021. "Documenting and denouncing violence at eastern European borders: the socio-legal relevance of refugee voices through the production of audio-visual material." In *Handbook on Human Security, Borders and Migration*, edited by N. R. Mateos and T. Dunn, 178–209. Cheltenham, UK: Edward Elgar Publishing.

Denaro, C. 2021. "Re-bordering policies and de-bordering practices in pandemic times: Offshore isolation as de facto detention." https://www.law.ox.ac.uk/research -subject-groups/centre-criminology/centreborder-criminologies/blog/2021/09/re -bordering.

Denaro, C. 2020. "Voice through exit: Syrian refugees at the borders of Europe and the struggle to choose where to live." In *Displacement*, edited by S. Pasquetti and R. Sanyal, 131–52. Manchester: Manchester University Press.

Denaro, C. 2016a. "The reconfiguration of Mediterranean migration routes after the war in Syria: narratives of the 'Egyptian route' to Italy (and beyond)." In *Migration, Mobilities and the Arab Spring*, edited by N. Ribas-Mateos, 71–104. Cheltenham, UK: Edward Elgar Publishing.

Denaro, C. 2016b. "We have the right to choose where to live: agency e produzione di materiale audio-visuale nei percorsi di fuga dalla Siria." *Mondi Migranti* 2/2016: 123–45.

Denaro, C. 2015. "The Mediterranean Sea as a transnational space and (struggle) field. Reflection on the critical sea-watching phenomenon as a new form of citizen-ship." *Feministisches Geo-RundMail* 64: 15–20.

Earl, J., and K. Kimport. 2011. *Digitally Enabled Social Change*. Cambridge, MA: MIT Press.

Gammeltoft-Hansen, T., and J. C. Hathaway. 2014. "Non-refoulement in a world of cooperative deterrence." *Columbia Journal of Transnational Law* 53: 235–84.

Georgiou, M. 2018. "Does the subaltern speak? Migrant voices in digital Europe." *Popular Communication* 16 (1): 45–57.

Gillespie, M., S. Osseiran, and M. Cheesman. 2018. "Syrian refugees and the digital passage to Europe: Smartphone infrastructures and affordances." *Social Media + Society* 4 (1): 2056305118764440.

Giuffré, M. 2017. "Access to asylum at sea? Non-refoulement and a comprehensive approach to extraterritorial human rights obligations." In *"Boat Refugees" and Migrants at Sea: A Comprehensive Approach*, edited by V. Moreno-Lax and E. Papastavridis, 248–75. London: Brill Nijhoff.

Goodwin-Gill, G. S. 2011. "The right to seek asylum: Interception at sea and the prin-ciple of non-refoulement." *International Journal of Refugee Law* 23 (3): 443–57.

Hamood, S. 2006. *African Transit Migration through Libya to Europe: The Human Cost*. Cairo: American University in Cairo, Forced Migration and Refugee Studies.

Hamood, S. 2008. "EU–Libya cooperation on migration: A raw deal for refugees and migrants?" *Journal of Refugee Studies* 21 (1): 19–42.

Heller, C., L. Pezzani, and S. Studio. 2012. "Report on the 'left-to-die boat.'" London: Forensic Architecture Project Goldsmiths University of London, 11.

Hess, S. 2017. "Border crossing as act of resistance. The autonomy of migration as theoretical intervention into border studies." In *Resistance*, edited by M. Butler, M. Mecheril, and L. Brenningmeyer, 87–100. Bielefeld: Transcript Verlag.

Hodzic, R., and D. Tolbert. 2017. "Media and transitional justice: A dream of sym-biosis in a troubled relationship." In *Research Handbook on Transitional Justice*. Cheltenham, UK: Edward Elgar Publishing.

Human Rights Watch. 2009. "Pushed back, pushed around. Italy's forced return of boat migrants and asylum seekers, Libya's mistreatment of migrants and asylum seekers." https://www.hrw.org/sites/default/files/reports/italy0909webwcover_0.pdf/

Isin, E. F., and G. M. Nielsen, eds. 2008. *Acts of Citizenship*. London: Zed Books Ltd.

Jones, R. 2016. *Violent Borders: Refugees and the Right to Move*. New York: Verso Books.

Leurs, K., and K. Smets. 2018. "Five questions for digital migration studies: Learning from digital connectivity and forced migration in(to) Europe." *Social Media + Society* 4 (1): 2056305118764425.

Lindgren, R., and M. Johnson-Glenberg. 2013. "Emboldened by embodiment: Six precepts for research on embodied learning and mixed reality." *Educational researcher* 42 (8): 445–52.

Kisiara, O. 2015. "Marginalized at the centre: How public narratives of suffering perpetuate perceptions of refugees' helplessness and dependency." *Migration Letters* 12 (2): 162–71.

Malkki, L. H. 1996. "Speechless emissaries: Refugees, humanitarianism, and dehistoricization." *Cultural Anthropology* 11 (3): 377–404.

Meikle, G. 2018. *The Routledge Companion to Media and Activism*. Andover: Routledge Ltd.

Mezzadra, S. 2001. *Diritto di fuga. Migrazioni, cittadinanza, globalizzazione*. Verona: Ombre Corte.

Mezzadra, S., and M. Stierl. 2019. *The Mediterranean Battlefield of Migration*. London: openDemocracy.

Mountz, A., and J. M. Loyd. 2014. "Constructing the Mediterranean region: Obscuring violence in the bordering of Europe's migration 'crises.'" *ACME: An International Journal for Critical Geographies* 13 (2): 173–95.

Mountz, A., K. Coddington, R. T. Catania, and J. M. Loyd. 2013. "Conceptualizing detention: Mobility, containment, bordering, and exclusion." *Progress in Human Geography* 37 (4): 522–41.

Nyers, P., and K. Rygiel. 2012. *Citizenship, Migrant Activism and the Politics of Movement*, volume 2. London: Routledge.

Papacharissi, Z. 2015. "Affective publics and structures of storytelling: sentiment, events and mediality." *Information, Communication & Society* 19 (3): 307–24.

Papadopoulos, D., and V. S. Tsianos. 2013. "After citizenship: autonomy of migration, organisational ontology and mobile commons." *Citizenship Studies* 17 (2): 178–96.

Papadopoulos, D., and V. Tsianos. 2007. "The autonomy of migration: The animals of undocumented mobility." In *Deleuzian Encounters. Studies in Contemporary Social Isues*, edited by A. Hickey-Moody and P. Malins, 223–35. Basingstoke: Palgrave Macmillan.

Pécoud, A. 2020. "Death at the border: Revisiting the debate in light of the Euro-Mediterranean migration crisis." *American Behavioral Scientist* 64 (4): 379–88.

Price, M., and N. Stremlau. 2012. "Media and transitional justice: Toward a systematic approach." *International Journal of Communication* 6 (23): 1077–99.

Rae, M., R. Holman, and A. Nethery. 2018. "Self-represented witnessing: the use of social media by asylum seekers in Australia's offshore immigration detention centres." *Media, Culture & Society* 40 (4): 479–95.

Rygiel, K. 2014. "In life through death: Transgressive citizenship at the border." In *Routledge Handbook of Global Citizenship Studies*, 84–94. New York: Routledge.

Scheel, S., and V. Squire. 2014. "Forced migrants as illegal migrants." In *The Oxford Handbook of Refugee and Forced Migration Studies*, 188–99. Oxford: Oxford University Press.

Silver, D., A. Massanari, and S. Jones. 2006. *Critical Cyberculture Studies*. New York: NYU Press.

Spivak, G. C. 2003. "Can the subaltern speak?" *Die Philosophin* 14 (27): 42–58.

Squire, V., A. Dimitriadi, N. Perkowski, M. Pisani, D. Stevens, and N. Vaughan-Williams. 2017. *Crossing the Mediterranean Sea by Boat: Mapping and Documenting Migratory Journeys and Experiences*. Coventry, UK: University of Warwick.

Stierl, M. 2019. "Migrants calling us in distress from the Mediterranean returned to Libya by deadly 'refoulement' industry." *The Conversation* 7.

United Nations. 2018. "Desperate and dangerous: UNSMIL/OHCHR report on the human rights situation of migrants and refugees in Libya." https://reliefweb.int/report/libya/desperate-and-dangerous-report-human-rights-situation-migrants-and-refugees-libya.

UN High Commissioner for Refugees (UNHCR). 2014. *Speaking for Ourselves: Hearing Refugee Voices, A Journey Towards Empowerment*. https://www.refworld.org/docid/537afd9e4.html.

Zelizer, B. 2002. "Finding aids to the past: Bearing personal witness to traumatic public events." *Media, Culture, and Society* 24 (5): 697–714.

NOTES

1. https://observers.france24.com/en/20180822-libya-migrants-rare-protest-eritrea-ethiopia.

2. See https://data2.unhcr.org/en/country/lby.

3. https://www.asylumlawdatabase.eu/en/content/ecthr-hirsi-jamaa-and-others-v-italy-gc-application-no-2776509.

4. https://eumigrationlawblog.eu/wp-content/uploads/2017/10/MEMORANDUM_translation_finalversion.doc.pdf.

5. Intervention carried out in the frame of Memorandum of Understanding between Italy and Libya, consisting of interventions carried out through the EUTF, North Africa window, Libya, can be synthetized as follows: technical trainings to 105 members of the General Administration for Coastal Security on issues like navigation skills and human rights, thirty sport utility vehicles and ten buses were delivered to the relevant Libyan authorities; two vessels belonging to the General Administration for Coastal Security have been rehabilitated. https://ec.europa.eu/trustfundforafrica/sites/default/files/eutf_libya_en.pdf.

6. https://www.statewatch.org/analyses/2020/mediterranean-as-the-fiction-of-a
-libyan-search-and-rescue-zone-begins-to-crumble-eu-states-use-the-coronavirus
-pandemic-to-declare-themselves-unsafe/.

7. The other two pillars of EUTF-funded activities are "protection and assistance
to those in need," which is being pursued through a total of €237.3 million, and the
"stabilization of Libyan Municipalities" to which €160.8 million have been devoted.

8. Watch the Med Alarm Phone was initiated in October 2014 by activist networks
and civil society actors across the Mediterranean. The project established a self-
organized and volunteer 24/7 hotline for people in distress in the Mediterranean Sea.
See also https://watchthemed.net and https://alarmphone.org/en/.

9. People were initially reported to be eighty-five, while after their autonomous
arrival in Pozzallo their number totaled 101.

10. The report is available at https://alarmphone.org/en/2020/05/20/maltas
-dangerous-manoeuvres-at-sea/.

11. The initial information shared by Alarm Phone, which reported only sixty-five
people onboard, was then rectified by survivors to eighty-two.

12. See report: https://alarmphone.org/en/2020/08/23/four-shipwrecks-in-one
-week-off-libya/.

13. https://sciabacaoruka.asgi.it/en/complaint-to-the-un-human-rights-committee
-over-the-role-of-italy-malta-and-libya-in-violating-the-right-to-leave-libya-resulting
-in-denial-of-the-rights-of-asylum-seekers/ and https://ecre.org/med-fight-for-justice
-over-pushback-case-amid-continuing-deaths-rescues-and-pullbacks-to-libya/.

Chapter 10

Autonomy of Migration in the Age of Deportation

Migrants' Practices against Deportation

Leandros Fischer and Martin Bak Jørgensen

INTRODUCTION

In light of the so-called refugee crisis, research in migration and critical border studies has emphasized migrants' agency in resisting repressive border regimes. Some recent studies within digital migration studies have emphasized the role of information and communication technologies (ICTs) in these practices (Dekker et al. 2018; Gillespie et al. 2018; Smets et al. 2019) and argued that the reconfiguration of platform and electronic devices has strengthened the agency of migrants, thus providing an argument for the "autonomy of migration" (AoM) approach. Most of these studies have examined movements from North Africa and the Middle East/Turkey and looked at migrants' routes into Europe, investigating how the European border regime has sought to restrict access (Brinkerhoff 2009; Diminescu 2008; Leurs 2014; Leurs and Smets 2018; Milivojevic 2019; Siapera 2014). In several European countries today, we can identify a paradigm shift from migrant integration to the securitization of migration and deportation (e.g., Banai and Kreide 2017). In Denmark, the government in 2019 changed the name of social benefits available for refugees from an "integration benefit" to a "return benefit" and has generally stepped up deportations. At the same time, we see an expansion of the category of deportable populations. This politicization of immigration in Denmark has caused enormous insecurity among migrants. Similar tendencies can be observed in Germany, where the end of an institutional *Willkommenskultur* (politics of welcoming as illustrated by Chancellor Merkel's statement "we can do this") has been met with an increase of deportations to Afghanistan and the Balkans (Hamman and Karakayali 2016; Smolarski 2018). This means that potential deportees and undocumented migrants increasingly have to develop survival strategies for if and when they are deported. Furthermore, migrants are starting to share information and strategies online on how to return to Turkey and the Middle East. In the case of Denmark, we see a still increasing number of people disappearing from the authorities and going to other European countries living as irregular migrants or trying to apply for asylum through loopholes in the Dublin agreement. We see, for instance, a larger number of rejected asylum seekers from Scandinavia applying for church asylum in Germany, Iraqi Kurds going to Italy, Afghanis going to France, and Palestinians going to Belgium due to networks or new policy practices (as informed and shown by solidarity activists in Denmark; also Bathke 2021). We are interested in *how decisions to stay on the move and resist being deported are shaped though digital practices and how such practices form digitized sites of care*. Our aim here is explorative. We cannot necessarily assume that the dynamics of ICT and digital practices are the same as when the same person or group made the journey to the countries that rejected their request for asylum. There may be other variables and risks at stake in this latter type of mobility and other types of knowledge involved, which may depend on other infrastructures of connectivity and (digitized) sites of care. Hence, our explorative focus in this article begins by investigating if the use of ICTs by potentially deportable subjects differs from those on the move. To this end, the methodology of our research consisted of both analogue and digital research.

This chapter is based on qualitative interviews with migrants within the asylum systems and solidarity activists conducted by the authors in Hamburg, Germany, and northern Denmark between late 2018 and the summer of 2019. We have done six formal and informal interviews at different sites in Denmark and four individual interviews as well interviews with two families in Hamburg. The contacts to our interlocutors were established through solidarity networks at both sites. In Denmark we also include one interview with a solidarity activist. The interviews were conducted by the authors of this chapter and research assistant Alaa Izzat Saleem Abu Almeiza. All names are anonymized. We deliberately include interlocutors from one city (Hamburg) and one region (northern Denmark). The sites represent different phases for people on the move. The selection of both case studies was based on the interconnectedness of their loci; during the "summer of migration,"

Hamburg was both a destination and a transit point for Balkan route migrants en route to Scandinavian countries such as Denmark. However, the closure of the German-Danish border in 2015 did not signal the end of all movement. Instead, we are witnessing movements (or desires thereof) in both directions and born out of various motivations. We therefore included interviews with interlocutors from Denmark being in the process of applying for asylum or having had their claims for such rejected to be able to examine how deportability becomes a factor in their daily lives. In addition to this analogue fieldwork, we discuss the role of an online Facebook group, here called Platform—an information-sharing portal of migrants, both of those on the move as well as those wishing to relocate to other European countries—that was mentioned by different interlocutors. We do not include any literal material from the group but will use examples of the same kind of topics that one will meet in the group. We did not make use of "media-device tours," as well coined by Mollerup (2020), where the researcher gets the informant to show the researcher digital practices and applications on their smartphone, but had our research assistant discuss the Platform with people who had used it. We are not interested in the technical aspects of the Platform as such but in the meaning it offers as an infrastructure of connectivity and a digitized space of care. The group—and other groups like this one—are important to understand how migrants exercise agency within and against the European asylum regime. We discuss this kind of digital resistance and connectivity to explore the latent tension between balancing an ethical approach to working with vulnerable groups, on the one hand, and not playing down AoM's focus on migrant agency, on the other (see in particular Fischer and Jørgensen 2022; Sandberg et al. 2022).

The chapter proceeds as follows. Initially, we discuss autonomy of migration in the age of deportation as an attempt to posit a theoretical and conceptual framework to guide our analyses. In terms of analysis, we first look at the case of Germany and in particular Hamburg as a main hub for people on the move. Second, we look at the sites in Denmark and discuss how the latest political and policy developments have amplified the reactions against deportation. Third, we discuss the role of digital spaces as examples of digitized sites of care, knowledge, and solidarity. We end the chapter with a brief conclusion.

AUTONOMY OF MIGRATION IN
AN AGE OF DEPORTATION

Our investigation of anti-deportation strategies is largely based on elements from the AoM approach, and specifically the concept of the "mobile commons" (Papadopoulos and Tsianos 2013; Parsanoglou, Trimikliniotis, and Tsianos 2014). Influenced by the Italian *autonomia* tradition, AoM emerged as a direct response to a "methodological nationalism" (Glick, Schiller, and Wimmer 2002) in migration studies and corresponding perceptions of migration as an objectifiable process conditioned exclusively by structural "push" and "pull" factors. Migration is theorized instead as linked to the agency of migrants themselves, specifically the desire for the freedom of movement, "an elemental and constitutive force in the ongoing unresolved struggles that are implicated in making and transforming our socio-political world" (Tazzioli et al. 2018, 243). In addition, the desire for movement should not be simply conceptualized as merely the need for social mobility, but as one also motivated by a condition of "stuckedness" and a lack of "existential mobility," the "sense that someone is going somewhere in life" (Hage 2009). Such conditions of stuckedness are proliferating within a context of deepening crisis, affecting both legal citizens and non-citizens alike.

Although early interventions by AoM stressed migrant autonomy against attempts by sovereign borders to classify them in legal categories, the European so-called refugee crisis has witnessed attempts at developing the concept further. Given a global turn toward the illegalization of migrants as deportable subjects, the latter are actively contesting their status as "refugees" as a form of "strategic essentialism" (Tazzioli et al. 2018, 245), denoting both a right to receive protection as well as the right to decide *where* to receive this protection; migrants do not simply desire the right to stay but want—like those enjoying full civil rights—to decide themselves where their place of settlement should be. This means that often migrants risk a secure existence in one state to live in another one, motivated by a sense of justice. The inherent subversiveness of such autonomous practices must be viewed in conjunction with the creation of "global deportspora" (Nyers 2003) consisting of illegalized and/or deportable subjects, a process accelerated since the "war on terror" in the early 2000s and the exponential increase in "irregular citizenship" (Nyers 2018) and threat of denationalization for unwanted citizens. In the case of Europe, some authors have located the creation of a "European space of circulation" (Karakayali and Rigo 2010) of deportable citizens, as co-constitutive of a growing tendency of externalizing borders (Casas-Cortes et al. 2015). As such, the production of deportable subjects must not be viewed as an aberration from otherwise liberal migration regimes, but co-constitutive of the creation of new exclusionary collective identities in times of crisis by invoking a "spectre of migrant illegality" (De Genova 2013).

The most concrete example of externalization combined with an increase in deportability within the European context can be chronologically situated in the period following the "summer of migration" in 2015. On the one hand, humanitarian (and sometimes paternalistic) discourses of welcoming deserving "refugees" were overnight transformed into their dialectical opposite, positing the figure of the "illegal" and potentially dangerous "migrant," resulting in an increase in the number of deportations in countries such as Germany. On the other hand, this process has gone hand in hand with measures, such as the 2016 EU-Turkey externalization agreement, the precedent of which can be found in similar agreements negotiated by the Italian government and the deposed Libyan regime some years earlier. A clear example of this reconfiguration concerns the physical border between our two case studies, Denmark and Germany. Whereas a train ride from northern Germany to Denmark is a mundane affair, passport controls imposed by Denmark since 2015 make the journey a stressful one, not just for migrants but also racialized European citizens, more likely to be viewed with suspicion by border police. This combination of events has seemingly suffocated the room for the freedom of movement of migrants, enclosing them in an unwelcoming European space, whose legal configurations seem to condemn them into a state of constant and sometimes clandestine mobility from one European country to another.

While research on migrant agency within and against the European border regime before 2015 appears to posit the existence of a single European space of mobility, current events challenge this perception, as we are witnessing a renationalization of border practices *within* Europe. It is indeed our contention that the various creative practices of migrants on the move reconfigure our understanding of "core" and "periphery" in Europe, especially when perceptions of linear migration flows from the former to the latter have been instrumentalized by regimes to generate ideologies legitimizing the exclusion of migrants, such as in present-day Hungary, where the government is using the specter of migration to present itself as a defender of "European values" (Kallius et al. 2016). Countries, such as Hungary or Greece, might be peripheral in our common understanding of geography, but in the context of the Dublin Regulation that condemns migrants to an existence at the margins of Europe, they can also represent a core one tries to leave from, or escape/return to. In addition, we ask what the decision of some migrants to return to transit countries like Turkey or even to Syria tells us about the periphery-core linear migration paradigm. Contrasting dominant discourses of a "migrant question," we conceptualize the practices of migrants as pointing to the existence of a "European question" (De Genova 2016) instead; new border restrictions within Europe respond to migrant agency, telling us more about "Europe" than about migration itself.

In exploring the way in which ICTs shape the various strategies of migrants circulating within Europe, we rely on the framework of the mobile commons, a concept that needs to be continuously updated and extended, and that encapsulates the innumerable uncoordinated but cooperative actions of mobile people that contribute to its making. People on the move create a world of knowledge, of information, of tricks for survival, of mutual care, of social relations, of services exchange, of solidarity and sociability that can be shared, used and where people contribute to sustain and expand it. (Papadopoulos and Tsianos 2013, 190)

Digital "infrastructures of connectivity" (Papadopoulos and Tsianos 2013, 190) constitute a basic component of the mobile commons, providing those on the move with useful information, whether in the form of navigation apps, social media, online for a, or simply as "hardware," such as battery-loading docks for smartphones present along the Balkan route prior to its closure. Likewise, they constitute digitized sites of care, where connections, safety, and knowledge are shared to offer alternative care structures for those in need. The digitality of the mobile commons points to the fact that border zones should not be understood primarily as geographically fixed points, but rather shaped by numerous power relationships, as well as the practices of migrants on the move (Tsianos 2015, 115). As such, agencies like Frontex make extensive use of data collection, biometric and otherwise, and surveillance technologies as do national authorities (see Meaker 2018), to which migrants respond with their own digital practices, such as strategically switching phones on and off to remain undetected, or by using social media to create solidarity relations with local activists.

GERMANY: A BRIEF WINDOW OF WELCOMING CULTURE

The so-called refugee crisis unfolded in a number of places. However, Germany's experience remains emblematic, owing to both the country's size and its location at the heart of Europe. Refugees fleeing wars in Syria, Iraq, and Afghanistan began arriving in the country at the start of the last decade. Nonetheless, the expansion of the "Islamic State," and the deteriorating conditions in Turkey, the most important transit country for Syrian, Iraqi, and Afghan refugees, combined to produce a mass exodus that began in 2014 and culminated in the "summer of migration" in 2015. Important here was Angela Merkel's decision to open the borders to refugees. This was probably after realizing that the Dublin II Regulation—requiring refugees to file asylum application in the first EU country they arrive to—was made null and void by their agency, specifically their crossing of the Balkan corridor. Merkel's decision accelerated this movement, leading to an unprecedented wave of solidarity among the local population (Hamman and Karakayali 2016).

However, the social repercussions, specifically a growing wave of racist attacks against accommodation centers, soon led Merkel to backtrack. Eager to win back conservative voters amid the rise of the right-wing populist Alternative for Germany, the government accelerated the pace of deportations, culminating in 25,375 deportations in 2016 (BPB 2021). This policy reversal reached a peak with the 2016 EU-Turkey agreement spearheaded by Merkel, and the forceful return of the paradigm of border externalization. In this case, the institutional framework matters in two senses. On the one hand, asylum applications are processed through the so-called Key of Königstein (*Königssteiner Schlüssel*), a mechanism that allocates refugees to the country's 16 states according to their population and financial capabilities. On the other hand, deportations have followed the same pattern, with North Rhine-Westphalia, the most populous state, and southern conservative Bavaria and Baden-Württemberg leading in numbers (Bundeszentrale für Politische Bildung 2021). Nevertheless, deportation is a real and existing danger even for refugees in more liberal states.

The German case study of our research focuses on the northern city-state of Hamburg, the country's second largest city, and a key transport link to Denmark and Sweden. Activists have made use of this geographical location; some solidarians mention knowledge of people who have transported people to the Danish borders in their cars, prior to its closure. Indeed, three of our interview partners mentioned the presence of a large number of volunteers at the city's main station, providing northbound refugees with train tickets to continue their journey. Despite being a transit destination in 2015, Hamburg was for many refugees a final destination, but also a point of *forced remigration*. This is a trend rather than an absolute rule. Denmark is still a preferred destination for certain politically active refugees, such as those from the ethnic Arab minority in Iran, who cite a better level of protection for their community there than in Germany. However, the overall trend has been one of securitization in Scandinavia, with Germany becoming a default country of destination. This constitutes a significant shift, placing more responsibilities on German solidarians, who in interviews mention their past admiration of Scandinavian asylum policies as more humane compared to those of Germany. In the following section, we focus specifically on the cases of Ali, Khaled, and Mohammad from Syria, as well as Khalida and two families from Afghanistan. Without extrapolating generalizations about the situation of all refugees in Hamburg, we wanted to find out the ways that led them to Hamburg, as well as the role played by ICTs in this decision.

While the Danish government's decision to close the border ended Hamburg's transit character, the different configurations of asylum policies in Scandinavian countries have forced some refugees to return to the city. The two Afghan families interviewed are symptomatic of this case. Both live together under church asylum in Hamburg, having previously lived in Sweden independently from one another and having their asylum applications rejected there. At the beginning, Germany was a transit destination for both families. The first family said they thought that the further north they traveled, the better, indicating that if possible, they would even go to Finland. Passing through the northern German port city of Rostock, they eventually came to Sweden by ferry, where the authorities forcibly took their fingerprints. The second family passed through Hamburg on their way to Denmark, which they avoided because they were told that their chances for asylum in Sweden were better. In both cases, knowledge of mobility as a mobile commons (where to go, where chances of asylum were better) fused with a cognitive geography of north as synonymous with prosperity and well-being. The prevalence of the second was strengthened by the families' relative lack of experience with technology; they both acquired their smartphones on the move and were dependent on information by smugglers along the way. In addition, both mention taking no safety precautions when using their phones. The same inexperience with ICTs is observed in the case of Ali, who comes from Damascus. Barely eighteen at the time of our interview, he traveled with his uncle from Turkey by boat from Greece and via the Balkan route to Germany. During his trip, they were relying on others who had access to navigation smartphone apps for information. Settling in Hamburg, Ali did not receive refugee status but subsidiary protection, which makes the task of bringing over his parents from Syria more difficult. At the same time, other refugees from Afghanistan like Khalida were more successful. Despite having relatives in Sweden, her family was told beforehand that the situation for Afghans was difficult there, so they arranged for a Schengen visa to Italy, to which they flew from Dubai, circumventing the Dublin system. From there, the family traveled to Hamburg, where they successfully applied for asylum.

In Sweden, the two Afghan families were sent to refugee accommodation centers while waiting for their applications to be processed. Eventually, the applications of both were rejected multiple times in the course of three years, on the grounds that not enough information was provided, in addition to Afghanistan being considered a "safe" country. However, they had spent a considerable amount of time in Sweden—three years—during which they had used their smartphones to navigate daily life there, even learning some Swedish. After being deported, they made their way back to Germany, where their applications were also rejected in two states, Bremen and Mecklenburg-Vorpommern, forcing them into church asylum in Hamburg. Church asylum is an ambivalent term. Churches do not enjoy, nor do they claim, extraterritorial status, and law enforcement agencies can theoretically access church premises anytime. However, church asylum supporters justify their actions with reference to the constitutionally guaranteed right to asylum, fighting an uphill battle as the state has increasingly rejected the validity of church asylum (MacGregor 2019). Nonetheless, it must be emphasized that the majority of deportations in Germany affect rejected applicants from the Balkans, specifically Albania, Kosovo, and Serbia. Deportations to Afghanistan have gained more notoriety. Despite not listed as a safe country of origin, the protection rate for Afghans has dropped from 77.6 percent in 2015 to 42.5 percent in 2020 (Flüchtlingsrat NRW 2021). Hamburg is known to deport Afghans solely in cases of crime, terrorism, or identity theft (ProAsyl 2019). The consequence for the two Afghan families is currently a life in limbo, where they have to tread extremely carefully in their daily lives amid a securitized discourse on migration, as to not be inadvertently criminalized.

Other refugees in Hamburg have been more successful with their goals, and some evidence suggests that this might be related to their greater proficiency in ICTs. Khaled from Syria came to Greece by boat from Turkey. His smartphone was his prime instrument of navigation. He mentions switching his phone off while on the boat to avoid detection, later switching it on every ten kilometers to download maps. His story is similar to that of Mohammad, also from Syria, who followed the same route to Germany, to avoid being drafted in the military. As a former employee at Syria's largest mobile provider, he had expert knowledge on what apps to use and which to avoid, as he witnessed the Syrian regime's use of surveillance technology firsthand at his workplace. Both interviewees had prior knowledge of Germany before embarking on their journeys. Khaled had studied there fifteen years ago and even had a job offer but could not get a visa at the German consulate in Istanbul. Mohammad did all his research on the internet while in Turkey and after being unable to find work in the Gulf states. Khaled mentions a mobile commons of knowledge among people on the move, whereby the Scandinavian countries are considered best for family reunifications, and Germany is seen as the best country for career advancement. Some professionals like doctors had better luck in having their diplomas recognized in Germany, sometimes bringing family from Sweden. Others have reconfigured their initial plans for Sweden and Denmark, following the harsher policies adopted by these countries. As in the case of the Afghan families and Khalida, structural factors—restrictive migration policies in Scandinavia—have transformed Germany from a transit to a destination country for refugees. However, ICTs and the "infrastructures of connectivity" can provide those on the move with agency and an advantage, the possibility to plan ahead, making knowledge ICTs a form of social capital.

DENMARK: THE ARCHITECTURE
OF DETERRENCE POLICIES

The "refugee crisis" arrived in Denmark the first Sunday of September 2015. Before that particular day, the crisis was something taking place on Greek islands, in Eastern Europe, or at German train stations. For the broad public and Danish politicians, it had little to do with Denmark. That perception changed abruptly on Sunday September 6, 2015. During the following week, fifteen hundred refugees entered the country, many of them with no intention of applying for asylum in Denmark as their destination was Sweden. This was the triggering event evoking the notion of "refugee crisis" in Denmark. The Sunday encounter had its own timeline and spurred different reactions from both the public and the authorities. That afternoon, the first large group of refugees and migrants arrived at Rødby on the island of Lolland. Five hundred refugees crossed the border within twenty hours and the situation was described as chaotic and out of control (Agustín and Jørgensen 2019; Róin 2016). The "long summer of migration" had also come to Denmark. On the following Wednesday night, the Danish police gave safe-conduct to all the refugees who stayed in Padborg and Rødby. They were allowed to leave the places they stayed to move on to Sweden, which was the desired destination for the vast majority of them. The police gave up detaining the hundreds of refugees refusing to cooperate and be registered. The refugees blocked trains and, in the end, the police issued a safe-conduct for people wanting to move on.

The decision to offer the Sweden-bound refugees safe-conduct to pass through the country led to criticism from other EU member states. The Swedish Prime Minister Stefan Löfven (from the Social Democrats) launched massive criticism, and the chairman of the Swedish Left Party (Vänsterpartiet) termed Denmark a "Hungary light" (Expressen, September 10, 2015).

The actions taken by the refugees refusing to be registered and insisting on moving where they want to in a post-Schengen European political reality (at the time) can be read through the AoM perspective. AoM makes mobility and migration the starting point of analysis and conceptualizes migrants as having agency. In this way, borders follow migration—and not the other way around—by constituting collective action that challenges institutional power to reshape the border regime. AoM "seeks to reinterpret the effects of seeing regular, irregular, transit and other forms of migration as constitutive factors of border policies, architectures, and practices" (Casas-Cortes et al. 2015, 897). In the words of Angela Mitropoulos, the "concept of autonomy was a way of thinking of the act of migration itself as a political act" (2010).

As mentioned in the introduction, different studies have shown how migrants circumvented the border regimes and managed to follow the different routes as they developed and transformed from Greece, through the Balkan corridor to Austria or Germany or further north to Scandinavia. In the interviews, we have several accounts on the role and use of ICT. Almost all of our informants used them to get access to smugglers. No one attempted to cross the Mediterranean without such. They have told us in detail when to hide your phone, when to turn it off, when to buy local SIM cards, and when not to. Often smartphones had mundane purposes, as they do for people not on the move (e.g., staying in touch with family and friends). Basically, they function as digitized sites of care. ICT becomes part of the mobile commons. They constitute "[v]irtual spaces such as chatrooms, Facebook, emails as well as the spaces of the camps and of migrant neighbourhoods [that] are the spaces that help one stay mobile, collect information about routes, possibilities for survival and learn tactics of existence" (Papadopoulos and Tsianos 2013, 190). What is interesting about the Danish case is that very few of the people we interviewed had the deliberate intention of ending up in Denmark. The first goal was reaching Greece or Italy. "When I arrived in Italy, I called many people and my friend. I asked which country was the best" (Amena, April 2019). Some of them arrived in southern Europe and when there tried to figure out where to go next—others had family in Sweden, which they hoped to connect to. Several of them were caught at the border and forced to apply for asylum in Denmark after the free-passage possibility had closed down. Knowledge of mobility is not static but always changing. The comments and experiences given here illustrate different dimensions—*knowledge of mobility* and *infrastructures of connectivity*—of the mobile commons.

Initially, thousands of people applying for asylum received it. However, looking at the rejection rate in 2018, it rose to 66.1 percent in Sweden and dropped to 44 percent in Denmark. However, the numbers of applicants vary between the two countries. In Denmark, 3,559 applied for asylum in 2018 whereas 21,502 applied in Sweden (Nyt fra Danmarks Statistik 2019; Asylumineurope.org 2019). The rejection rates likewise differ for different nationalities, with some groups like the Afghans having a high rejection rate in both countries. The push by different member states to get the European Commission to force the Afghan government to accept rejected Afghan asylum seekers may see a new turn with the Taliban takeover of the country in August 2021. However, the political ambition of deporting rejected asylum seekers is strong, and just one week before the complete takeover by the Taliban the Danish government tried to get the Afghan government to accept the deportation of Afghans from Denmark (Høj et al. 2021). The consequence, regardless of the differences (of national background), is a situation with more than fifteen thousand applicants rejected just in 2018. On top of these, we can add the undocumented migrants, the over-stayers, and other categories. We know from studies on irregular migration and studies on deportation regimes that people who have had their claim for asylum rejected rarely just return to their home countries. Hence, the emerging questions are the increasing threat of deportation (i.e., both the decision and the actual act of deporting): What kind of autonomy is possible under the deportation regime, and how do the mobile commons adjust accordingly?

Fast forward to 2019 and 2020. In the Danish case, a growing number of rejected asylum seekers are placed in deportation camps such as Kærshovedgård and Sjælsmark. The local deportation regime does not enact deportations as much as making conditions for the people placed here intolerable in order to make them accept return (Freedom of Movements Forskningskollektiv 2018). Rejected asylum seekers, who for different reasons remain undeportable, have become the center of a series of repressive government policies aiming to "make their life intolerable," in the words of then-Minister of Immigration, Integration and Housing Inger Støjberg (quoted in Skærbæk and Klarskov 2016), thus making forced deportation into voluntary return. Very few people placed in the camps accept this. In November 2019, 419 deportees had disappeared from Kærshovedgård (Skærbæk 2019). Some 773 disappeared from Sjælsmark over a five-year period, amounting to one-fourth of the total number placed there (Søndergård Ingvorsen 2020). Not only people at risk of deportation are disappearing, though. We also know from our interviews that people still in the process, for instance with an open case in for appeal, are disappearing. For some people, Denmark was never the imagined end destination or has turned out to be impossible to remain in. The decision to disappear necessitates a different kind of analysis able to understand the changing dynamics of mobility and immobility and power relations within multiple intersecting geographic scales (Glick Schiller and Salazar 2013). The mobility regime (the right to enter a country and apply for asylum) here is defined by immobility (the rejection of the claim and placement in deportation camps), but for some met with practices of mobility. People disappearing do not reject the asylum system but use information to organize mobility and knowledge on where to re-apply. As such, following Papadopoulos and Tsianos (and their reading of Rancière), this kind of politics should not be seen as "acts of resistance but as attempts to create a new situation that allows those who have no part—to enter and change the conditions of social existence altogether" (2013, 188). Here we see sharing of information being pivotal and ICT playing an important part as an infrastructure of connectivity. Our informants tell us about several families they know of who have left Denmark to seek asylum in other European countries. Some people have succeeded in getting asylum in England. A common statement is "in Denmark, there is nothing" (Reem, March 2019). These windows change all the time as the mobility regime is reconfigured. For a period in 2018 and 2019, a larger number of deportees made it to Germany where they sought church asylum on special humanitarian grounds. When this opportunity closed down during 2019 (MacGregor 2019), people changed strategies. In 2021, it again became possible to apply for church asylum in Germany (Bathke 2021), and we have later heard of people going to Germany to try to avoid deportations in Denmark. One solidarian tells us how she helped a rejected asylum seeker to get from Kærshovedgård to Germany and later in 2019 got a call on Viber from the person who had been successful in getting asylum in Scotland (Grethe, February 2019). Living with the risk of deportation makes people plan to disappear from Denmark. Another informant told us in detail how her case was rejected five times and that she received deportation orders twice. Still she is in Denmark (Maya, February 2019). Last time the police offered to book her a ticket to Cairo and give her pocket money to make it to Gaza, where she is from. This was not a possibility for her. It is too dangerous to cross Sinai. Instead, she started gathering counter-information through her extended network and discovered that Belgium (in 2019) was taking up claims for asylum from Palestinians. If she could make it to Belgium and live there for half a year irregularly, it would be possible to get a new case opened in Belgium. She had planned everything and found a safe place to stay in the Palestinian network but ultimately had to let go of the plan as it required her to pay six hundred euros a month to cover costs.

The different stories show how the mobile commons—as knowledge, infrastructure of connectivity, solidarity and claims for justice, and digitized sites of care—are essential to navigate the mobility regime. Migrants like the ones we talked to not only follow the development of the policies, but their actions also shape them. It was autonomous acts and practices of solidarity that created the church asylum opportunity. The authorities (Federal Office for Migrants and Refugees) closed it down, but people find new ways of staying mobile and seeking protection.

THE PLATFORM: AS A MOBILE COMMONS

In the communication and interviews with our informants, it became evident that ICT plays different roles and purposes in different stages of one's life. All of the informants had used ICT when they were on the move but often for very mundane purposes (e.g., keeping contact, chatting with friends). Mundane does not mean unimportant, but as an important aspect of these digitized sites of care ICT served a purpose of both providing information but also creating a kind of normality. Some informants told us about specific sites that they had used to gather information about routes, or finding connections that could help them onward. Some had used social media sites to find information about destination countries. One such site, which we call Platform, was formed on Facebook in 2015. All posts are written in Arabic. As of early 2021, it had more than 330,000 members. According to one of the founders, it "relates to the fact that you don't have a home, you're lost, tired, etc. A group that only helps with finding a route/way to flee and not e.g., getting legal papers. It's a closed group, as no human smugglers are allowed to join" (interview with founder, YouTube, October 2015; translation Alaa Izzat Saleem Abu Almeiza). The group is one of several that all have the aim of supporting people who need information and support to navigate the European border regimes. Other groups offer information on sea conditions (write and share about the sea, weather conditions), but the Platform is by far the biggest of such groups. The group has been mentioned in newspapers around the world and as such is no secret. Here we nonetheless refrain from mentioning the name or any source that would make it identifiable.

In the openly accessible without membership introduction text to the group, the "refugee crisis" is mentioned as the reason for having such a group despite being formed in 2014. Syrian refugees are mentioned specifically: "No embassy opened its doors to them, and none of them, except for proceeding in 'illegal' ways that pose many risks" and "many Syrians chose to proceed with these deadly risks, and full of dangers and adventures, but they are unaware of these methods and their steps, and it is necessary to advise someone who has tried this before them. From here came the idea of our group" (Facebook description 2020; our translation).

We are not members of the group ourselves, but got the information about the dynamics and topics discussed in the group from a member of the group. It seems that people use both their own profiles and profiles made for the occasion to post questions. Often a post is made to ask a question, and it will be deleted soon after answers have been given. The group is a closed group where one has to apply for membership that is approved by one of the admins. However, a group with more than 330,000 members is de facto open, and it is easy to see how anyone could gain access if they wanted to, including police and border agencies. This is probably a reason why the rules of the group stipulate that human smugglers have no access, nor may deals be made with smugglers or brokers.

The site is both a constantly evolving knowledge base of mobility and an infrastructure of connectivity. Often the questions relate to routes, "Good evening. Is there a way for a person to travel from Turkey to Germany or from Syria to Germany? It has to be a guaranteed way and not too expensive." Posts can receive hundreds of comments with experiences and suggestions. Questions posted reflect the migrants' perception of having the right to decide *where* to receive protection. Some questions, moreover, express the stuckedness and motivation spurred by this to claim justice through mobility. As stated by Papadopoulos and Tsianos, people on the move create a world of knowledge, information, tricks for survival, mutual care, social relations, services exchange, and solidarity and sociability (2013, 190). Although the rules of the group stipulate that smugglers are not allowed, nor should the use of such be encouraged, many posts relate directly to getting access to people who can facilitate mobility (sometimes referred to as smugglers, sometimes in other terms "I know a person"), asking into the quality and integrity of specific smugglers, prices, speed, and security. The answers to these posts often warn against the proposed plan (e.g., answers like "it is too dangerous traveling on your own as a woman," "that route is closed," and "even if you make it there is no chance you will get asylum, go to Germany, brother") but almost all support the decision to cross borders. Immobility and lack of security is considered immoral—border crossing is not. The shared knowledge on routes, openings, people, and resources in the group is constantly updated and constitutes a mobile commons.

The borders of Europe are not only geographical and physical; they are also digital and expansive. The border authorities and agencies apply digital surveillance and screening tools as well as creating comprehensive databases shared between the EU countries. Although one element of these also is internal (i.e., making sure that the receiving countries keep the responsibility), other elements are external and set up to keep the borders closed and only penetrable by the ones assessed "worthy." People on the move know this and seek to disrupt the system. The border struggles are also fought online through knowledge sharing and disruptive tactics. When the European Union and Frontex configure the access to the European Union in one way (as with the EU-Turkey agreement from 2015 and the establishment of the "hotspots" in Greece), people insisting on mobility reconfigure the border in another.

Several posts on the platform relate to screening procedures and databases. Some examples could be posts like "if a person has a visa to country A, can he go to another country to seek asylum and which country can 'break fingerprints' from country A?" and "does Spain break Greek fingerprints and accept asylum from Palestinians from Gaza?" Some posts inquire about low-tech strategies to counter high-tech border control (the passport and central and verified registration), whereas other posts ask query techniques, procedures, and legal frameworks. The answers often are followed by assessments of the country in question (e.g., "There is no country that can break country A's fingerprints. People in country A flee from there"). We hear that people are often given correct information (at the time of posting) but also misinformation. This type of organic knowledge bank collects both facts and experiences but also wishful thinking. However, the shared knowledge of the platform does reveal the cracks, loopholes, and counter-information.

The Dublin I–III Regulations are not flawless, and member states act differently within the regulations. Such practices are notified and shared by the users here. At the time of collecting data, Belgium had opened up for re-assessing Palestinians' claims for asylum instead of returning them to the member state where the asylum seeker had first claimed asylum. Or the fact that Belgium at the time had much higher approval rates for Palestinians applying for asylum made other Palestinians leave the country they were in, live irregularly in Belgium for the required months it takes for the prints to be deleted from the Eurodac database, and apply anew (see also Lemberg-Pedersen and Halpern in this volume). Prior to this, Afghan deportees had sought to get to France and re-apply as France at the time had started re-assessing claims for asylum from Afghans. Others have tried to get to Spain where the regions have discretionary powers in regularizing irregular migrants if they have had a job and a place to stay for a specific period. These practices can from the perspective of the state be seen as illegal, but from the perspective of the poster and people denied mobility they are perceived as justifiable. Some were forced to apply for asylum in a country they had no desire to reside in; others had given up hope for a normal life and decided their claims for protection were better fulfilled elsewhere.

In late 2019 and the first months of 2020, we heard about an increase of posts relating to deportation and questions asked how to navigate within the deportation regimes. People seek information on what do to when deported (new routes, places to avoid, time to pass before it is possible to apply again). People share experiences of having been deported and now seek to return to Europe again. Europe's borders do not start in Greece. For people on the move, they are faced strategically already in Syria. People here know of the dangers and risks and still pursue mobility. The existential immobility is harder to accept than the concrete dangers and risks. Connectivity and counter-knowledge help them navigate the border spectacle (cf. De Genova 2013, 2016).

Similar dynamics characterize the choices and wish for mobility for people already being deported or facing deportation. There is a proliferation of posts inquiring into safe spaces, procedures, cracks, and loopholes in 2019 and onward. The Platform in this stage is a mobile commons comprising knowledge, care, and connections.

As with examples of people asking about routes, procedures, and practices the previous years, the answers given to these contain both accurate and wrong information. As such, anti-deportation strategies and mobility in the "global deportspora" (cf. Nyers 2018) are an example of what autonomy of migration looks like in the age of deportation and how migrants are a constitutive force in reconfiguring both the external and internal border regimes.

Mobile commons, like the Platform, play an important role for that type of agency in everyday strategies. Returning to Papadopoulos and Tsianos:

> The mobile commons, that is the real world of moving people, is assembled and materialised in these fields of everyday life. . . . In fact, the autonomy of migration approach is only possible if it contributes to creating conditions of thick everyday performative and practical justice so that everyday mobility, clandestine or open, becomes possible. This is a form of thick justice which creates new forms of life that sustain migrants' ordinary movements. The sustaining of such forms of life is driven by the immediacy of the quest for justice. And from the perspective of migration justice is the making of daily social relations, connections and conditions that evade the control of mobility. (2013, 192)

CONCLUSION

In this contribution, we presented a brief outline of the contemporary experience of deportation by focusing on the experience of migrants in Germany and Denmark, as well as online. In doing so, we attempted to ask the question if the digital practices of migration differ qualitatively from those threatened with deportation. The short answer is that there is a tremendous degree of overlap between the two, because migration in itself is not a linear process leading from an imagined periphery to a center. "Center" and "periphery" lose their significance in the shadow of a permanent European regime of mobility and immobility that structures the lives of a growing number of migrants. Migrants post-2016 are caught within a continuously evolving and nationally structured border regime, where repression and deportations have reasserted themselves as the norm, following the aberration of the "summer of migration." The German-Danish frontier is a perfect example of how an otherwise inconspicuous border has for migrants become an impenetrable wall one tries to cross or cross again in search of a better life. Nevertheless, migrants claim not only a right to asylum but also the right to choose where to receive this asylum. By reconfiguring their asylum and bordering practices, European states are reacting to the agency of migrants, not the other way around.

There are many continuities between the use of ICTs while making a journey to a desired destination and their use when threatened with deportation or seeking "escape routes" (Papadopoulos, Stephenson, and Tsianos 2008) out of forced immobility. Whether crossing a border or "disappearing" from the authorities, migrants use ICTs as a mobile commons providing crucial information on the formulation of future survival strategies.

If there is a vital difference, it is quantitative: the growing sophistication with which migrants use ICTs *after* they have reached what is at the time perceived as their final destination. Migrants do not only face restrictive border and deportation regimes, but additionally have to confront false perceptions ("the further north, the better") as well as disinformation. The examples of the Afghan families in Hamburg and the Platform stand out as two chronically opposed extremes. Whereas the families acquired proficiency in ICT use during the journey, thus suffering from a lack of information that was detrimental to their quest of asylum, the Platform acts as an increasingly sophisticated community of mutual care.

REFERENCES

Agustín, Ó. G., and M. B. Jørgensen. 2019. *Solidarity and the "Refugee Crisis" in Europe*. Cham: Springer.
Asylumineurope.org. 2019. "Overview of statistical practice." https://asylumineurope .org/reports/country/sweden/statistics/.
Banai, A., and R. Kreide. 2017. "Securitization of migration in Germany: the ambivalences of citizenship and human rights." *Citizenship Studies* 21 (8): 903–17.
Bathke, Benjamin. 2021. "Germany eases restrictions on church asylum." January 15. *InfoMigrants*. https://www.infomigrants.net/en/post/29675/germany-eases -restrictions-on-church-asylum.
Brinkerhoff, Jennifer M. 2009. *Digital Diasporas: Identity and Transnational Engagement*. Cambridge: Cambridge University Press.
Bundeszentrale für Politische Bildung. 2021. "Abschiebungen in Deutschland." https:// www.bpb.de/gesellschaft/migration/flucht/zahlen-zu-asyl/265765/abschiebungen.
Casas-Cortes, M., S. Cobarrubias, and J. Pickles. 2015. "Riding routes and itinerant borders: Autonomy of migration and border externalization." *Antipode* 47 (4): 894–914.
De Genova, N. 2016. "The 'crisis' of the European border regime: Towards a Marxist theory of borders." *International Socialism* 150: 31–54.
De Genova, N. 2013. "Spectacles of migrant 'illegality': the scene of exclusion, the obscene of inclusion." *Ethnic and Racial Studies* 36 (7): 1180–98.
Dekker, Rianne, Godfried Engbersen, Jeanine Klaver, and Hanna Vonk. 2018. "Smart refugees: How Syrian asylum migrants use social media information in migration decision-making." *Social Media + Society* 4 (1): 205630511876443.
Diminescu, Diana. 2008. "The connected migrant: An epistemological manifesto." *Social Science Information* 47 (4): 565–79.
Expressen. 2015. "Löfven: Der finns en bred samsyn." Expressen.se, September 15. https://www.expressen.se/nyheter/darfor-bjuds-inte-sd-in-till-flyktingmotet/.
Fischer, Leandros, and Martin Bak Jørgensen. 2022. "Impossible research? Ethical challenges in the (digital) study of deportable populations within the European border regime." In *Research Methodologies and Ethical Challenges in Digital Migration Studies. Caring For (Big) Data?*, edited by M. Sandberg, L. Rossi, V. Galis, and M. B. Jørgensen. London: Palgrave.

Flüchtlingsrat NRW. 2021. "Fakten zu Flucht und Asyl." https://www.frnrw.de/top/fakten-zu-flucht-und-asyl-2020-21.html.

Freedom of Movements Forskningskollektiv. 2018. *Stop Killing Us Slowly. En forskningsrapport om de motivationsfremmende foranstaltninger og kriminaliseringen af afviste asylansøgere i Danmark.* Copenhagen: Freedom of Movements Forskningskollektiv.

Gillespie, Marie, Souad Osseiran, and Margie Cheesman. 2018. "Syrian refugees and the digital passage to Europe: Smartphone infrastructures and affordances." *Social Media + Society* 4 (1): 2056305118764440.

Glick Schiller, N., and N. B. Salazar. 2013. "Regimes of mobility across the globe." *Journal of Ethnic and Migration Studies* 39 (2): 183–200.

Hage, G. 2009. "Waiting out the crisis: On stuckedness and governmentality." *Anthropological Theory* 5: 463–75.

Hamann, U., and S. Karakayali. 2016. "Practicing Willkommenskultur: Migration and solidarity in Germany." *Intersections. East European Journal of Society and Politics* [S.l.] 2 (4): 69–86.

Høj, Emil, Ulrik Dahlin, and Sebastian Gjerding. 2021. "Til det sidste pressede regeringen på for at få sendt asylansøgere tilbage til Afghanistan." *Information*, August 18. https://www.information.dk/indland/2021/08/sidste-pressede-regeringen-paa-faa-sendt-asylansoegere-tilbage-afghanistan?fbclid=IwAR2DQx4H8xb7XvjL9hc9QQLjw3XLeFEEZYUO05OtuPpYjkIE8SkqUtPJhmY.

Kallius, A., D. Monterescu, and P. K. Rajaram. 2016. "Immobilizing mobility: Border ethnography, illiberal democracy, and the politics of the 'refugee crisis' in Hungary." *American Ethnologist* 43 (1): 25–37.

Karakayali, S., and E. Rigo. 2010. "Mapping the European space of circulation." In *The Deportation Regime. Sovereignty, Space, and the Freedom of Movement*, edited by Nicholas De Genova and Nathalie Peutz, 123–44. Durham, NC: Duke University Press.

Leurs, Koen. 2014. "Digital throwntogetherness: Young Londoners negotiating urban politics of difference and encounter on Facebook." *Popular Communication* 12 (4): 251–65.

Leurs, Koen, and Kevin Smets. 2018. "Five questions for digital migration studies: Learning from digital connectivity and forced migration in(to) Europe." *Social Media + Society* 4 (1): 205630511876442.

McGregor, Marion. 2019. "Almost zero chance of church asylum in Germany." *Infomigrants*, October 7. https://www.infomigrants.net/en/post/19994/almost-zero-chance-of-church-asylum-in-germany.

Meaker, Morgen 2018. "Europe is using smartphone data as a weapon to deport refugees." *Wired*, July 2. https://www.wired.co.uk/article/europe-immigration-refugees-smartphone-metadata-deportations.

Milivojevic, S. 2019. "'Stealing the fire,' 2.0 style? Technology, the pursuit of mobility, social memory and de-securitization of migration." *Theoretical Criminology* 23 (2): 211–27.

Mitropoulos, A. 2010. "Interview with Angela Mitropoulos." *Shift Magazine* 18–20.

Mollerup, N. G. 2020. "Perilous navigation: Knowledge making with and without digital practices during irregularized migration to Öresund." *Social Analysis* 64 (3): 95–112.

Nyers, P. 2018. *Irregular Citizenship, Immigration, and Deportation.* London: Routledge.

Nyers, P. 2003. "Abject cosmopolitanism: The politics of protection in the anti-deportation movement." *Third World Quarterly* 24 (6): 1069–93.

Nyt fra Danmarks Statistik. 2019. *Nyt fra Danmarks Statistik* 27. marts 2019 - Nr. 116.

Papadopoulos, D., and V. S. Tsianos. 2013. "After citizenship: autonomy of migration, organisational ontology and mobile commons." *Citizenship Studies* 17 (2): 178–96.

ProAsyl. 2019. "Übersicht: Abschiebepraxis Afghanistan." https://www.proasyl.de/wp-content/uploads/2015/12/%C3%9Cbersicht-Abschiebepraxis-Afghanistan-Stand-Februar-2019-konvertiert.pdf.

Róin, Philip. 2016. "Da medborgere blev menneskesmuglere." *Information*, May 13, 14, section 3.

Sandberg, M., L. Rossi, V. Galis, and M. B. Jørgensen. 2022. *Research Methodologies and Ethical Challenges in Digital Migration Studies. Caring for (Big) Data?* London: Palgrave.

Siapera, Eugenia. 2014. "Diasporas and new media: Connections, identities, politics and affect." *Crossings: Journal of Migration & Culture* 5 (1): 173–78.

Skærbæk, Morten. 2019. "419 udlændinge er forsvundet fra Udrejsecenter Kærshovedgård." *Politiken*, November 6. https://politiken.dk/indland/art7481765/419-udl%C3%A6ndinge-er-forsvundet-fra-Udrejsecenter-K%C3%A6rshovedg%C3%A5rd.

Skærbæk, Morten, and Kristian Klarskov. 2016. "Støjberg vil »utåleliggøre« tålt ophold." *Politiken*, June 1. https://politiken.dk/indland/art5624285/St%C3%B8jberg-vil-%C2%BBut%C3%A5leligg%C3%B8re%C2%AB-t%C3%A5lt-ophold.

Smets, Kevin, Koen Leurs, Myria Georgiou, Saskia Witteborn, and Radhika Gajjala, eds. 2019. *The Sage Handbook of Media and Migration.* First edition. Thousand Oaks, CA: SAGE Inc.

Smolarski, C. 2018. "Fluid identities and navigating integration: The politics of solidarity in contemporary Germany." *Crossings: Journal of Migration & Culture* 9 (1): 45–59.

Søndergård Ingvorsen, Emil. 2020. "773 udlændinge fra Sjælsmark er forsvundet fra myndighederne." *Information*, January 29. https://www.dr.dk/nyheder/indland/773-udlaendinge-fra-sjaelsmark-er-forsvundet-fra-myndighederne.

Tazzioli, M., G. Garelli, and N. De Genova. 2018. "Autonomy of asylum?: The autonomy of migration undoing the refugee crisis script." *South Atlantic Quarterly* 117 (2): 239–65.

Trimikliniotis, N., D. Parsanoglou, and V. Tsianos. 2014. *Mobile Commons, Migrant Digitalities and the Right to the City.* New York: Springer.

Tsianos, V. S. 2015. "FeldForSchung in den 'MoBile coMMonS.'" *Zeitschrift für Medienwissenschaft* 7 (1): 115–25.

Wimmer, A., and N. Glick Schiller. 2002. "Methodological nationalism and beyond: nation-state building, migration and the social sciences." *Global Networks* 2 (4): 301–34.

Chapter 11

Migration and Counter-Information Practices

Enhancing Mobility while Subverting the Mainstream Media

Vasiliki Makrygianni and Vasilis Galis

FROM CORPORATE MEDIA TO COOPERATIVE GRASSROOTS MEDIA CULTURE

There is a growing critique within media studies regarding the democratic deficits embedded in a corporate-dominated, highly commercialized media system. Particularly, these deficits refer to inequalities of access, issues of representation and political/ideological power, economic and structural alignment with globalizing capitalism, and proliferation of consumer culture (Carroll and Hackett 2006). Moreover, mainstream media has been accused of reproducing migration critical and xenophobic discourses (d'Haenens et al. 2019; Titley 2019). At the same time and to counter these deficits and discourses, social movements, and people in solidarity with migrants, have taken advantage of the spectacular technological changes since the popularization of the internet and digital media. They are early adopters of digital technology, and they use digital media in creative and alternative ways for inclusive organizing and to encourage alternative forms of participation in democratic politics (Uldam and Vestergaard 2015). Activists also build these digital media collectives in hopes of counteracting the commercial influence and racist politics of mainstream media and for creating a space for solidarity actions (Downing 2001; Atton 2004; Fuchs 2010). In the same manner, digital media have been utilized by solidarians and migrants for the preparation of migratory trips as they are strongly linked to the decision of departure and facilitate aspects of organization (Gillespie et al. 2016).

There is a growing number of self-organized digital collectives created and used by migrants and people in solidarity to provide *counter-information*. Counter-information, that is, the diffusion of information on social struggles and solidarity from below, is among the most important and widespread practices of contemporary grassroots movements (Dalakoglou and Vradis 2011; Metropolitan Sirens 2011). Various digital platforms, both commercial and self-organized, that act as spaces of solidarity have been created or appropriated by solidarity communities that provide counter-information, and they challenge both discursively and materially the idea of borders and actively facilitate freedom of movement. In this chapter, we will empirically describe and conceptualize how counter-information digital platforms become a lens and a tool for shared decision-making, information spreading, and navigation among solidarians and migrants crossing the borders and entering Europe through the Greek-Turkish borderland. Crucially, the ways in which migrants and people in solidarity appropriate and repurpose these platforms, rather than simply use them, have received less attention. In the following, we will present our theoretical framework focusing on the concepts of counter-information, *detournement*, and counter-citizenship, our methodological toolkit, and finally the analysis of our interview material.

THE EMANCIPATORY POTENTIAL OF COUNTER-INFORMATION

Counter-Information: An Act of Detournement

The concept of counter-information is not an officially recognized term, that is, corporate media and mainstream journalists do not accept this form of news broadcasting and information sharing as valid, orthodox, and reliable (even if they often and unofficially use counter-information as a source). On the other hand, counter-information opposes institutional ways of providing information to the public sphere; therefore, it is a counter-praxis. There are grassroots movements that are competitive and hostile toward state control and organize their own channels of information to promote their own interests and communication practices. Spreading the news on alternative channels, bypassing mainstream channels of information, and creating crucial knowledge for vulnerable groups are some of the main goals of counter-information practices. Often, counter-information derives from people's mistrust of the official channels that leads to "system avoidance," that is the state *where individuals choose unofficial or non-monitored channels and services over those that are official and generate data* (Brayne 2014 in Latonero and Kift 2018, 7). Ever since such practices entered the digital sphere, solidarity has been greatly reinforced. According to Metropolitan Sirens (2011), counter-information consists of two basic elements: "[F]irst, it is organized from below and, second, it serves the needs of the movement that is competitive and hostile toward authority and by extension, it stands in competition with mainstream media since the latter serves the interests of authority" (134–35).

Moreover, counter-information relates to the ways technology can be adapted or shaped by activists to serve purposes other than those intended by its designers (Jordan and Taylor 2004; Coleman and Golub 2008). For us, this constitutes an act of *detournement*. The Situationists defined detournement as "rerouting spectacular images, environments, ambiences and events to reverse or subvert their meanings, thus reclaiming them" (Lasn 1999, 103). Regarding media culture, Holt and Douglas (2012) suggest that it is about "turning expressions of the capitalist system and its media culture against itself." Grassroots movements have a long tradition of reclaiming media technologies, divorcing them from their corporate originators, and reinventing media's uses in ways not intended by their designers (Croeser 2014; Rodríguez et al. 2014; Tufekci 2017). Thus, the praxis of counter-information also involves detourning media technologies to mobilize civil society across the political spectrum, organize protest, enable information sharing, communicate a cause, and deconstruct racist, authoritarian, and liberal rhetoric (Galis and Neumayer 2016). Counter-information is also an act of refusal to corporate news broadcasting (Metropolitan Sirens 2011), moving toward solidarity through information sharing.

Counter-Information: An Act of Enhanced Mobility

When it comes to mobile populations, counter-information practices not only facilitate people's mobility around the globe, but they also deconstruct corporate media's biases about the newcomers and challenge sexism and racist rhetoric (Gemi et al. 2013; Stolic 2019). They enforce the distortion of boundaries imposed by identity and place and question dipoles such as those of legality/illegality and migrant/refugee. At times, they act as a "digital lifeline" (Maitland 2018), that is, (a) the use of digital media by migrants to ensure their physical mobility in terms of getting informed, planning their journeys, and staying in contact with smugglers and solidarians (Newell and Gomey 2015; Gillespie et al. 2016; Dekker et al. 2018); and/or (b) a "hotline" for travelers who find themselves in emergency situations when crossing borders toward Europe (see, for example, Stierl 2016; Heller et al. 2017). Counter-information also entails dangers and problems. Broadcasting news from below does not always guarantee the validity of the information or prevent the spreading of false information and fake news through corporate social media (Gillespie et al. 2018; McCabe and Harris 2021). On several occasions (2016, 2019), false information was spread about new routes to western Europe through Greece and the so-called Balkan corridor, leading to clashes between migrants and the Greek police.[1] Another example is the propagandistic attempt by German right-wing websites to raise alarm that Germany was facing an alleged storm of sexual assaults committed by migrants, fueling panic about the recent influx of newcomers and the safety of women in the country. As we will show in the empirical section of the paper, migrants and solidarians have developed counter-information media projects not only to facilitate the migratory journey at every point of the journey—in their country of origin, along the route, or in the places where they hope to start a new life—but also to counter misinformation and racist propaganda (see also Farkas and Neumayer 2017). From a political economy perspective, digital media (especially corporate social media) *recuperate* solidarians' and migrants' production of content, which contributes to the social media industry's corporate power instead of challenging it. Consequently, radical and anti-hierarchical political and migrant projects demand creative and inventive appropriation of digital media to turn them into agents of political change and solidarity with migrants (Galis and Neumayer 2016).

Counter-Information: An Act of Resistance against Bordering Practices

In this context, counter-information constitutes an act of resistance through detournement of bordering practices, racialized spaces, and racist corporate media rhetoric as it enables transnational movement of populations and counters stereotypes built upon the identity of the migrant. According to Hands (2010, 97), "acts of resistance ensure the maintenance of a space of collective interaction, of coming together, of creating recognition and solidarity and thus enabling all sorts of other forms of multiple communication and collective action, and for 'the scream' to be spread." In this respect, counter-information as a resistance practice is about sharing and accelerating the spread of information among those in need. Moreover, counter-information practices are enabled to overcome "information precarity" (Wall et al. 2017) and mean to subvert the power of hidden information and misinformation. It is common that counter-information pursuit derives from people's mistrust of the official channels that leads to "system avoidance," that is the state *where individuals choose unofficial or non-monitored channels and services over those that are official and generate data* (Brayne 2014, quoted in Latonero and Kift 2018). As solidarity practices very often entail a form of disobedience, it is about subverting the current *state of affairs*. Counter-information creates a digital space for migrants to navigate the complex landscape of information and border regimes en route to Europe (Borkert et al. 2018), an encounter and commoning (Trimikliniotis et al. 2014) formed by people in solidarity and people on the move. Counter-information practices enable people's movement and transform from a means of communication to a means of mobility.

Moreover, counter-information also subverts borders and enclosures paused by commodification processes. Counter-information practices question the role of information as a commodity as very often they subvert the commercial purpose of the digital spaces and information itself. Thus, in our case, the social media engaged for counter-information processes transform momentarily from accelerators of the circulation of capital (see Manzerolle and Kjøsen 2012) into means of enhancement of human mobility. Both groups and individuals participating in the arena of counter-information stand against commodification of information, as they provide it in solidarity with refugees and not in exchange for money. All our informants made it clear that the sharing and circulation of information was not mediated by money or any other exchange currency. In a world where capital moves easier than certain people (Gillespie 2018), counter-information is not only a means of people's unconditional transnational circulation but also a means of subverting the dominant role of social media platforms.

A NOTE ON METHOD

This chapter mainly draws from research conducted in the framework of the research project DIGINAUTS (2018–2020), which was accomplished by eight researchers of different disciplines based at the IT University of Copenhagen, the University of Copenhagen, and the University of Aalborg operating in three different sites (Danish-Swedish borders, Danish-German borders and Hamburg, and Greek-Turkish borders and Athens). While the wider research experience informed our data, this chapter focuses on research conducted on the Greek site. We conducted twenty-five semi-structured interviews in Athens, Lesvos, and Chios during the period 2019 to 2020 and twelve semi-structured interviews during our preliminary research in Athens and Thessaloniki in the summer of 2016. In total, we interviewed forty-one people of different genders and sexual orientations. At the time of the research, the informants belonged to the age group of twenty to forty years old. Most of the interviewees had recently migrated from countries of the Middle East and Africa; five of them (also recently migrated) had both conducted the trip and were actively involved in solidarity and counter-info grassroots groups and practices; six of them were European citizens, born and raised in Europe, who acted as solidarians with the mobile populations. We interviewed people who had migrated from Syria, Egypt, Iran, Iraq, Palestine, Cameroon, and Afghanistan for various (and many times overlapping) reasons, like gender violence, sexual discrimination, war conflicts, poverty, and racism. There are significant ethical and practical difficulties when conducting research regarding solidarity acts. Given the fact that such acts were and still are persecuted by state authorities, we carefully selected our questions in order not to draw any type of information that could ultimately endanger any vulnerable subjectivities, although in several cases the interviewees were more than willing to share information on their practices led by the belief that these practices were just. To protect our sources, we used pseudonyms and we filtered the information taken before it was exposed to the public view. We recruited some of our informants by meeting them randomly in public space, and we also used academic contacts to get in touch with people in solidarity and migrants participating in grassroots initiatives. Both sources led to more informants (snowball effect). In the beginning of the fieldwork, it was not difficult to find people on the move on the Greek site as during the time of the research most of them were using the Greek public space as a site of leisure and as an escape from their residencies (nongovernmental organization [NGO] apartments and camps). Due to ethical concerns, we did not interview any people residing in public space (out of respect for their personal sphere) and we did not conduct any research with people detained. All our informants had access to information and communication technologies. They shared with us videos, pictures, and online pages as they were describing online counter-information practices.

COUNTER-INFORMATION PRACTICES: FROM MEANS OF COMMUNICATION TO MEANS OF MOBILITY

Counter-information in the digital sphere involves a set of human and non-human actors: it consists of devices, cables, and antennas, and groups and individuals that position themselves in solidarity with mobile populations. In migrants' case, smartphones are of the most used devices throughout the journey, and they are part and parcel of a set of tools and tactics that facilitate communication and enable migrants' mobility. The summers of 2015 and 2016 confirmed that digital media play a significant role in the management of migrants' mobility (Sajir and Aouragh 2019). As Noori (2020) argues, "from the perspective of 'via politics' this is not merely an instrument but in itself a disobedient intervention and part of an irreducible zone of knowledges, tactics and politics" (quoted in Walters 2016, 435).

Counter-information is essential for the migration trajectories, since it (a) facilitates navigation—for accessing and exchanging information on routes and destinations; identifying, mapping, and navigating safe/unsafe passages; and circumventing and resisting border controls—(b) promotes networking and negotiating—for contacting various actors (smugglers, temporary contacts, networks of support, etc.); and (c) provides care and contact—for keeping in touch with family and friends; monitoring the routes of others; being able to access "digital care" by volunteers, solidarity workers, and organizations; and translation tools—(d) constitutes a lifeline during the trip—for sending alarms while at sea and for seeking protection from (or revealing) abuse.

Facebook and Twitter constitute dominant spaces of information exchange among migrants and of propaganda of solidarity acts, whereas WhatsApp is broadly used for direct communication between the mobile populations (Frouws et al. 2016; Sánchez-Querubín and Rogers 2018). Social media are key players in counter-info practices along with (self-organized) digital collectives like those of "Lesvos Solidarity," "Refu.com," "Are you Syrious," "Borderline Europe," "Aegean Boat Report," and the Watch the Med Alarm Phone Project. An assemblage of different technologies (platforms and devices, hardware and software) is used, depending on the geographic area, the accessible means by migrants and solidarians, etc. Alex, a member of the Alarm Phone group, explains:

> We receive a lot of emergency notifications via Facebook, via WhatsApp. So, we use different technologies through which we can be reached although the front hotline is our main way to circulate our number . . . since October 2014 we have assisted in about 2,500 emergencies at sea and the majority came from the Aegean Sea, about 1,500 boats. (Interview with Alex, November 2018)

Most of these groups and collectives in solidarity with migrants were formed to respond to the urgent need for information regarding survival and navigation for both the sea and land borders. Another informant who was involved in sharing news briefings for the "Are you Syrious" group notes that his group started by spreading information on means of transportation: "In the late 2015, one of the founders of 'Are you Syrious' started to publish . . . I think it started with train timetables . . . of the trains that were going from Serbia to Slovenia, going through Croatia" (interview with John, December 2018).

At that time, there was an urgent need for information regarding different trajectories, ways, and means of transportation that these grassroots groups tried to fulfill by employing several platforms. In this effort to enhance human mobility, they attempted to trespass barriers of communication (often coming from institutional/mainstream sources) such as those of language, misinformation, lack of information, or even excess of information. Overcoming language barriers is a crucial task to make information accessible to non-locals and to all non-English or Greek speakers as it seems that in the Greek context during the period of 2015 and 2016 there was a high demand of information in Arabic languages that formal institutions were not able to fulfill. Many of the groups and individuals that promoted counter-information practices dedicated much time to translating news and documents to make them accessible to the non-western language speakers (interview with John, December 2018).

However, it is not only the movement toward Europe that is at stake but also the counter-/reverse-movement due to the numerous illegal pushbacks that take place in borderlands (Amnesty International 2020; Border Violence Monitoring Network 2019; Protecting Rights at Borders 2021). Such groups make use of migrants' testimonies and personal stories to highlight racist actions (coming from state institutions) and deconstruct the anti-migration neoliberal rhetoric. These groups disrupt state misinformation, like for example declarations of nation-state representatives denying the pushbacks (see European Council on Refugees and Exiles 2021) that even mainstream media report as false allegations (see, for instance, Stevis-Gridneff 2020). This means that by providing valuable information to those on the move and by revealing secret and violent pushbacks, counter-information tactics attempt to highjack the trajectories ordered by the hegemonic European regimes. These counter-information practices open the path for the detour of the directions of human movements in favor of migrants, whether this detournement concerns enhancing (and accelerating) movement toward the desired (for migrants) destinations or the obstruction of authorities' attempts to perform illegal pushbacks (by raising the issue in the public debate).

Counter-Information in Action en Route to Europe

Counter-information is spread beyond borders and in various scales starting from a molecular level (e.g., someone's device) and spreading to larger audiences. Access to such information facilitates surpassing physical boundaries posed against human mobility. While migrants navigate, they need different types of information according to the different phases of their trip. Counter-information sites provide help for those wishing to cross the borders but also for people reaching European territories either in camps or in urban environments. In a not necessarily linear sequence, information is crucial: (a) before the trip and during the decision-making process, (b) during the trip and the navigation, and (c) during settling down, either in camps and deportation centers or in the urban cores. One informant, Rosa, both a member of a rescue team but also as a person who used these practices to cross the borders, describes the different people, types of information, and geolocations that were involved during the first days of her trip:

> There is a team in Mytilene that provide the first aid . . . and if they need a lawyer. In my case, I contacted them because I needed a lawyer . . . and they told me "because you are a refugee in Greece and you live in Athens, we have a lawyer in Athens, we have a lawyer in Thessaloniki" and I was in contact with the lawyer. (interview with Rosa, April 2018)

As Rosa explains, different people are involved in rescuing actions, using social media to secure migrants' survival. Moreover, in most cases, counter-information practices entail the simultaneous involvement of various geolocations when it comes to solidarians. Rosa explains that people who use the same type of technologies while residing in different geolocations manage to join forces and collaborate toward a common goal, that is, being in solidarity with people on the move (interview with Rosa, April 2018). This digital collaboration is also affected by physical space and its materialities as it involves devices, cables, antennas, groups, and individuals that position themselves in solidarity with mobile populations. Technologies used in accessing and spreading information differentiate according to different geolocations. For example, when crossing different borders throughout the Mediterranean, access to networks varies according to reception availability. One of our informants, a member of the Alarm Phone group, described the ways they had to adapt to different conditions of the geographical sphere:

> We work differently in the different regions on the Mediterranean Sea because just the modalities of crossings are so complex and different . . . in the Aegean Sea because of the reception is nearly everywhere. . . . It's very different in the central Mediterranean where the distances are much longer so that you don't have coverage in that area and so . . . most boats, although this has changed and now it seems like it's more normal again to have a satellite phone on boat . . . so there are like different fluctuations. (Interview with Alex, November 2018)

Demographics of the mobile population are connected both with different accessibility in technologies as well as with different levels of technological literacy and habits. Practically, that means employing different technological artifacts while adjusting to the different geographies of technology in the Mediterranean. As Alarm Phone Alex notes:

> And it's also different demographic mostly, like a lot of Syrians, people from Iraq, Afghanistan . . . they usually have smartphones or at least some of the people on the boats have smartphones so that they could reach out to us very

easily through Facebook, WhatsApp and phone calls. People coming from Morocco, they used to have old mobile phones so you couldn't transmit a GPS signal. So, we had, like, to try and base our search for the location on the things they could see around them. The condition of the sea, whether they had used an engine or just paddles, when they had left, of course from where and so on . . . how many people they were on board . . . so that was a bit of a guessing game . . . this has changed because more and more people now use smartphones, also from Morocco, which is a really important shift. (Interview with Alex, November 2018)

Moreover, the spreading of counter-information is not exhausted in digital space but also relies on analogue modes of exchange. Leaflets and word of mouth are crucial and complementary to digital practices. The analogue sphere merges with the digital world creating a hybrid of digital/analogue routes and networks of information. Alex mentions:

A woman who came from Syria . . . had discovered our phone number written on the arm of another person wanting to cross and she didn't know anything about the Alarm Phone but she just called the number because she could speak English . . . and so she reached out to us and we stayed in touch with her and *then* we basically followed her as she was walking along the Balkan route in 2015 and then we met her in Germany. (Interview with Alex, November 2018)

Geographies of counter-information spread in the analogue and digital spheres. In some cases, the digital connectivity promotes the geographical expansion of solidarity and counter-information projects. Such expansions are curved and usually follow mobile populations' trajectories. Counter-information sites not only spread accordingly to mobile populations' primal routes but also flourish the moment these populations reach European ground. As we will show in the next section, on these sites information is still valuable to survive in racialized and exclusionary territories such as the camps and detention centers or the new to them urban environments.

COUNTER-INFORMATION: A SITE OF CONTESTATION AND A PLACE OF DIGITAL ENCOUNTER

Counter-information practices create a contestation site against mainstream politics as they promote autonomy and independence of mobile populations. In the current digital age, migrants not only have the possibility of arranging their journey more independently, but they are also empowered to conduct their everyday lives in the western context. In this respect, Zijlstra and Van Liempt (2017) mention the importance of knowledge of the availability of welfare payments and services, such as unemployment benefits and state support for migrants. Basic everyday information such as city spaces and neighborhoods friendly to newcomers and shops that provide migrant-related supplies and services (such as telecommunication services) is circulated through counter-information networks that operate in their native languages.

One of our informants, Muhammad, in his forties, coming from Syria, along with three other migrant friends, created a Facebook page to facilitate migrants' access in the job market. As Muhammad mentioned, his motivation was to create a space where Arab-speaking migrants could exchange information directly without having to be mediated by informal job agents. In his case, he found his first job through another migrant, whom he had to pay twenty euros. Thus, his motivation was to surpass such mediations and to self-organize one of his basic needs. In his own words:

> I ended up having this page because of a situation that happened to me. When I had arrived in Athens, I met someone and I asked him about jobs, so he asked me "what is your profession?" and I told him that I am a tailor and the guy told me that "I know someone that could hire you but in order to connect you to this guy you have to give me twenty euros." So, I gave him the money and I found a job and I thought that it is not nice to blackmail someone to find a job. So, I thought about making this group where the guy who has the job put his number, so people can find immediately what they are looking for, without people in the middle. (Interview with Muhammad, November 2018)

Muhammad and his friends attempted to surpass mainstream channels of information precarity in their effort to contest their precarious state as unemployed migrants. They managed to some extent to surpass mediators that used to exploit them. In this case, mediators were not coming from state authorities or big corporations but were also migrants withholding (and commodifying) valuable information. Such counter-information practices contest actively power relations by promoting solidarity among the subalterns while breaking the circulation of the capital coming from blackmailing practices.

Issues of visibility and invisibility are also at stake within counter-information practices. On the one hand, gaining visibility and therefore being heard and present is a core issue among mobile populations. That includes visibility in the public sphere by spreading information regarding migration and breaking the monopoly of information held by state authorities. For instance, one of our informants, Petros, a Greek solidarian from Lesvos, describes how difficult it was for migrants and solidarians to share information before the wide use of smartphones. As he explains, there used to be very strict policies against spreading photos of the refugee camps before 2010 as migrants were deprived of their devices when entering the camp of Pagani in Lesvos, and

NGO workers were under strict surveillance from police officers and guards in order not to shoot photos. According to Petros, an incident in 2007 during a No Border camp manifestation was a viral moment for spreading information with the use of digital technology:

> During the No Border during one of the first contacts between migrant prisoners and solidarians, the latter gave them from a window a camera . . . it was in the children's space [a space in the camp where children were placed] . . . and this was the first time that images of Pagani came out, images from inside a cell. . . . So, a very good connection was made, and technology was used so to reproduce images to the world outside. . . . The video was very intense. . . . It went viral. (Interview with Petros, January 2019)

Petros's narration shows that social media use that is nowadays often taken for granted was an issue at stake back in the day. While we do not perceive in this chapter media technology as manna from heaven, such cases highlight social media as a powerful weapon against authorities' efforts to impose a totalitarian control in spaces like migrants' camps. In Pagani, people's disobedience turned expressions of the capitalist system against itself as mobile devices were turned into "dangerous artifacts" for the cohesion of the nation-state and its racist propaganda. Visibility of counter-information processes and groups might also serve as a protection shield against persecution. It is a strategy for creating safe spaces and allies in the public sphere. At the same time, anonymity provided by such practices offers the necessary invisibility to vulnerable subjects that would be endangered if exposed to media. Accumulation of testimonies, images, and facts toward a counter-information project (personal or collective) might put at risk certain people or their relatives and friends left behind. However, as some informants point out, the social media sphere often creates an illusion of safety, and several people choose to expose their identities and cases. Another informant, a Greek solidarian named Sara, member of an LGBTQ group located in Greece, comments on the ways migrants often disclose personal information in social media and she describes the ways and strategies to surpass such dangers:

> Members get confused . . . and write in the open group about their medical issues. . . . For example, a child went to the hospital in the emergency room and uploaded pictures from the ambulance. And we have told them countless times in the assemblies: do not upload these things when you enter the hospital. . . . That was one reason I blocked the group [as she was one of the administrators] so as not being able to post such things . . . because they were confused. . . . So, I blocked the wall and check who is posting what. (Interview with Sara, November 2018)

Due to such events, measures of precaution and control are taken to protect anonymity and personal data of the users. Moreover, Sara also explains how they are trying to deal with the constant change of members due to the dynamic character of such groups.

> The LGBTQ group has two Facebook groups. . . . We have a Facebook group for all members who come to the meetings, to communicate and another that is open to members who have been at some point in the meetings. We did this so that previous members who no longer are active won't read about the closed procedures. Because when new members come who do not know the previous members, a little chaos is created. The group is to post the minutes of the assembly and events and for us to get organized. (Interview with Sara, November 2018)

Such dialectics between the benefits of information sharing among counter-info processes (such as commoning knowledge) and the dangers that lurk behind the circulation of information reveal the asymmetries of power in the information terrain and in the digital space. Latonero and Kift (2018, 7) explain that

> it is important to interrogate, then, whether networks serve to proactively connect and aid refugees or whether they instead (or also) make them dangerously accessible to harmful systems, policies, or individuals. . . . However, once collected, data on vulnerable populations can be abused at a later stage, after political winds have changed or public opinion has shifted.

Digital space is a battlefield where counter-information subjects fight against institutional and state mechanisms of enclosures like the official surveillance databases (such as Eurodac or Eurosur). In fact, digital space has largely been occupied by European authorities for discipline, control and surveillance purposes, and migration management and control (see, for instance, Gammeltoft-Hansen and Sørensen 2013; Torpey 2000). Counter-information practices challenge risks and power asymmetries and create multiple sites of contestation. Many grassroots initiatives, aware of the dangers that may invoke exposure to popular digital platforms, take various precautions. John from "Are you Syrious" notes:

> We are very careful with the sources that arrive to us. Like, if someone contacts us through Facebook, we try to bring the conversation somewhere else. Everyone has their own way of doing that . . . and then we bring back on Facebook, I don't know, the material that will be published or we think could be interesting, like we never publish names of the sources that we use. (Interview with John, December 2018)

And while system avoidance or detouring of platforms are very common reactions, at the same time channels of counter-information are hosted in the digital space formed by corporations that empower this system. Corporations like Google or Yahoo[2] have even developed technologies in favor of the mobile populations. Scholars like Latonero and Kift (2018) point to these contradictions and comment on the repurposed digital infrastructures of the private sector: "It remains to be seen whether a digital infrastructure that remains part of a global, privatized, and commercial space and is primarily geared toward making profit can, at the same time, be repurposed for the protection of fundamental rights." Although via different technologies nowadays, it is not the first time that capital intends to recuperate counter-actions to commodify them. While our informants use to a large extent these corporate platforms, there is a crucial repurposing when spreading and sharing counter-information. Moreover, these digital acts have at their core the negation of exchanging information with any sort of currency.

We remain skeptical in the view of this site of contestation where, on the one hand, actors are the most prominent representatives of today's "society of spectacle" (see Debord 1967) that tries to accumulate the efforts of numerous activists and, on the other, vulnerable and precarious subjectivities who choose to fight against all odds. That said, issues of trust are of great importance to people on the move. In this vast terrain of contradictions there might be trust of information and a parallel mistrust of platforms. The distinction between useful information and fake news is a difficult task and the triangulation of data to enhance the credibility sometimes seems almost impossible. People's decisions are often based on rumors and are motivated more by hope and empathy than by reasoning processes of validation. At the same time, trust between people that were either on the move or participated in counter-information as volunteers had been growing strong. Rosa, commenting on how she trusted the first person she contacted to get involved with a solidarity group, notes:

> I didn't know him, and he is not from my city . . . but I gained his trust through social media . . . and when we were taking the step to take the baleen boat from Turkey, the moment that I heard the sound of the wave I got a little bit afraid. But whatever happens I knew that there are my friends they are going to help me. Whatever will happen they will send the rescue team for me to be alive. And of course, I trust them. (Interview with Rosa, April 2018)

In this huge set of people, mutual trust was unavoidable. Digital space and counter-information practices enhance the trespassing of national boundaries and promote transnational synergies between migrants who choose or are forced to trust unknown individuals with their lives. Those who have survived the border crossing owe their lives partly to this condition of random trust to unknown individuals. On the other hand, mistrust of social media platforms often leads groups and individuals to take certain precautions such as encryption and proxy systems. The private sector, state authorities, and counter-information activists, which attempt to ensure their anonymity in the digital sphere, are playing hide and seek. Alex explains:

> Most of our members are skeptical to digital platforms such as Facebook and WhatsApp. So, some of our own communication is encrypted so we use different platforms when we communicate amongst ourselves. And then we have this phone number which seems fairly secure but obviously we change the passwords and so on regularly but, you know, we are such a big network. . . . Most of the people I know communicate via Facebook or WhatsApp and this is just how information circulates among migrant communities who do not belong to one place. Of course, we accept Facebook messages, and we must open a Facebook channel to be reached if this is the dominant way of communication. I mean, you cannot really encrypt Facebook, and WhatsApp is something in between. Ideally people do not give their names or like correct names. What we need is just the location, the accuracy of the informational receive mark which obviously you cannot verify in the first moment, but we can ask certain questions that are based on people who are crossing. (Interview with Alex, November 2018)

However, most of our informants who had already accomplished the trip appeared to delegate a high level of trust to information sharing and the use of social media. Meanwhile, access to valuable information (like during border crossing) generates multiple power asymmetries. It is then that hierarchies and contestations between vulnerable subjects sharpen. Counter-information access appeared to be the breaking point while people were navigating in the Aegean Sea. Rosa describes her experience while on the boat heading to the Greek shores:

> I was responsible at that time and I was in contact with my rescue team. And one person, he had a knife and he threatened me. . . . And me and my brothers sent my mum [to talk to him]. We tried to cool him down in a way that we said that "if you are going to do some mistake, foolish mistake, we are all in the sea . . . we cannot help each other. So we are going all to die, together." . . . Generally, the smugglers that are on a boat don't want a person to be in contact with the rescue team. (Interview with Rosa, April 2018)

Being involved in counter-information practices is also about questioning the dipole of legality and illegality. Many activists, even if they are aware of the illegal status of their actions, are willing to take the risk, and others do not consider even themselves performing illegal actions. After all, whatever is legal is not necessarily ethical and aligned with mobile populations' survival.

As Rosa puts it: "I can say that the team it's not something illegal. It's a team, a rescue team. We have no one to support us. We are volunteers there. And we support them from our pocket money. Until now I didn't get one cent because it's a volunteer job" (Interview with Rosa, April 2018). These contestation sites have as a result persecution of solidarity and repression, coming from state authorities. Spreading the news, providing valuable information for those who wish to cross borders, and empowering vulnerable populations is often considered a criminal act. The last few years, both the Greek state and mainstream media launched a whisper campaign against solidarity with migrants. Self-organized collectives and counter-information projects were criticized, discredited, and criminalized by government officials and reporters/journalists who sympathized with the regime (Rozakou 2017; Gordon and Larsen 2020). Risks and threats come also from non-institutional sources. As John notes about the Croatian "Are You Syrious" site:

> The Croatian group has been very active in reporting on police brutality on the border, publishing reports and stuff. . . . And their offices have been attacked a couple of times by fascists, throwing stones at the window, breaking the windows of the vans so they had to do the work . . . and at the same time, we've seen that we've started to receive many racist and fascist comments or bad reviews on the website . . . on the Facebook page. (Interview with John, December 2018)

Despite the risks, threats, and contestations coming from multiple sites, counter-information practices have been forming a (digital) place of encounter of various subjectivities. The counter-information landscape is constituted by several pages, blogs, groups, and accounts on the web. Synergies between subjects in solidarity groups (like the Facebook group of which Rosa is a member) create hybrid subjectivities, that is people with floating identities between migration solidarity and activism while breaking the dipoles of refugee and migrant, beneficiary and provider, solidarian and migrant. An informant coming from the "Are You Syrious" collective describes the process of information gathering that happens daily and involves various activists from around Europe who have been involved in various geolocations of contestation. In his words:

> There are people from all over the place and we write about all of Europe so it's people that have been involved in Greece, in the Balkan route or in France, in Paris, in the UK, in Scandinavia. . . . The info gathering collective goes through personal contacts and Facebook groups and Twitter and e-mail . . . sometimes people contact us to give us information about activists' and volunteers' groups in different parts of Europe. These are people that have been involved in solidarity movements throughout Europe and then for different reasons got to know "Are you Syrious" and got involved. So we've got people living in Turkey, in

the US, in Norway, Sweden, in Spain. . . . This is how it works. (Interview with John, December 2018)

There are also significant synergies between individuals and groups. Alarm Phone Alex describes how certain individuals became an inspiration for collective solidarity work. These synergies resulted in the empowerment of individual solidarians and the strengthening of the collectives. In his words:

> And the intention was to . . . in some ways, support individuals like father Mussie Zerai[3] who has done this work individually but of course he couldn't . . . you know, he had received calls every day from the center Mediterranean. . . . As the idea was really to support people like him. . . . And the intention was to have a way to be reached from the sea in all the different Mediterranean regions. . . . And then a lot of activists from various places in Africa and Europe came together and there we decided that we really wanted to have a more direct way to engage in the Mediterranean Sea and so for the first time the idea came up to maybe use a phone. (Interview with Alex, November 2018)

Meanwhile, hybrid spaces are formed between semi-institutional and grass-roots initiatives. However, such encounters face several issues due to the different nature of the participants. One of our informants, a member of the Alarm Phone collective, describes one of these coalitions:

> I think Boats4People (an offline network that wanted to do solidarity work in place after many drownings in the Mediterranean) was composed of NGOs and activists. And then it, somehow, inevitably led to some issues, you know, we felt that some of the NGOs, although we trust them and cooperate with them, they had a different decision-making process which usually took longer than one activist had to make decisions. (Interview with Alex, November 2018)

Therefore, even synergies in good faith in crisis times do not always ensure fruitful and efficient collaborations. Structure issues, such as the level of self-organization or the complexity of the articulation of each group, constitute differentiating factors regarding decision-making processes along with the management of practical issues. Furthermore, grassroots initiatives and solidarity processes differentiate from charity and philanthropy traditions. Counter to NGOs and institutionalized groups, they break the barriers between beneficiaries and authorities and reestablish relations between people on the move and those in solidarity.

CONCLUSION: COUNTER-INFORMATION—A DIGITAL PLACE OF ENCOUNTER AND SUBVERSION

Counter-information practices are about creating alternative channels for spreading the news, surpassing mainstream channels of information, and creating crucial knowledge for vulnerable groups. Within this spectrum, there is a double role of digital technologies of information and communication as they act both as persecutors of mobile populations and as facilitators of people's mobility across the globe. As shown, technology can be adapted or shaped by activists to serve purposes other than those intended by its designers. First and foremost, counter-information practices are about detournement as they subvert the mainstream politics of platforms like Facebook or Twitter. Groups and individuals use these social media platforms to facilitate human mobility and border crossing. In this way, they turn surveillance technology against itself as they appropriate infrastructures, recontextualize the distorted messages of power mechanisms, upgrade the characteristics of existing platforms, and escape momentarily state control.

Counter-information also involves appropriating media technologies to mobilize civil society across the political spectrum, organizing protests, enabling information sharing, and deconstructing racist, authoritarian, and neoliberal rhetoric. Such practices empower vulnerable subjectivities like in the cases of the "sans-papiers," LGBTQ people and so many others on the move. In this respect, they enhance human mobility as they either reverse the communication passages and thresholds of mainstream media (Facebook, Google, etc.) or use "underground" passages for subverting power structures and border crossing. While spreading the news, they question the dipole of legality and illegality, and they oppose the commodification of information while they enact empowering tactics that enhance people's unconditional transnational circulation. For many on the move, counter-information processes are a matter of life and death. All in all, digital space of counter-information constantly implies the creation of conditions of possibility for making the journey.

REFERENCES

Al Jazeera. 2020. "Google launches 'Crisis Info Hub' to help refugees." https://www.aljazeera.com/news/2015/10/24/google-launches-crisis-info-hub-to-help-refugees.

Amnesty International. 2020. *Greece: Violence, Lies, and Pushbacks.* London: Amnesty International Ltd.

Atton, Chris. 2004. *An Alternative Internet.* Edinburgh: Edinburgh University Press.

Borkert, M., K. E. Fisher, and E. Yafi. 2018. "The best, the worst, and the hardest to find: How people, mobiles, and social media connect migrants in(to) Europe." *Social Media+ Society* 4 (1).

Brayne, Sarah. 2014. "Surveillance and system avoidance: Criminal justice contact and institutional attachment." *American Sociological Review* April 4.

Carroll, William K., and Robert A. Hackett. 2006. "Democratic media activism through the lens of social movement theory." *Media, Culture & Society* 28 (1): 83–104.

Coleman, E. Gabriella, and A. Golub. 2008. "Hacker practice: Moral genres and the cultural articulation of liberalism." *Anthropological Theory* 8 (3): 255–77.

Croeser, Sky. 2014. *Global Justice and the Politics of Information: The Struggle Over Knowledge*. London: Routledge.

Debord, Guy. [1967] 2013. *The Society of the Spectacle*. Berkeley, CA: Bureau of Public Secrets.

Dekker, R., G. Engbersen, J. Klaver, and H. Vonk. 2018. "Smart refugees: How Syrian asylum migrants use social media information in migration decision-making." *Social Media+ Society* 4 (1).

d'Haenens, Leen, Willem Joris, and François Heinderyckx. 2019. *Images of Immigrants and Refugees in Western Europe*. Leuven: Leuven University Press.

Downing, John D. H. 2000. *Radical Media: Rebellious Communication and Social Movements*. New York: Sage.

European Council on Refugees and Exiles. 2021. "Greece: Authorities deny problems in Moria 2.0 amid record winter, disregard pushbacks as fake news, and continue to violate safe-guards of vulnerable asylum seekers |19 February]." https://www.ecre.org/greece-authorities-deny-problems-in-moria-2-0-amid-record-winter-disregard-pushbacks-as-fake-news-and-continue-to-violate-safe-guards-of-vulnerable-asylum-seekers/.

Farkas, Johan, and Christina Neumayer. 2017. "'Stop fake hate profiles on Facebook': Challenges for crowdsourced activism on social media." *First Monday*.

Frouws, B., M. Phillips, A. Hassan, and M. Twigt. 2016. "Getting to Europe the 'WhatsApp' way." http://www.regionalmms.org/images/briefing/Social_Media_in_Mixed_Migration.pdf.

Fuchs, Christian. 2010. "Alternative media as critical media." *European Journal of Social Theory* 13 (2): 173–92.

Galis, Vasilis, and Christina Neumayer. 2016. "Laying claim to social media by activists: A cyber-material détournement." *Social Media + Society* 2 (3).

Gammeltoft-Hansen, Thomas, and Ninna Nyberg Sørensen, eds. 2013. *The Migration Industry and the Commercialization of International Migration*. New York: Routledge.

Gemi, Eda, Iryna Ulasiuk, and Anna Triandafyllidou. 2013. "Migrants and media newsmaking practices." *Journalism Practice* 7 (3): 266–81.

Gillespie, Marie, Lawrence Ampofo, Margaret Cheesman, Becky Faith, Evgenia Iliadou, Ali Issa, Souad Osseiran, and Dimitris Skleparis. 2016. *Mapping Refugee Media Journeys. Smartphones and Social Media Networks*. Paris: The Open University/France Médias Monde.

Gillespie, Marie, Souad Osseiran, and Margie Cheesman. 2018. "Syrian refugees and the digital passage to Europe: Smartphone infrastructures and affordances." *Social Media + Society* 4 (1).

Gordon, Eleanor, and Henrik. K. Larsen. 2020. "'Sea of blood': The intended and unintended effects of the criminalisation of humanitarian volunteers rescuing migrants in distress at sea." *Disasters*.

Hands, Joss. 2010. @ *Is for Activism: Dissent, Resistance and Rebellion in a Digital Culture*. London: Pluto Press.

Heller, Charles, Lorenzo Pezzani, and Maurice Stierl. 2017. "Disobedient sensing and border struggles at the maritime frontier of Europe." *Spheres: Journal for Digital Cultures* 4: 1–15.

Holt, Douglas B., and Douglas Cameron. 2012. *Cultural Strategy: Using Innovative Ideologies to Build Breakthrough Brands*. Oxford: Oxford University Press.

Jordan, Tim, and Paul A. Taylor. 2004. *Hacktivism and Cyberwars: Rebels with a Cause?* Hove, East Sussex, UK: Psychology Press.

Latonero, Mark, and Paula Kift. 2018. "On digital passages and borders: Refugees and the new infrastructure for movement and control." *Social Media + Society* 4 (1): 2056305118764432.

Lasn, Kalle. 1999. *Culture Jam: How to Reverse America's Suicidal Consumer Binge—And Why We Must*. New York: HarperCollins.

Maitland, Carleen F., ed. 2018. *Digital Lifeline? ICTs for Refugees and Displaced Persons*. Cambridge, MA: MIT Press.

Manzerolle, Vincent, and Atle Mikkola Kjøsen. 2012. "The communication of capital: Digital media and the logic of acceleration." *TripleC* 10 (2): 214–29.

McCabe, A., and K. Harris. 2021. "Theorizing social media and activism: where is community development?" *Community Development Journal* 56 (2): 318–37.

Metropolitan Sirens. 2011. "The (revolt) medium is the message: Counter-information and the 2008 revolt." In *Revolt and Crisis in Greece*, edited by Antonis Vradis and Dimitris Dalakoglou, 133–50. Chico, CA: AK Press.

Newell, Bryce Clayton, and Ricardo Gomez. 2015. "Informal networks, phones and Facebook: Information seeking and technology use by undocumented migrants at the US-Mexico border." *iConference* 1–10.

Noori, Simon. 2002. "Navigating the Aegean Sea: Smartphones, transnational activism and viapolitical in(ter)ventions in contested maritime borderzones." *Journal of Ethnic and Migration Studies* 1–17.

Protecting Rights at Borders. 2021. *Pushing Back Responsibility. Rights Violations as a "Welcome Treatment" at Europe's Borders*. European Programme for Integration and Migration.

Rodríguez, Clemencia, Benjamin Ferron, and Kristin Shamas. 2014. "Four challenges in the field of alternative, radical and citizens' media research." *Media, Culture & Society* 36 (2): 150–66.

Rozakou, Katerina. 2017. "Solidarity# humanitarianism: The blurred boundaries of humanitarianism in Greece." *Etnofoor* 29 (2): 99–104.

Sajir, Z., and M. Aouragh. 2019. "Solidarity, social media, and the 'refugee crisis': Engagement beyond affect." *International Journal of Communication* 13: 28.

Sánchez-Querubín, Natalia, and Richard Rogers. 2018. "Connected routes: Migration studies with digital devices and platforms." *Social Media + Society* 4 (1).

Stevis-Gridneff, Matina. 2020. "E.U. border agency accused of covering up migrant pushback in Greece." *The New York Times,* November 26, sec. World. https://www .nytimes.com/2020/11/26/world/europe/frontex-migrants-pushback-greece.html.

Stolic, Tijana. 2019. "Media representations of migration and racism." *European Journal of Communication* 34 (6): 691–97.

Stierl, Maurice. 2016. "A sea of struggle–activist border interventions in the Mediterranean Sea." *Citizenship Studies* 20 (5): 561–78.

Titley, Gavan. 2019. *Racism and Media.* London: SAGE Publications Limited.

Trimikliniotis, Nicos, Dimitris Parsanoglou, and Vassilis Tsianos. 2014. *Mobile Commons, Migrant Digitalities and the Right to the City.* London: Springer.

Torpey, John. 2000. *The Invention of the Passport: Surveillance, Citizenship, and the State.* Cambridge Studies in Law and Society. Cambridge: Cambridge University Press.

Tufekci, Z. 2017. *Twitter and Tear Gas: The Power and Fragility of Networked Protest.* New Haven, CT: Yale University Press.

Uldam, Julie, and Anne Vestergaard, eds. 2015. *Civic Engagement and Social Media: Political Participation beyond Protest.* London: Springer.

Vradis, Antonis, and Dimitris Dalakoglou. 2011. *Revolt and Crisis in Greece: Between a Present Yet to Pass and a Future Still to Come.* Chico, CA: AK Press.

Wall, Melissa, Madeline Otis Campbell, and Dana Janbek. 2017. "Syrian refugees and information precarity." *New Media & Society* 19 (2): 240–54.

Walters, William. 2016. "The flight of the deported: Aircraft, deportation, and politics." *Geopolitics* 21 (2): 435–58.

Zijlstra, Judith, and Ilse Van Liempt. 2017. "Smart(Phone) travelling: Understanding the use and impact of mobile technology on irregular migration journeys." *International Journal of Migration and Border Studies* 3: 174.

NOTES

1. See for example Euronews (2016) "Desperation in Idomeni - false information spreads about new route to western Europe" and BBC (2019) "Greek police clash with migrants after 'fake news' border movement."

2. See for instance Al Jazeera's (2015) "Google launches 'Crisis Info Hub' to help refugees."

3. Mussie Zerai is a Catholic priest known for his work with migrants crossing the Mediterranean Sea from North Africa to Europe during the recent migration crisis. Zerai was nominated for the Nobel Peace Prize in 2015 for helping save migrants' lives. In 2017, he was under investigation accused of smuggling, in a state attempt to criminalize people helping refugees. More information on his case is available at https://www.bbc.com/news/world-africa-40949062.

PART V

Epilogue

Chapter 12

Afterword

Counter-Mapping the Technology Hype in Migration Studies

Martina Tazzioli

A political genealogy of migration controls cannot be disjoined, historically, from a genealogy of identification technologies. In fact, as the historian Adam McKeown has argued in his seminal book *Melancholy Order* (2008), the emergence of border controls in the nineteenth century went in parallel with, and has been consolidated through, the development of "photography, fingerprinting and anthropometric measurement" (McKeown 2008, 12). Such a historical insight into the longstanding intertwining of mobility controls and identification technologies enables dealing with the (partial) digitalization of the border regime without falling in the trap of presentism. Indeed, the implementation of algorithmic-driven systems in migration governmentality and the systematic use of biometric technologies at the border and in some refugee camps does not come out of the blue. In particular, as critical migration scholars we should be cautious, I suggest, in not reproducing states and private actors' narrative on "digital innovation" in migration and refugee governance. Yet to avoid the trap of presentism in research on migration and technology does not mean stating a full continuity between past and contemporary modes of control. Rather, building on Michel Foucault's understanding of genealogy, it is a matter of foregrounding partial continuities alongside ruptures and transformations on the other (Foucault 2021).

The book *The Migration Mobile: Border Dissidence, Sociotechnical Resistance, and the Construction of Irregularized Migrant*s follows a similar methodological approach, by not conflating the study of technologies at the border with the high-tech and refraining from techno-fetichism. In their intro-duction, Martin Bak Jørgensen and Vasilis Galis point to

> the co-construction of border technologies, sociotechnical resistance to borders and (irregularized) mobility first can help us understand how the global migra-tion regime is changing in the twenty-first century, and secondly to raise critical questions regarding the implications of those technologies and how they poten-tially can remake migration and mobility.

Thus technology is taken in the book as an analytical lens for grasping the restructuring of the border regime and, at once, to question how through border technologies new migrants subjectivities and categories are made up (Hacking 1986). In order to carry on such a research agenda and counter the techno-fetichism that is growing both in academic and non-academic debates on migration and technology, it is key to reverse and disrupt the state-based gaze on migration, or to say it with James Scott, to "stop seeing like a State" (Scott 1998).

This involves, first, disjoining (reflections on) migration from the gov-ernmental reason; that is, it entails not to craft migration as a "problem" and not assuming the position of states that interrogate how to govern migration better. Second, seeing like a state means not reproducing the *technology hype* enhanced by states, humanitarian and migration agencies, as well as by high-tech companies about the use of algorithmic-driven systems for control-ling and supporting refugees (Valdivia and Tazzioli 2021). In fact, the border regime is (still) based on multiple papers and non-digitalized documents that asylum seekers need to keep and show upon request, to confirm their own identity and prove their right to stay. Hence, nowadays it becomes key to study the entanglements of paper-based migrants' identity and the scat-tered data doubles. How does our understanding of sociotechnical systems change if we overturn the gaze and start seeing like a migrant? What does it mean, methodologically, to take stock of the history of technologies at the border, on the one hand, and of the recent transformations occurred through algorithmic-driven systems and through systematic use of digital technology, on the other? Here I engage with these questions advancing what I call a counter-mapping approach to the technology hype in migration studies.

UNDOING PRESENTISM THROUGH
COUNTER-MAPPING

A counter-mapping approach apt at challenging the technology hype in migration studies essentially consists in reversing the states' sovereignty gaze on border technologies. Importantly, counter-mapping should not be confused with techno-pessimism nor with analyses that expose technology as the cause of migrants' exclusion. More concretely, it involves undertaking four methodological moves. First, the "counter" of a counter-mapping approach in this context refers to an analysis that investigates what an insight on technology helps us seeing and what it partially invisibilized about the racialized bordering mechanisms and of border violence. For instance, an exclusive focus on "techno-humanitarianism" (Morozov 2012) and on the technologization of borders detached from the carceral economies in which these are embedded ends up overshadowing the heterogeneity of violent modes of migration containment. In fact, while asylum seekers might be surveilled and tracked inside refugee camps, their lives are simultaneously chocked by bureaucratic hurdles and by being turned into detainable and deportable subjects (De Genova 2020). Saying this does not mean downplaying research on border technologies nor the containment effects that these might produce on migrants. Rather, the theoretical and political stake consists precisely in findings ways of analyzing the entanglements between carceral spaces, digitalized modes of control, and bureaucratic violence and how they mutually reinforce each other.

Second, counter-mapping as a method entails shifting attention from how states and non-state actors uphold the technologization of migration governance and the *care-and-control* narrative they mobilize toward an inquiry on how biometric technologies and algorithmic systems do actually work, not work, and their outcome.

Elsewhere, I have introduced the concept of technologies of expulsion to foreground that digital technologies are mostly adopted in refugee governmentality for obstructing migrants from claiming asylum and getting financial and humanitarian support: "an exclusive focus on how technology enhances surveillance, monitoring and tracking overshadows," I argue, the multiple disruptions and forms of debilitation that asylum seekers experience as forced techno-users (Tazzioli 2021). Technologies are in fact used for both monitoring migrants closely and tracking them at a distance. And yet surveillance is not the only nor the major purpose, as this is often turned into a further obstacle or into a deterrence for migrants to get access to rights, asylum, and financial support. A case in point is represented by the use of digital technologies in the field of asylum, where these work as forced technological intermediations between asylum seekers and humanitarian or state actors.

For instance, since 2016, in Greece people who seek asylum are obliged to book an appointment with the Ministry of Migration and Asylum through a Skype call system, in order to lodge their asylum claim. Moreover, in order to receive update from the authorities or to communicate with humanitarian actors, asylum seekers cannot but use apps—like Viber and, to a lesser extent

WhatsApp. These are often promoted by migration agencies as a way for streamlining the communication channels between asylum seekers and non-governmental organizations or state authorities. In reality, they often become digital barriers that disrupt migrants' access to rights and increase the physical distance with humanitarian actors.

Third, counter-mapping the techno-hype in migration studies involves coming to grips with the methodological quandary between the risk of de-historicization, on the one side, and the importance of studying emergent configurations of the border regime, on the other. In other words, how to trace a genealogy of technologies of migration control in history without overshadowing modes of control, exploitation, and exclusion that are enforced through algorithmic-driven systems or through technologies that where not used in the past? This question confronts us with the interrogation about how, to what extent, and for which purpose a "history of the present"—of contemporary migration governmentality—has to be situated within a genealogy of border technologies, foregrounding its colonial legacies.

In fact, a counter-mapping approach resists the flattening of the analysis of the current context into a homogenous past-present, which gives rise to another form of de-historicization. To the contrary, tracing a history of border technologies means unfolding the legacies of the current mobility regime and, at once, highlighting the moments of rupture, novelty, and subtle recombination enforced (also) through technologies that were not used before or that were used for other purposes. For instance, as a growing scholarship has pointed out, biometric technologies, and fingerprinting in particular, have a clear colonial legacy that traces back to the second half of the nineteenth century (Arora 2019; Browne 2015; Maguire 2009).[1] Subsequently, at the end of the nineteenth century they started to be incorporated into border control practices (McKeown 2008). However, since then the function and goal of biometric technologies at the border has changed over time: as well explained by Brigitta Kuster and Vassilis Tsianos in this volume, migrants' fingerprints are essentially taken in Europe for enforcing the Dublin Regulation, which imposes restrictions on migrants' choice about where they can claim asylum and stay. For this reason, as Ana Valdivia and colleagues have rightly remarked, "a critical questioning of the use of fairness in biometrics systems should also be focused on the historical, political and social contexts in which biometrics are deployed," and not narrowed to struggles over bias (Valdivia et al. 2021, 2). Counter-mapping as a method does not only consist in forging methodological tools for analyzing border technologies without seeing like a state: It also pursues transformative goals. That is, the "counter" of counter-mapping does not exclusively refer to a deconstructive move; it is also about building up, creating, and re-purposing.

Counter-mapping draws on, and is partly narrowed by, the epistemic structure and the original function of the map; for this reason, it can be considered a situated practice, that acts within and against the mapping codes (Casas-Cortes et al. 2017; Pickles 2012). As Martin Bak Jørgensen and Vasilis Galis observe in this volume, "migrants repurpose, rather than simply use these technologies." Thus counter-mapping appears as the political tactical tools par excellence in practices of tech-resistance, silent subversions, as well as in collective mobilizations in support of migrants in transit. In particular, I suggest, it helps unsettling the techno-hype in migration debates from within—that is, by navigating the interstices and the leeway of maneuver of border technologies and, as Stephan Scheel argued in relation to biometrics, by "appropriating mobility" (Scheel 2018). Counter-mapping is in fact enacted by twisting, re-coding, and re-purposing scripts and technologies of mobility control. Far from implicating high-tech technology, counter-mapping activist practices, as other contributors illustrate in this volume, are based on technologies that are used daily (see Creta and Denaro, Galis, Makrygianni). More precisely, they are often enacted through non-digital tools, including cartographic counter-maps, for instance, for helping migrants to move on by visualizing the dangerous crossing points and safe shelters. It is not the purpose of this chapter to disclose these cartographic counter-maps, and some of these are meant to remain secret. What matters is to highlight that counter-mapping is not only a method for unsettling the techno-hype in migration studies but also a practice adopted both by migrants and people who mobilize in solidarity, which consists in appropriating, twisting, and re-purposing mapping technologies.

ON SEEING BORDER TECHNOLOGIES
LIKE A MIGRANT

The border regime and the multiple bordering mechanisms it is formed of—asylum procedure, visa system, deportation processes, identification system, data circulation, etc.—are nowadays partly shaped by a series of sociotechnical assemblages. It is in fact not an exaggeration to say that in the present context we can no longer imagine border procedures enforced without technology. However, we cannot even imagine these without a multiplicity of papers, and paper-based documents that migrants are giving or are requested, as well as data shared on paper among authorities. Going back to Adam McKeown's genealogy of the globalization of borders, the question to raise is "what do we mean by technology when we speak about the technologization of border controls?" In other words, if the history of the global border regime is also the history of technologies of identification and control, it is important to incorporate both digital and non-digital technologies in present analysis of sociotechnical assemblages, as the diverse contributions collected in *The Migration Mobile* do. In fact, in order to de-fetishize techno-humanitarianism, it is key to deconstruct the high-tech and the constellation of notions that pivot around "digital innovation," taking into account assemblages of papers, biometric technologies, non-digital data, and human interactions that shape the infrastructures of migration containment. In place of narrowing down the inquiry to pilot projects and experiments of algorithmic-driven systems used at the border, it is a question of widening and re-framing the analysis around assemblages of routinized "low-tech" technologies, non-digitalized documents, and more "high-tech" systems. Undoing the techno-hype in migration studies entails, as I argued earlier, giving up and challenging a sovereignty gaze on migration. This is the case for any analysis of migration that deems to be critical, and more specifically for reflections about border technologies and the so-called techno-humanitarianism.

Indeed, a critical and situated analysis should refrain from endorsing and reiterating narratives on technologization of the border regime and of refugee governmentality promoted by both states and non-state actors. Narratives on techno-humanitarianism do mobilize a state-based gaze on migration even when they are crafted by non-state actors such as humanitarian agencies or high-tech companies, because they center on three main aspects. First, they assume a governmental gaze on migration by debating the extent to which digital and biometric technologies allows managing asylum seekers and migrants "better" and identifying "suspect" subjects. Second, new biometric technologies and artificial intelligence automated decision-making systems are promoted as part of a problem-solving logic apt at tackling the so called migration crisis. Third, algorithmic-driven systems are assumed to be efficient and to streamline identification and asylum procedures, as well as to facilitate the work of humanitarian actors. A critical analysis of border technologies should be careful in not surreptitiously or involuntarily replicating ideas of efficiency, better migration management (through technology), and problem-solving. So does not seeing like a state imply reversing the gaze and start seeing like a migrant (Hardt and Mezzadra 2020)? Seeing like a migrant is not conceived here in abstract terms of an ideal positionality, but as an analytical gaze that pays attention to the claims that migrants raise for and against technologies and that is grounded in the materiality of struggles for movement.

Both academic and non-academic contentious debates mainly focus on surveillance, data collection, and privacy. Instead, an insight into migrants' struggles and claims reveals other priorities and thorny problems connected to intrusive technologies, such as the multiplication of techno-bureaucratic hurdles they encounter to claim asylum, the disruptions and delays in receiving the monthly financial support, and the digital barriers they face for renewing the permit to stay. Indeed, after being fingerprinted for the first time in a European country, migrants are aware of the digital trap enforced through the Dublin Regulation and the Eurodac database. For this reason, being tracked within or outside refugee camps or being an object of data extraction is often not the main concern and struggle of migrants stranded at Europe's borders. Therefore, I suggest, seeing like a migrant involves re-articulating the debate on border technologies building on the contestations, collective claims, and silent refusals that those who are racialized and governed as "migrants" enact within and against the infrastructures of mobility containment. The "tech" of migration governmentality is only in part made of cutting-edge high-tech systems and only partly used for surveilling and tracking. Thus, if the goal of critical knowledge on migration is to support struggles for "mobility justice" (Sheller 2018), acts of re-purposing and twisting need coming to grips with a heterogeneity of paper-based, digital, and non-digital technologies that disrupt, delay, and hamper migrants from staying, moving, and accessing rights.

REFERENCES

Arora, Payal. 2019. "Politics of algorithms, Indian citizenship, and the colonial legacy." *Global Digital Cultures: Perspectives from South Asia* 37–52.

Browne, Simone. 2015. *Dark Matters*. Durham, NC: Duke University Press.

Casas-Cortes, Maribel, Sebastian Cobarrubias, Charles Heller, and Lorenzo Pezzani. 2017. "Clashing cartographies, migrating maps: The politics of mobility at the external borders of EU rope." *ACME: An International Journal for Critical Geographies* 16 (1): 1–33.

De Genova, Nicholas. 2020. "The economy of detainability." In *The Bureaucratic Production of Difference: Ethos and Ethics in Migration Administrations*, edited by Julia M. Eckert, 155–74. Bielefeld: transcript-Verlag.

Foucault, Michel. 2021. "Nietzsche, genealogy, history." In *Language, Counter-memory, Practice*, 139–64. Ithaca, NY: Cornell University Press.

Hacking, Ian. 1986. "Making up people." In *Reconstructing Individualism: Autonomy, Individuality, and the Self in Western Thought*, edited by Thomas C. Heller, Morton Sosna, and David E. Wellbery, 161–71. Stanford, CA: Stanford University Press.

Hardt, Michael, and Sandro Mezzadra. 2020. "Introduction: Migrant projects of freedom." *South Atlantic Quarterly* 119 (1): 168–75.

Maguire, Mark. 2009. "The birth of biometric security." *Anthropology Today* 25 (2): 9–14.

McKeown, Adam M. 2008. *Melancholy Order: Asian Migration and the Globalization of Borders*. New York: Columbia University Press.

Pickles, John. 2012. *A History of Spaces: Cartographic Reason, Mapping and the Geo-coded World*. London: Routledge.

Scheel, Stephan. 2018. "Real fake? Appropriating mobility via Schengen visa in the context of biometric border controls." *Journal of Ethnic and Migration Studies* 44 (16): 2747–63.

Scott, James C. 2008. *Seeing like a State*. New Haven, CT: Yale university Press.

Sheller, Mimi. 2018. *Mobility Justice: The Politics of Movement in an Age of Extremes*. London: Verso Books.

Tazzioli, Martina. 2021. "Technologies of expulsion: Rethinking refugees' carceral economies beyond surveillance." https://www.law.ox.ac.uk/research-subject-groups /centre-criminology/centreborder-criminologies/blog/2021/11/technologies.

Valdivia, Ana, Júlia Corbera-Serrajòrdia, and Aneta Swianiewicz. 2021. "There is an elephant in the room: Towards a critique on the use of fairness in biometrics." *arXiv preprint arXiv:2112.11193*.

Valdivia, Ana, and Martina Tazzioli. 2021. "Una crítica a la inteligencia artificial más allá de los sesgos." E~l Salto Diario. https://www.elsaltodiario.com/paradoja -jevons-ciencia-poder/critica-inteligencia-artificial-sesgos.

Vinsel, Lee. 2021. "You're doing it wrong: notes on criticism and technology hype." *Medium*. February 1. https://sts-news.medium.com/youre-doing-it-wrong-notes-on -criticism-and-technology-hype-18b08b4307e5.

NOTE

1. As Marck Maguire pointed out, it is notable that biometrics "offered 19th-century innovators more than the prospect of identifying criminals: early biometrics promised a utopia of bio-governmentality in which individual identity verification was at the heart of population control" (Maguire 2009).

Index

About the Authors

Sara Creta is an award-winning journalist and documentary filmmaker with extensive experience investigating human rights abuses. Over the past years, she has reported from Sudan, Ethiopia, Bangladesh, the Democratic Republic of the Congo, Libya, Chad, Cameroon, Morocco, Tunisia, the Gaza Strip, and a rescue ship in the Mediterranean. Currently, she is pursuing her PhD at the School of Communications of Dublin City University under the Future of Journalism Institute. With an academic background in international cooperation and protection of human rights, she focuses much of her research on how dissident actors use internet technologies in affecting political action vis-à-vis the Horn of Africa region and politics. For her research, she has received funding from the European Union's Horizon 2020 research and innovation program under the Marie Skłodowska-Curie Action.

Chiara Denaro is a postdoctoral researcher in sociology at Trento University on the project "PRIN-2017, Debordering activities and citizenship from below of asylum seekers in Italy." She is a social worker and legal expert, working with migrants and refugees. Her sociolegal research work concerns asylum and migration policies in the Mediterranean space, border control policies, human rights, right to asylum, as well as the practices and strategies of resistance put in place by people on the move. As part of WatchTheMed Alarm Phone, Chiara focuses on the central Mediterranean route.

Leandros Fischer is an assistant professor of international studies at Aalborg University and part of the Democracy, Migration and Society Group (DEMOS). In the last years, he has conducted research on migration and refugee solidarity movements in Cyprus and Hamburg. Other research interests include German politics, international solidarity movements, political parties of the left, populism, as well as questions of race and class. His work has appeared in numerous edited volumes and peer-reviewed journals, such as the *Journal of Palestine Studies*, *Citizenship Studies*, *Mobilities*, and

Antipode. He has worked in the past as visiting teaching fellow at the Philipps University of Marburg, as well as adjunct faculty at the University of Cyprus in Nicosia.

Vasilis Galis is an associate professor in the Technologies in Practice (TiP) group at the IT University of Copenhagen. Galis's research is interdisciplinary, and it is impregnated by a strong epistemological solidarity with social movements. Galis has published on social movements, migration, and sociotechnical systems from a science and technology studies (STS) perspective. He is co-investigator for the interdisciplinary project *DIGINAUTS: Migrants' Digital Practices in/of the European Border Regime.*

Oliver Joel Halpern has worked as the research assistant for Martin Lemberg Pedersen for the past two years alongside completing his master's degree at the University of Copenhagen. His interdisciplinary approach takes particular interest in bureaucratic state-forming practices, deportation, and biometric technologies. His publications include *Uncertain, Illegible, Incomplete: Exploring Categorization in Police Bureaucracy of Deportable Migrants from Denmark* (2021), and co-publishing *EU Exit Regimes in Practice: Case Studies from the Netherlands, Spain, Germany and Denmark* (2021) and *Frontex and Exit Governance: Dataveillence, Civil Society and Markets for Border Control* (2021).

Martin Bak Jørgensen is a professor in processes of migration at DEMOS at the Department for Culture and Learning, Aalborg University, Denmark. He works within the fields of sociology, political sociology, and political science. He has published *Politics of Dissent* (2015), *Solidarity without Borders: Gramscian Perspectives on Migration and Civil Society Alliances* (2016), and *Solidarity and the "Refugee Crisis" in Europe* (2019), all co-authored with Óscar García Agustín. He has published articles in journals like *Internal Migration Review, Critical Sociology, Journal of International Migration and Integration,* and *British Journal of International Politics.*

Brigitta Kuster is an assistant professor at the Department of Cultural History and Theory, Humboldt-Universität zu Berlin. She holds a PhD in philosophy from the Academy of Fine Arts, Vienna. Kuster specializes in film/media and gender/queer studies, with a particular emphasis on postcolonial and border studies. Her current research focuses on issues of biometric technologies and the EU border, as well as on continuations of considerations, practices, and concerns of so-called Third Cinema, "cinéma militant," and contemporary radical/artistic practices in post-cinematic realms. Her recent publications include several articles in international journals on the digitization of the border and on post-cinematographic media assemblages (e.g., cinema of care).

Martin Lemberg-Pedersen is an honorary associate professor at the University of Warwick, and head of policy and society for Amnesty International, Denmark, with a PhD in political philosophy from the University of Copenhagen. His work involves interdisciplinary analyses of Western refugee ethics and policies, and deportations and military-industrial relations, with a focus on EU politics in Afghan, Greek, Turkish, and Libyan contexts. He has examined postcolonial trajectories between Western colonialism and current displacement politics. Book publications include *Postcoloniality and Forced Migration: Migration Management, Surveillance, Agency* (lead editor, 2022), and journal articles in *Forced Migration Review* (2021), *Journal of Borderlands Studies* (2020), *Citizenship Studies* (2020), *Global Affairs* (2019), *Questions of International Law* (2019), and *Etikk i Praksis* (2018).

Claudia Lintner is a junior professor of sociology at the Faculty of Education, Free University of Bolzano (Italy). She received her MA in migration studies from the University Ca' Foscari of Venice and her PhD from the Free University of Bolzano. Her research interests focus on the concrete border experiences of refugees, the understanding of agency as a relational process, the digitalization in the refugee context, as well as policies and practices of exclusion. Currently, she coordinates the project "Digital border experiences of refugees: Understanding the use of ICT in the context of forced migration at the Brenner border-Italy (DIBO)," a cooperation between the Free University of Bolzano (Italy-Internal research fund CRC 2019), the University of Innsbruck (Austria), and the Technical University of Munich (Germany).

Vasiliki Makrygianni has a background in architecture and engineering, and her PhD research focuses on migrants' emancipatory spatial practices in Athens, Greece. She has worked in various research projects on migration and spatial practices. Her primary research areas include critical urban theory, feminist methodologies, and the theory of intersectionality, while current research interests focus on digital space, feminist technoscience, and practices of solidarity and care.

Nina Grønlykke Mollerup is an associate professor of ethnology and affiliated with the Centre for Advanced Migration Studies at University of Copenhagen. She was trained as an anthropologist and holds a PhD in communication. Her research focuses on practices around visual documentation of violence and questions of truthfulness, temporality, and spatiality. She has worked extensively on the uprisings and ensuing violence in Egypt and Syria and has also conducted fieldwork in northern Europe. She has published in journals such as *Social Analysis*, *International Journal of Communication*, and *Journalism*. She is chair of the EASA Media Anthropology Network E-seminar series.

Evie Papada is a human geographer based at the School of Geography & Sustainable Development, University of St Andrews, Scotland, United Kingdom. Her research interests intersect border studies, asylum seeking, with a particular interest in the sociology of law. Prior to joining the academic community, Papada worked as a policy adviser within international human rights organizations in the United Kingdom, Spain, and Greece. She has since acted as the impact coordinator for the ESCR-funded Mediterranean Migration Research Programme and has completed her PhD thesis on the question of vulnerability designation in the Greek hotspots. She is the co-author of *New Borders: Hotspots and the European Migration Regime*. Her work is driven by her passion for social and climate justice.

Luca Rossi is an associate professor of digital media and networks at the Department of Digital Design of IT, University of Copenhagen. He coordinates the Human Centered Data Science research group, and he is member of the Networks Data and Society (NERDS) research group. He teaches network analysis and digital media analysis. His interdisciplinary research applies computational methods to the study on online social phenomena such as online participation, online activism, political campaign, and election studies. He has a track of publication into both media and communication as well as computer science venues such as *New Media & Society*, *Information Communication & Society*, *Social Science Computer Review*, *ACM Computing Survey*, and others. He has been active in the development of two packages for the R statistical software: coornet—to detect online coordinated behavior—and multinet—to analyze multi-layer social networks.

Marie Sandberg is an associate professor, PhD, in European ethnology and director of the Centre for Advanced Migration Studies (AMIS) at the University of Copenhagen. Sandberg's ethnographic research expertise focuses on European borders, migration practices, and everyday life Europeanization. She studies how borders in/of everyday life are continuously negotiated, overcome, and rebuilt in interactions such as volunteer work in support of refugees coming to Europe during the 2015 "refugee crisis." She has published several peer-reviewed articles in high-ranked journals such as *Journal of European Studies*, *Nordic Journal of Migration Research*, and *Identities*. Sandberg serves as the president of the International Society for Ethnology and Folklore and is a member of the IMISCO board of directors and is thus vividly engaged in discussions within international as well as Nordic fields of ethnology, migration, and border studies.

Martina Tazzioli is a lecturer in politics and technology at Goldsmiths. She is the author of *The Making of Migration: The Biopolitics of Mobility at Europe's Borders* (2020), *Spaces of Governmentality: Autonomous Migration and the Arab Uprisings* (2015), and co-author of *Tunisia as a Revolutionised Space of Migration* (2016). She is co-editor in chief of the journal *Politics*.

Vassilis S. Tsianos is a professor at the University of Applied Sciences, Kiel, where he teaches theoretical sociology, migration studies, social policy, and methods in qualitative social research. He has published numerous books, including, most recently, the co-authored monographs *Mobile Commons, Digital Materialities and the Right to the City: Migrant Digitalities and Social Movements in Three Arrival Cities – Athens, Istanbul, Nicosia* (2015); *Escape Routes: Control and Subversion in the 21st Century* (2008); the co-edited "Racism in post-migrant society. Movements" (2016); *The Art of Being Many: Towards a New Theory and Practice of Gathering* (transcript, 2016); *Empire and the Biopolitical Turn* (2007); as well as *Turbulent Margins: New Perspectives of Migration in Europe* (transcript, 2007).

Vasilis Vlassis is currently a postdoctoral researcher in the IT University of Copenhagen. He holds a bachelor's degree in mathematics from the University of Crete, a master's in philosophy and history of science and technology from the National and Kapodistrian University of Athens, and a PhD from the business information technology department of the IT University of Copenhagen in 2019. His thesis, titled "Registration of irregularised migrants in the EU in times of 'crisis,'" focused on practices of border guards and their use of technologies in the identification and registration process, as it occurred in the border between Greece and Turkey, and is placed in the intersection between science and technology studies (STS), surveillance studies, and critical border studies. His current work focuses on Big Data policing methods in Denmark, as part of the Welfare after Digitalization (WaD) project, funded by the Velux Foundation.

Antonis Vradis works at the School of Geography & Sustainable Development, University of St Andrews, Scotland, United Kingdom. He has acted or acts as principal investigator for Nutricities (British Academy) and Transcapes (ESRC), lead organizer of The Welcoming City and Decolonising the City (both Urban Studies Foundation), and co-investigator of CUPP (Nordforsk) and PURSI (ESRC). He is an associate editor at *Political Geography* and an editorial collective member at *CITY*. Vradis is a geographer with an urban focus and a migration inclination. More than anything, through his work with colleagues and comrades within and beyond academia, he is driven by the inherently political urge to make sense of our turbulent times: how we got into this mess to begin with and what ways there might be for us to stop it.

www.ingramcontent.com/pod-product-compliance
Lightning Source LLC
Chambersburg PA
CBHW051957270326
41929CB00015B/2684